Leadership, Gender and Culture in Education

Leadership, Gender and Culture in Education

Male and Female Perspectives

Edited by
John Collard and Cecilia Reynolds

Open University Press

Open University Press
McGraw-Hill Education
McGraw-Hill House
Shoppenhangers Road
Maidenhead
Berkshire
England
SL6 2QL

email: enquiries@openup.co.uk
world wide web: www.openup.co.uk

and Two Penn Plaza, New York, NY 10121–2289, USA

First published 2005

Copyright © John Collard and Cecilia Reynolds 2005

A catalogue record of this book is available from the British Library

ISBN 0 335 21440 1 (pb) 0 335 21441 X (hb)

Library of Congress Cataloging-in-Publication Data
CIP data applied for

Typeset by YHT Ltd
Printed in the UK by MPG Books Limited, Bodmin, Cornwall

Contents

List of Contributors

Sandra Acker is Professor and former Chair of the Department of Sociology and Equity Studies in Education, Ontario Institute for Studies in Education of the University of Toronto. She is a sociologist of education whose research interests include women and education, teachers' work and academic careers and cultures. She has taught in the USA, Britain and Canada. Currently she is Principal Investigator of a study funded by the Social Sciences and Humanities Research Council of Canada of transitions over time in teacher education institutions, especially with regard to the research culture, which increasingly shapes the work of academics. She is the author of a book on elementary school teachers' workplace culture entitled *The Realities of Teachers' Work: Never a Dull Moment* (Continuum, 1999).

Marie Battiste is a Mi'kmaw educator, Professor in the College of Education, and Coordinator of the Indian and Northern Education Program within the Department of Educational Foundations at the University of Saskatchewan. Her historical research of Mi'kmaw literacy and education as a graduate student at Harvard University and later at Stanford University where she received her doctorate degree in curriculum and teacher education provided the foundation for her later writings in cognitive imperialism, linguistic and cultural integrity, and decolonization of aboriginal education. A recipient of two honorary degrees from St Mary's University and from her alma mater University of Maine at Farmington, she has worked actively with First Nations schools and communities as an administrator, teacher, consultant and curriculum developer. Her research interests are in initiating institutional change in the decolonization of education, language and social justice policy and power, and post-colonial educational approaches that recognize and affirm the political and cultural diversity of Canada and the ethical protection and advancement of indigenous knowledge. A technical expert to the United Nations, she has most recently written *Protecting Indigenous Knowledge and Heritage: A Global Challenge* with J. Youngblood Henderson (Purich Press, 2000) and edited *Reclaiming Indigenous Voice and Vision* (UBC Press, 2000). She was senior editor with Jean Barman for *First Nations Education in Canada: The Circle Unfolds* (UBC Press, 1995).

Jill Blackmore is Professor, School of Social and Cultural Studies, Faculty of Education, Deakin University, Australia. She has researched and published on organizational change, leadership, globalization, educational restructuring, teachers' work, school governance, gender equity reform, the parental movement, and citizenship education. She has co-edited *Gender Matters in Educational Administration and Policy: A Feminist Introduction* with Jane Kenway and has co-authored with Jane Kenway, Sue Willis and Leonie Rennie in *Answering Back: Girls, Boys, Education and Feminism*. She is author of *Troubling Women: Feminism, Leadership, and Educational Change*.

Cryss Brunner is Associate Professor of Educational Policy and Administration at the University of Minnesota and joint director of the UCEA Joint Program Center for the Study of the Superintendency. Her research on women power, the superintendency, and the gap between public schools and their communities has appeared in many well-known professional journals. She has published a number of books on the superintendency: *The New Superintendency* (Elsevier, 2001); *Principles of Power: Women Superintendents and the Riddle of the Heart* (SUNY Press, 2000); *Sacred Dreams: Women and the Superintendency* (SUNY Press, 1999). She is also one of the co-authors of the *American Association of School Administrators' Ten Year Study of the School Superintendency* (AASA, 2000).

John Collard is the Head of Graduate Programs in the School of Education and Community Studies University of Canberra, Australia. His previous appointment was as Program Co-ordinator of the Centre for Lifelong Learning at Australian Catholic University. He has published many articles on leadership and policy in prominent refereed journals, has worked as a consultant to state and national governments in Australia, and been active in national and international professional associations. Prior to entering higher education Dr Collard was a teacher of English, principal of a large multicultural secondary school and a senior official in one of the largest school systems in Australia where he was specifically responsible for school leadership. This led him to undertake a PhD at the University of Melbourne in the 1990s. His current research interests include leadership and gender, leadership and intercultural understanding, and student and community leadership. In 2002 he introduced the Master of Educational Leadership Degree from the University of Canberra to China using intercultural frameworks and bilingual pedagogy.

Marian Court is a Senior Lecturer in the Department of Social and Policy Studies in Education, Massey University, Aotearoa/New Zealand. Her current research is focusing on alternative approaches to educational leadership in secondary schools, especially bi-cultural and male/female co-principal partnerships. Her published articles and her doctoral thesis 'Sharing school leadership: narratives of discourse and power' reflect her abiding research interest in issues around gender, culture and leadership and finding ways to build more inclusive organizing practices in schools.

Anna Davis is a research assistant and graduate student. She works on various projects at the Centre for Principal Development, Umeå University.

Karin Franzén is a PhD student in the Department of Education at the University of Umeå in Sweden. Her research interests focus on the construction of school leadership from a gender perspective. She is interested in how school leaders describe their educational leadership and the discursive rules that frame the ways that men and women speak about their leadership. Her work looks at gender within the discourses of both leaders and teachers.

Margaret Grogan is currently Professor and Chair, Department of Educational Leadership and Policy Analysis, University of Missouri-Columbia. Originally from Australia, she received a bachelors degree in ancient history and Japanese language. She taught at a high school in Australia and was a teacher and an administrator at an international school in Japan where she lived for 17 years. During that time she received her masters degree in curriculum and instruction from Michigan State University. She moved to the USA in 1992. After graduating from Washington State University with a PhD in educational administration, she taught in principal and superintendent preparation programmes at the University of Virginia for eight years. She has published many articles and chapters and has authored, co-authored and edited three books. Her current research focuses on women in leadership, the superintendency, the moral and ethical dimensions of leadership, and leadership for social justice. She also edits a series on women in leadership for SUNY Press.

Olof Johansson is an Associate Professor of Political Science and Director of the Centre for Principal Development and Director of the National Head Teachers Training Programme at Umeå University, Sweden. Dr Johansson also holds an appointment as a Visiting Fellow of the International Institute for Educational Leadership at the University of Lincoln, UK. His main research interest is implementation of educational policies, organization, leadership and values. Most of his research has a clear comparative profile.

James Koschoreck is Assistant Professor in Educational Administration at the University of Cincinnati. Dr Koschoreck received his doctorate in educational administration from the University of Texas at Austin in 2000. Before arriving at the University of Cincinnati, Dr Koschoreck served as the managing editor of the *International Journal of Qualitative Studies in Education*. He has published numerous book chapters, articles and book reviews. Additionally, he has presented papers and conducted symposia at national conferences on such diverse topics as gender and sexuality, state educational policy, and educational equity in urban districts. Dr Koschoreck is currently engaged in a significant evaluation project that seeks to examine the effectiveness of a model for community engagement in the facilities decision-making process of Cincinnati public schools. He remains active in various service projects, which include his roles as co-founder and co-facilitator of the Gay and Bisexual Men's Support Group, the newly elected president of the College Faculty Senate Committee, and editor of the Point/Counterpoint feature of the *UCEA Review*. His most recent achievements include having been chosen as a recipient of the Dean's Faculty Incentive Award and the Faculty Development Council Individual Grant. As an instructor, he regularly teaches educational policy analysis, programme evaluation, introductory and intermediate statistics, and economics of education.

Betty Merchant is Associate Professor and Chair of the Department of Educational Leadership and Policy Studies at the University of Texas, San Antonio. Her research interests focus on educational policy, equity, student diversity and school leadership. She has taught in public schools, preschool through high school, and in tribally controlled Native American schools in the southwest.

Cecilia Reynolds is Dean of Education at the University of Saskatchewan and has been writing, teaching and researching about gender and education for approximately two decades. Following a teaching career of 17 years in both elementary and secondary Ontario schools, she completed doctoral studies at the Ontario Institute of Studies in Education in the field of educational administration. Her work has been published in several international scholarly journals and books. She is also co-editor, with Dr Beth Young, of *Women and Leadership in Canadian Education* (Temeron Press, 1995). Her latest books are *Women and School Leadership: International Perspectives* (SUNY Press, 2002) and *Equity and Globalization in Education* with Alison Griffith (Temeron Books, 2002).

Acknowledgements

Several of the authors presented earlier versions of their chapters at the Commonwealth Conference on Educational Administration in Umeå, Sweden, in 2002. Some of these papers were published in a special issue of *Leading and Managing* (2002) 8(2), and are reproduced here with permission.

We wish to thank Rebecca Cittadini for her excellent work as editorial assistant on this project. Thanks as well to Fiona Richman and Melanie Smith at Open University Press for their assistance on this book.

Foreword

This rich explorative book examines the intricacies of gender, sexuality, ethnicity and class and how these complex influences weave their patterns in the daily lives of leaders. What shapes the perceptions and beliefs of leaders in particular education settings? What drives them to behave in different ways? What perceptions do their 'followers' have? What makes them the leaders they are, or want to be?

In answering these questions a commentator like Edward Said would have argued against oversimplifications, pointing to the interrelationship between politics and culture and suggesting that people have been encouraged to believe that they are only, mainly, exclusively white or black, western or oriental, male or female. Cultures and traditions exist, he argued in *Culture and Imperialism* (1993 pp 407–408) but 'there is no reason except fear and prejudice to keep insisting on their separation and distinctiveness'. 'No one today is purely one thing and labels like Indian, woman or American are no more than starting points, which if followed into actual experience for only a moment are quickly left behind'.

And this is where John Collard's and Cecilia Reynolds' edited collection comes into its own. The contributors achieve the difficult balance between acknowledging the differences: the distinctiveness not only of culture and beliefs but also of gender and sexuality, as well as the unifying elements. They confront some of the stereotypes about women and leadership and challenge prevailing 'gung-ho' models which focus on heroic individuals who achieve narrowly defined goals.

The power of stereotypes is pervasive and limiting. It is as hard for the male leader to resist the pressure of becoming the 'Chief Executive' as it is for his female counterpart to avoid being the 'Prom Queen'. But confronting the stereotypes is one of the most difficult leadership challenges. Selma James (*The Ladies and the Mammies: Jane Austen and Jean Rhys*: 1983 pp.94–95) has taught us much about how to challenge those stereotypes, such as the 'Mammy, the mythologized Black woman...portrayed as a large woman with a round face and a scarf tied around her head...someone whom a white child was able to turn to for everything.' An image which 'suggests that in the midst of the mess of the white family, the plantation master's family, there was a Black woman who was a pillar of stability, who kept everything together, and who was always good-tempered'.

In the field of education we are always offered widely different models of women leaders. In late nineteenth century England, we had the Misses Beale and Buss. The former founded Cheltenham College and sought to promote the Victorian feminine ideal, and the latter founded both North London Collegiate and Camden Girls' School where, by contrast, she strove to encourage young women to develop academically and to be economically independent.

The book also raises many questions about the context for leadership. The institutional context creates the boundaries in which leaders function. A competitive, individualistic climate inevitably works against collaborative leadership models and generates fragmentation or isolated pockets of colla-boration that are semi-detached from the prevailing culture. How do leaders create different models against the backcloth of the institutional weight?

Discussions within the book on mentoring, for example, raise some of the tensions. On the one hand, mentoring can be a powerful tool to en-courage underrepresented groups into leadership positions. One the other hand, mentoring models tend to have a view of how leaders ought to lead, based on existing models

This leads back to the central issues of: leadership for what? What are leaders there to do – and for whom? To ensure that students achieve higher examination scores, or to promote equity and social justice? This book offers many fresh insights into these and other important questions.

Professor Kathryn Riley
Institute of Education
University of London, July 2004

Introduction

John Collard and Cecilia Reynolds

This edited collection contains chapters by some of the world's leading scholars on gender and educational leadership. The chapters draw on research on men and women leaders in elementary, secondary and post-secondary schools in Australia, Canada, New Zealand, Sweden, the UK and the USA. The authors counter essentialist claims based on biological, psychological and sociological theories stressing differences across gender groups. Differences within gender groups are presented in a variety of ways and more sophisticated understandings of gender relations and leadership discourses are developed than has characterized this field in the past.

The book challenges, or 'troubles' (Blackmore 1999) rationalist traditions such as the separation of mind and body and the superiority of objectivity. Rooted in post-positivism, many of the chapters employ techniques such as discourse analysis, to move beyond mere descriptions of women leaders' experiences and consider such things as intrasubjectivity, heteronormativity, and the social construction of multiple forms of masculinity and femininity. The early work on gender and leadership is supplemented with more nuanced theories and explanations of how gender, race and class, for example, operate in connected and changing ways for both men and women leaders in different educational settings. Drawing upon recent sophisticated developments in the field of gender studies (Connell 1995), the authors argue that social and institutional contexts both shape and differentiate the leadership of male and female administrators in schools and universities.

The past decade has witnessed an increased degree of sophistication in the discourse about gender and educational leadership. This has involved a movement away from the essentialist typecasting which characterized the literature of the 1970s and 1980s where men and women were often depicted as polar opposites. There is now a greater awareness of multiple forms of masculinity and femininity that interact with economic, social, corporate and even minority cultures (Connell 1995). Culture, whether described as broad social mores, institutional histories or geographically bounded belief systems, shapes and mediates socially constructed gender identities.

An awareness of the concept of multiple femininities and masculinities is just beginning to appear in the discourse on educational leadership. In this respect, the field is beginning to catch up with the more advanced thinking in the field of women/gender studies. It is time to shed misleading stereotypes of male and female leaders that have assumed a mythic orthodoxy in popular discourse. The most prevalent evidence is a worldwide epidemic of training courses which presuppose that there is a distinctive 'women's way of leading'. Such assumptions gravely understate diversity among women and men. Discussions of gender and leadership also need to include understandings of how multiple interactions in societies, systems and institutions work to shape beliefs and practices. It is time to challenge notions that culture is simply 'the way we do things around here' (Caldwell and Spinks 1988, 1998). Such a definition concerns itself only with the manifest level of organizational culture such as patterns of language, behaviour, symbols and rituals. Recently articulated concepts in the organizational literature (Lundberg 1988) identify how such things as assumed values, institutional histories, power structures and pathologies coalesce to produce manifest levels of organizational culture. The chapters in this book provide new and complex understandings about the links between leadership, gender and culture.

Part I: Leadership discourses and gender

The chapters in Part I offer a critical analysis of current leadership theories that fail to adequately acknowledge the complex negotiations of individual men and women as they take up leadership roles in schools. All of these authors suggest that gender does not 'determine' leadership style or performance even though there are powerful stereotypes that do affect leadership work. Each chapter provides data from specific contexts. Taken together, these data provide a detailed picture of a variety of ways that men and women can and do work as school leaders.

In Chapter 1, 'Negotiating and reconstructing gendered leadership discourses', Marian Court from New Zealand demonstrates how discourse analysis can be used to illuminate how people understand and negotiate sociopolitical processes associated with gender and leadership in schools. A case study of a New Zealand primary school co-principalship is used to explore how three women constructed themselves as collaborating leaders. The discussion shows that they positioned themselves differently within professional collaborative, managerial and feminist discourses, yet negotiated some common understandings across these differences to build successful shared leadership. The chapter offers a critique of the role theory paradigm and delineates the strengths of discourse analysis.

In Chapter 2, 'Does size matter? The interaction between principal gender, level of schooling and institutional scale in Australian schools', John Collard from Australia reports on a broad-scale study of a balanced sample of male and female principals in Australia. Using questionnaire, interview and historical data, he explores relationships between the perceptions and beliefs of male and female principals and key contextual factors. Previous claims that

there are important and frequently overlooked differences in the cognitive frameworks of male and female leaders are confirmed. However, essentialist stereotypes are challenged by the findings. Factors such as level of schooling, institutional scale and student gender interact with and modify gender predispositions. Institutional scale was found to be a less important source of differences than other factors. However, it was a source of significant differences in the areas of staff management, self-image and personal wellbeing. This chapter challenges the field to develop a nuanced theoretical perspective that acknowledges the interactive nature of principal gender and the scale of organizations.

In Chapter 3, 'Gender and school leadership in Sweden', Anna Davis and Olof Johansson from Sweden discuss the many recent changes in the way that municipalities in Sweden organize their school sectors. Nearly all have merged boards, and leaders such as principals and superintendents are now responsible for day care centres as well as schools. One effect of this change, since the 1980s, has been an increase in the participation of women leaders. Today, over 70 per cent of all principals are women. The chapter explores the effects of this rapid change in school leadership and draws on data from three different Scandinavian studies that used the same questionnaire.

In Chapter 4, 'Gender and school leadership discourses: a Swedish perspective', Karin Franzén from Sweden offers a very different analysis of the leadership situation in Sweden today. Using a discourse approach, she describes in detail how individual men and women approach their leadership work. She argues that while men and women showed few differences in their approaches, teachers reacted differently to their male and female principals. Stereotypes based on gender seem still to have an impact on how teachers perceive their leaders. The discourses described in this chapter echo much of what is presented in Collard's earlier chapter in a very different context in Australia. Together, these chapters provide exciting glimpses into the complexities of leadership work in schools by both men and women.

Part II: Leadership practices amidst global and local change

The second part of this book brings together three chapters that focus on women leaders. Each author draws upon data in different contexts to argue that not all women respond to changing contexts in similar ways. Women are, however, affected by global and local changes, and such changes have an impact upon how they can do their leadership work. In Chapter 5, 'Steel magnolias in velvet ghettoes: female leaders in Australian girls' schools', John Collard from Australia provides historical information about a number of girls' schools and the various women who led them. Against that backdrop,

he draws on questionnaire and interview data from the present day to describe the attitudes and practices of women leaders in various sorts of schools. He argues that simple portrayals of women leaders mask complexities and need to be replaced by deeper questions about leadership activities and their relation not only to gender but also to such factors as the structure, history and size of particular schools and the class backgrounds of the students in schools where women have led.

In Chapter 6, 'Influences of the discourses of globalization on mentoring for gender equity and social justice in educational leadership', Margaret Grogan from the USA argues that there is a dark side to mentoring as a mechanism for preparing school leaders. By reinforcing the status quo, mentoring can fail to promote critical leadership or to advance gender equity or social justice. The current globalization discourse is also potentially dangerous to equity and equality ideals, but, it does offer the promise of diversity and hybridization that might enhance reform efforts aimed at serving those who have not benefited from educational policies and practices in the past.

In Chapter 7, 'Gender, leadership and change in faculties of education in three countries', Sandra Acker from Canada reports preliminary results of a small, comparative study based on in-depth interviews with women managers in faculties of education in Canada, Australia and Britain. Six women from each country, who held positions such as dean, associate dean, department head, associate head of department, or programme director, participated. The research examined how the women met two major challenges: (1) being part of the first generation of women to be involved in university management in any significant numbers; and (2) operating within a context of global change that makes the work of management more difficult than in the past. The particular focus in this chapter is on the paradox of feeling in/out of control. By definition these women had major responsibilities and a certain amount of power. Yet much of what they had to do was not of their own choosing: rapid change and university or government dictates meant that they felt that their agendas were not under their own control. Participants in all three countries reported struggling with cutbacks in resources, increases in workload and pressures towards accountability, although there were variations in degree and detail. These trends are often associated with globalization, but they are filtered through national and local practices. Many of these women had feminist commitments and were trying to make a difference in the university in terms of bringing about greater equity for women and other equity-seeking groups and accomplishing improvements in general. They found it difficult to reconcile their feelings of marginalization and isolation (as there are still not many women in management) with their sense of agency.

Part III: Disrupting the normative discourse of leadership

Picking up on the theme of marginalization from Part II, the chapters in Part III push the boundaries of previous work on gender and leadership by incorporating aspects such as sexuality, embodiment, race, ethnicity and professionalization into discussions about how men and women work as leaders in educational settings. Expanding our notions of both gender and leadership, we are challenged to consider normative conceptions of power, the body work of leaders, and the impact of heteronormativity, racism and globalized patterns, such as the recent emphasis on performativity. Themes such as decolonization and social justice perspectives are set out for our consideration in light of the findings and discussions of the previous chapters in this book. Informed by the past, cognizant of the complex interplay of gender with race, class and sexuality, and sensitized to the importance of contextual effects upon the leadership work of women and men, this final section lays down the gauntlet to the field of educational administration. What are the important research questions regarding gender and leadership? How can we better prepare school leaders? These important questions are given some surprising answers in the chapters of Part III.

In Chapter 8, 'Women performing the superintendency: problematizing the normative alignment of conceptions of power and constructions of gender', Cryss Brunner from the USA highlights the illuminations and limitations that researchers face when they choose to study the experiences of women in the superintendency. Given the low numbers of women in the role, problems related to research methods and design abound. This chapter provides examples of what can and cannot be learned from two distinctly different theoretical perspectives: post-positivism (emancipatory perspectives) and positivism (functionalist perspectives). The examples are grounded in research studies that the author conducted. The focus, however, is on methodology and theory creation rather than on the findings of such studies of women leaders.

In Chapter 9, 'Leadership, embodiment and gender scripts: prom queens and chief executives', Cecilia Reynolds from Canada challenges us to break from the Cartesian mind/body split and consider how feminist insights about embodiment can provide a new lens for considering leadership work in schools. She draws on her inter-generational interview study of school leaders in Canada to describe two dominant and gendered images – the prom queen and the chief executive officer. Both of these images have definite 'body' connotations and are related to sexuality. While individual men and women in this study were arguably not limited to only these two gender scripts, there is evidence that they were affected by the presence and power of such scripts within the culture of the schools in which they did their leadership work. The chapter also looks at examples of the 'body work' of school leaders in several international studies. While there is no single male or female response to doing the body work of leadership, dominant and marginalized discourses about that work affect us all in many important ways.

In Chapter 10, 'Transgressing heteronormativity in educational administration', James Koschoreck of the USA argues that the overwhelming heteronormativity presumed in the field of educational administration poses challenges both for scholars and practitioners who strive to transgress the societal expectations that constrain the expression of sexually diverse populations. In this chapter he uses a combination of autobiographical data and information gathered through personal interviews to examine multiple ways in which the normalization of sexuality might be interrogated. He argues that lesbian, gay, bisexual and transgendered faculty and administrators can more effectively contravene the normalizing practices of heterosexism by refusing to remain silent about issues of sexuality. Additionally, he indicates some implications for practising researchers and administrators who are seeking to challenge heterosexist norms.

In Chapter 11, 'Leadership and aboriginal education in contemporary education: narratives of cognitive imperialism reconciling with decolonization', Marie Battiste of Canada describes four narratives that currently operate in school cultures at elementary, secondary and post-secondary levels and that limit aboriginal peoples. Rather than focus on capacity, these discourses serve to colonize and marginalize students and teachers who are aboriginal or who try to work to improve or decolonize aboriginal knowledge and peoples. Post-colonial theories of Indigenous education are discussed and the complex process of educational reform that is needed is delineated. Stereotypes and images are shown to work not only through gender but also through categories such as 'Aboriginal'. In 'racialized' environments such as schools, tremendous challenges exist for leaders who wish to work for change and social justice.

In Chapter 12, 'Bridge people: leaders for social justice', Betty Merchant of the USA picks up the themes from the chapter by Battiste and applies them in another setting: her study of leaders in San Antonio, Texas. Based on interviews with eight individual men and women who were recognized by their peers as 'bridge people' or leaders for social justice and equity, this chapter describes the shared characteristics of these people. The passages from the interviews reveal the factors, past and present that have encouraged these leaders to work for the children and families in their communities who have few benefits from mainstream society. The participants detail their own experiences of marginalization and they offer advice for the preparation of school leaders who can make a difference for Hispanics or others who will benefit from leaders who work for social justice.

In Chapter 13, '"The emperor has no clothes": professionalism:

performativity and educational leadership in high-risk postmodern times', Jill Blackmore, of Australia casts yet another critical gaze on the issue of leadership. She mounts a critique of (1) how leadership has been treated as the solution and not the problem, and (2) how the technologies of management dominate over substantive ethical and educational issues. Good leadership has become, in 'best practice' discourse, the signifier of successful educational organizations in ways that ignore how the fundamental and core work done by teachers is what produces educational improvement for students. Ironically, the failure to recognize and support this professional expertise is in the context of a shift to a performative state and the demise of public advocacy models of professionalism. The performative state increasingly seeks to 'manage professionalism', to quieten critical voices within organizations by positioning it as disloyal, and to dumb down the professional's advocacy role in relation to 'the public' (as opposed to the client) and their respective constituencies. Discourses of professionalism and leadership are therefore at odds, as discourses of professional activism put organizations at risk, because they are based on extra-organizational principles and loyalties, and different parameters and fields of action. This chapter emerges from recent experiences and literature on universities and schools around leadership 'issues'. Theoretically, it calls upon literature about the new professionalism and a risk society, and around notions of performativity and what constitutes the public, and how this has implications for feminist practices in leadership.

PART I

LEADERSHIP DISCOURSES
AND GENDER

1 Negotiating and Reconstructing Gendered Leadership Discourses[1]

Marian Court

In her groundbreaking study of women in educational leadership, Shakeshaft (1987: 171–191) used a woman-centred approach to document differences in women's and men's work environments and styles of leadership, communication, decision-making and conflict resolution. She posited that a female culture (based in an ethic of relational response and care) was characteristic of women in educational administration. This female world in schools was conceptualized as having five main features. Relationships with others were central for women administrators; teaching and learning were their major foci; building community was an essential part of their style; sexism marginalized them; and in their daily work the line separating the public world from the private was blurred (Shakeshaft 1987: 197–198). This conceptualizing combined a cultural feminist 'female difference' argument with a radical feminist analysis of male domination.

These analyses have provided some useful insights into the nature of gendered leadership, but they have limitations for a feminist politics of change (Blackmore 1999). In this chapter I explain how a feminist post-structuralist approach can offer a more complex and dynamic analysis of women's agency in educational leadership. I illustrate this from a case study of a New Zealand primary school co-principalship (Court 2001). The proposal for this initiative was developed by two seemingly very similar 'Pakeha'[2] middle-aged women teachers. Their commitment to shared leadership had developed, however, out of some very different life and work experiences and different feminist positionings. A discourse analysis of their co-principal proposal reveals how the latter differences had been blended in an argument that was constructed within and against the grain of the new public management (NPM) discourse and different versions of professional collaborative leadership.

I begin these discussions by explaining and critiquing a cultural feminist approach.

Cultural feminism and 'women's ways of leading'

Cultural feminist discourse, as it has developed in the USA, Australia and New Zealand, is an offshoot of radical feminism, following its arguments that within patriarchal male domination, women, as an embattled sisterhood, need to support each other against men, as the enemy (Jones and Guy 1992: 305). Cultural feminism asserts that women have superior allegedly life-giving, innately female values that have been suppressed by men and their 'allegedly innately male, destructive values' (James and Saville-Smith 1989: 60). For example, Firestone (1971) argued that a gendered expressive/technological dichotomy (constructed by men) has stunted women's creativity and contribution to political life. According to Daly (1979), a revaluing of women's special qualities is essential as these are not only distinct from men's, but also *morally* superior. Gilligan's (1982) analysis maintained that as part of their different upbringings, girls experience a different moral development to boys and women develop a female ethics that centres on care, connection and contextual thinking, in contrast to an ethic of rights and justice developed by men. Ruddick's (1989) descriptions of women's forms of 'maternal thinking' have built on these arguments and Belenky's analysis of 'women's ways of knowing' (Belenky *et al.* 1986).

In the field of women in leadership, these analyses and Nodding's (1992) development of the ethic of care have influenced many studies (Blackmore 1999). While some researchers have been careful to distinguish differences in women's approaches (see, for example, Strachan 1999) many cultural feminist analyses tend to develop a universalizing discourse that treats all women as 'naturally' using 'feminine leadership', or a 'women's way of leading' (Rosener 1990). For example, Rogers (1988) described women as orientated towards caring, nurturing and inclusive participatory management practices as part of a 'female ethos', and Helgeson (1991) said that women's biology gave them a 'female advantage' in management. Women educational leaders have been advised to 'use their naturally collaborative and supportive style to elicit other's feelings about their ideas' (Albino 1992: 35). Some cultural feminists discount these kinds of biologically essentialist arguments, favouring instead explanations that gender differences emerge out of socially constructed roles for men and women. Robins and Terrell (1987: 207), for example, argued that '[w]omen learn to share, show compassion, be caring and nurturing ... to co-operate through networking and sharing resources. Men learn to win at all costs ... to compete according to the "old boys'" club rules'.

Whatever the understanding of the origin of gender differences, the effect of most cultural feminist analyses of women in leadership is a slide into an oppositional discourse of masculine versus feminine leadership, such as that constructed by Loden (1985). This presented masculine leadership as competitive, hierarchical, rational, unemotional, analytic, strategic and controlling, and feminine leadership as cooperative, team working, intuitive/rational, focused on high performance, empathetic and collaborative.

In the face of the historical silencing of women's experiences and contributions in leadership in most western societies, it is understandable that some feminists remain very attracted to a cultural feminist analysis. A significant problem in them, however, is that they reinforce 'the feminine as a monolithic, universal category' (Hennessy 1993: 130), privileging gender over other modes of difference, such as those of class, ethnicity, sexuality, personality, values (Weiner 1995; Smulyan 1999; Strachan 1999). The effect is to 'solidify' gender difference, rather than to enable any effective challenge to the practices that construct discriminatory gender dichotomies and hierarchies (Blackmore 1999). While aiming to counter masculinist gender difference discourse, which in western cultures has devalued and marginalized woman as 'other' to man as 'human', cultural feminism's valorizing of 'women's ways of leading' risks merely creating a 'reverse sexism' (Blackmore 1999).

As part of their attempts to develop more effective analyses and strategies for change, feminist post-structuralists influenced by Foucault have focused on the links created in language and other social practices between discourse, knowledge and power.

Introducing a feminist post-structuralist approach

Feminist post-structuralists argue that rather than 'natural' biological differences, or monolithic oppressive structures such as patriarchy, it is 'the range and social power of existing discourses, our access to them and the political strength of the interests they represent' that shape our lives and practices (Weedon 1997: 26). Discourses are understood here as being historically, socially and culturally specific bodies of meaning and knowledge (Foucault 1980a; Davies 1989; Weedon 1997). They are not just language, or ideas and beliefs, or theories about the world. They exist in, produce and are produced by social practices, such as the way we make meanings with words and actions and the ways we organize institutions.

As well as offering a range of competing and often contradictory ways of giving meaning to the world, discourses constitute historically and culturally specific ways of *being* in the world, through constructing different subject positions that individuals can take up. This understanding of discursively shaped subjectivity replaces universalizing and essentialist notions of identity, such as that constructed within a cultural feminist presentation of a woman leader. Feminist post-structuralists argue that a person's subjectivity (her sense of who she is) shifts and changes, as she has new experiences, encounters new discourses and takes up different subject positions (Davies 1989). Subjectivity is thus multiple and fragmented, marked at times by conflict and contradiction as an individual negotiates the differing positions available to her (Court 1995).

These theoretical ideas open up ways of illuminating differences between individual women, as well as enabling analysis of how people shift in their understandings of themselves in relation to others. As such, they provide a helpful alternative to a neo-liberal understanding of 'self' as constructed in an opposition between the 'self' and the 'other', between individual and community (Young 1990; Frazer and Lacey 1993; Mouffe 1995; Fraser 1997). In new public management discourse, for example, the 'self' is understood as autonomous and opportunistically self-interested and social interactions are seen as contractual forms of agreements between individuals (Boston *et al.* 1996). Society is conceived in this discourse as made up of 'atomized, competitive and acquisitive' individuals primarily focused on seeking opportunities and making choices that will better their social, economic and political situations (Middleton 1998: 10). This view gives little importance to 'the ways that individual lives might be lived in the light of something that transcended these [such as] collective goals or aspirations' (Grimshaw 1993: 68). In contrast, within a feminist post-structuralist understanding of individual subjectivity as constructed within discourse and in meaning-making interactions with other people (Davies 1993; Weedon 1997), *mutuality* is foregrounded. As recognition both of and by another, mutuality and inter-subjectivity are understood as a precondition for the constituting of subjectivity *and* for the building of social collectivity (Frazer and Lacey 1993: 175).

These ideas have provided me with useful ways of thinking about why and how some individual women became co-principals and worked with others to build collective co-principalships that challenged dominant discursive understandings and regulations for educational leadership.[3]

The study of women co-principals

In the late 1980s in Aotearoa/New Zealand,[4] within a new right restructuring of educational administration, the principal's role was reconstituted from being a collaborative instructional leader, to being a chief executive, entrepreneurial manager (Department of Education 1988a). The Employment Contracts Act 1991 introduced separate and tightly specified individual contracts for principals and senior school managers, defining their managerial tasks, accountability lines and performance standards in ways that heightened existing divisions between principals and teachers. The possibility of developing flattened, more democratic forms of shared decision-making and leadership seemed increasingly remote. Yet it was in this context that a small number of co-principalships were initiated around the country. This seeming paradox was one of the catalysts for my study of why and how the three primary school co-principalships were initiated. The other was that women initiated these shared leaderships. I wanted to explore how traditional gender power dynamics might be impacting on their ideas and approaches.

During five years' fieldwork, I visited each of the three schools, interviewing the co-principals, board chairpersons, board members, teaching and support staff, and parents, and in one school, students. I also interviewed personnel in the State Services Commission, the Ministry of Education, the School Trustees Association and the New Zealand Educational Institute (NZEI, the primary teachers' union). Further information was gathered within the schools from documents (including Education Review Office school review reports) and from observations of school meetings, class lessons and wider activities. State-level policy, legislative documents, and academic texts about educational leadership and management were also collected and perused to discover what kinds of issues were emerging around and within these shared leadership initiatives.[5]

I focus here on the Hillcrest Avenue co-principalship, drawing on Liz and Jane's stories to assist my discourse analysis of their proposal for initiating a shared leadership.

Initiating change through discursive dis-articulation and re-articulation: Liz and Jane's proposal for a shared leadership at Hillcrest Avenue School

In 1992, Hillcrest Avenue School was a small inner-city school with a top socio-economic decile rating of 10, three teachers and a roll of 64 children. At the end of the year, when two of its teachers left, Karen, the remaining teacher, applied for the principal's position. At the same time, Liz and Jane applied for the vacant positions of principal and senior teacher, proposing that they share them and work towards incorporating Karen (whom they did not know at that stage) into a three-way teaching co-principalship.[6]

When they applied for the positions at Hillcrest, Liz (aged mid-40s) and Jane (mid-50s) were deputy principals in different primary schools. Although they were not close friends, they had worked together teaching a professional development middle management course that drew on their study of professional leadership literature and their own successful experience in positions of responsibility. They had worked together also for the Department of Education, developing gender equity resources for teachers. This work grew out of their (separate) involvement during the 1980s in activist women's groups and Jane's university study of gender issues in education. They told me that these professional and feminist experiences fed into their development of their co-principalship proposal.

Their main goal was to initiate a change in the structure and the power dynamics of the principalship to enable it to be more focused on learning and teaching. They presented their argument as follows.

The proposal (1992)

- That Liz Nicholson and Jane Gilmore job-share the positions of principal and senior teacher.
- That the collaboration involves the third teaching member, support staff and behavioural objectives teacher.

Philosophical issues:

- The proposed collaboration transforms power from a single to a collective base.
- It is a structural change that validates a collaborative school culture.
- It supports a greater degree of consultation and collaboration with the school community.
- It increases responsibility and accountability of all involved.
- It depends on collective vision.
- It acknowledges differences and sameness.
- It is more likely to be focused on learning and teaching and less on trends and personality of the leaders.

Protocol issues:

- Priority is given to establishing clear systems of communication at both high and low levels.
- Sharing administrative tasks.

What are the links?

- Shared vision enhances commitment (ownership), motivation (meaning to the job), and high-level needs through work, teaching skills, school problem-solving.
- Shared vision results in high quality learning and teaching.
- It is an alternative management model for pre-service trainees and the wider educational community.
- Regular review of management structures – staff and board.
- Three-way teaching collaboration.

Their proposal also set out for the board (and for review in two years' time) their goals for learners and a school management approach that emphasized:

- collaborative planning, shared decision-making and collegial work in a framework of experimentation and evaluation;
- school self-review;
- school and teacher development and appraisal systems;
- parent and community consultation and decision-making;
- monitoring and evaluation of children's progress;
- people feel welcomed and involved.

Reflecting or challenging managerial, bureaucratic and professional leadership discourses?

At first glance, Liz and Jane's proposal seems merely to be reflecting a combination of the dominant discourses of educational leadership that were in circulation in Aotearoa/New Zealand in the early 1990s. I want to show, however, how the two women were both taking up *and* challenging different elements of these discourses.

Foucault (1980a) argued that in struggles over meaning-making, ruling groups are able to incorporate other knowledges into their discursive formation. Other discourses are sifted for elements that can be lifted out and re-forged in new configurations that no longer contradict, but support the prevailing 'regime of truth' (Foucault 1980a). The commonsense, universal appeal of such 'truth' (or a hegemonic formation) emerges as a consequence of the ways that elements from a wide range of discourses are appropriated and reshaped into a 'coherent frame of intelligibility' (Hennessy 1993). Liz and Jane's proposal and stories show how this kind of discursive sifting can occur also in resistant practices.

As I noted earlier, Liz and Jane were working in an education system that was regulated within the 'market managerial discourse' of new public management (introduced in New Zealand the late 1980s (Boston *et al.* 1996)). This positioned the school principal as a chief executive officer, requiring her/him to work with the board of trustees to define a 'hierarchy of objectives and priorities at all levels of the administrative structure' and to establish 'clear lines of accountability' to ensure the driving up of standards (Department of Education 1988a: 42).[7] An echo of this discourse appears in Liz and Jane's statement that a shared leadership 'increases the responsibility and accountability of all involved'. The NPM hierarchical and individualist managerial meanings of this phrase are altered, however, in their linking of accountability to collective responsibility and collaborative practices.

This linking is not surprising. Collaborative teamwork has remained a commonly accepted practice in schools, despite the new right revolution. Indeed, reformers into their arguments for change incorporated some elements of professional collaborative leadership discourse. Consequently, in the *Review of Educational Administration* (Picot Report), there is a somewhat contradictory constitution of the principal as a chief executive officer with managerial powers of control *and* as a 'professional and instructional leader, whose collaborative relationship with staff must be protected and enhanced' (Department of Education 1988a: 51). What critics of the new managerialism often overlook, however, is that within the 'bureaucratic discourse of professional educational leadership', collaboration was constituted and widely understood as enacted within clearly defined roles and mechanisms for collegiality (Cardno 1990). As an instructional leader, the principal was responsible for overseeing 'in-class supervision, in-service training and observation opportunities' for staff (Department of Education 1984). As a team leader, s/he was positioned at the head of a chain of influence and control, holding veto power and final accountability for all management decisions.

Liz and Jane's co-principal proposal was aiming to undo also these largely unproblematized professional hierarchies of influence and control. They envisioned instead a mutually influencing sharing of instructional leadership roles and responsibilities with each other and with Karen, the third teacher in the school, whom they proposed should join them in a fully flat, three-way teaching co-principalship.

Their proposal statement that such a shared leadership would transform power from a single to a collective base suggests that they were taking up a transformational leadership discourse. Promoted in education by theorists such as Foster (1989) and Sergiovanni (1992), 'transformational leadership discourse'[8] constructs the principal's role as an ethical educational leader engaged in a form of servant leadership, distributing leadership throughout the school. The aim of transformative leadership is to raise both leader and followers to a higher moral plane of shared commitment to educative principles and democratic collegial participation. In Aotearoa/New Zealand, Stewart and Prebble (1993: 188–189) married this discourse to a cultural management approach, presenting the reflective principal as centrally concerned with 'identify[ing] a set of core values, beliefs and practices and socialis[ing] teachers into these ... through collaborative decision making, shared planning and evaluation ... and constant discussion'. They argued that the main role of the principal should be encouraging organizational members to develop a 'passionate commitment' to the core culture, thus transforming it into a learning community. Liz and Jane had read some of Sergiovanni's writing on collaborative servant leadership and they had both attended David Stewart's reflective principal courses. Rose Fleming, who was a lecturer on this course, said:

> Some of the key ideas in the leadership courses were about trans-
> formational leadership and having a kind of diffused leadership so
> that all the teachers in the school were sharing that role. We were
> talking about it in theory, but I knew that Jane and Liz were doing it
> in practice – already – in their work as deputy principals in their own
> schools.

While their proposal does seem to echo elements of cultural management
and transformative leadership discourses, on a closer reading it also decon-
structs some elements. For example, the principal is commonly presented in
these discourses as a charismatic individual who personifies the school
(Stewart and Prebble 1993: 189) and 'shapes and shares a vision which gives
point to the work of others' (Handy 1992). Liz was critical of these ideas. She
told me, 'I used to think that good principals were charismatic visionaries. I
don't think that any more. Vision is important, but no one individual is more
important than anyone else.' She and Jane argued instead that a co-principalship would be focused less on trends and the personality of the leader and
more on teaching and learning.

Their statement that a co-principalship would 'transform power from a
single to a collective base' is worth further examination in relation to arguments put forward in a critical discourse of democratic leadership. Angus
(1989: 87), for example, maintained that in a democratic approach to school
leadership, 'power and authority would be regarded as reciprocal, relational
concepts ... and reform can be asserted from below by participants'. The
statement that reform can 'be asserted *from below*' (my emphasis) indicates
how a structural hierarchy persists even in this social justice organizational
discourse. It was this structural hierarchy between leaders and followers that
Liz and Jane set out to change.

What, though, had brought them to this point?

Liz: drawing on radical and cultural feminist discourse to argue for a structural change

Liz told me how her feminism had influenced her decision to initiate a co-
principalship as an attempt to change organizational hierarchy and unequal
power relations. She described how during the early 1980s she had worked
with NZEI women activists who were challenging the government's broken
service policy[9] and proposing a retraining scheme for teachers who had had
time out of full-time teaching. Liz was inspired by this NZEI group of women,
saying 'they gave me a strong analysis of myself as a woman and as an activist'. She said she came to 'realize how powerful women can be if they group
together – they can be really good at thinking through a strategy, and can be

really cunning and wise'. She believed also that women have 'feminine qualities of being interconnective, sensitively listening, caring and nurturing', but she said that her feminism was more than this: it was 'about a change in a power structure in society and a belief in the importance and power of women in the world', While she said, 'I would probably be a reasonably radical feminist in my personal beliefs', her comments reveal how cultural feminist discourse had also strongly influenced her.

Liz said that she tried out her feminist beliefs about collectivity and power sharing during the time she was seconded into a school liaison team as an advisor and while she worked in a very collaborative deputy-principal/principal partnership. She further tested her ideas in relation to transformational leadership literature when she participated in the reflective principal course, developing there her own critique of visionary leadership. It was her stories about these experiences that alerted me to the way that the co-principal proposal contains echoes of her discursive agency. In the proposal, the word 'transform' had been disarticulated from professional transformative leadership discourse and re-articulated within a combination of radical and cultural feminist discourses, which aim to 'transform power from a single to a collective base'.

In the early radical feminist collectives, an important aim was to 'transform' bureaucratic organizational structures and power relations that were seen as endorsing singular, masculinist forms of leadership (Rothschild 1994). Indeed, individual leadership was eschewed, on the assumption that it would lead inevitably to hierarchy and the capture of power and control by an individual, destroying group cohesion.[10] Instead, egalitarianism was stressed as a fundamental value, with the aim of every member having equal status and rights of participation. Singular power was assumed to be 'bad' and collective power 'good'. Both assumptions have underpinned a radical feminist understanding of power as exercised oppressively by men (as individuals in personal relationships and collectively through patriarchal systems) to subordinate women within a male-dominated society. Whereas men's collective power was analysed as oppressive, within a cultural feminist discourse, women's collective power was constructed as beneficial, enabling individuals to support one another's development of personal potential and to contribute to building a sisterhood for political change in patriarchal gender relations.

Liz was drawing on these kinds of ideas in her understanding of the co-principalship as a woman-centred collectivity that could challenge a masculinist managerialist system.[11] 'I have a strong commitment to women, as a group,' she told me. 'I suppose, for me, women are the most important thing in the world. I like the way they work, I feel more in tune with them philosophically.'

A cultural feminist could cite these comments as evidence that Liz's initiation of the co-principalship was founded in a women's approach to leadership. In another of her stories, however, Liz told me how she had observed some rather destructive struggles in a women's centre around identity politics and the correct feminist way to build a sisterhood. She described how some 'lesbian feminists challenged some other women with questions like, "Why on earth aren't you a lesbian if you like women?" It was so ugly and unpleasant.' Her commitment to feminism and her (still fairly uncritical) belief in women survived this experience, but she said that she had learned how differences between women could result in nasty struggles over power. She wanted instead to value women's differences. In the proposal's statements that the co-principalship would acknowledge differences and sameness, there is an echo of these experiences and Liz's beginning to unpick cultural feminist essentialism.

Jane: drawing on professional and liberal feminist discourse to 'validate' collaboration

The stories Jane told me about her experiences show that, like Liz, she respected and valued people's differences and that, for her also, the co-principalship was about power-sharing. Her ideas about this had developed in the first instance not within feminism, however, but within her professional experience, when she had worked with a collaborative male principal. She said:

> [H]e involved all the staff in a review of the school. This was quite innovative then. Young teachers' ideas were considered equally to those who held positions of responsibility. There was a lot of power sharing. As a relieving Scale A teacher, I was made the leader of a three-teacher syndicate. That was quite influential for me.

Jane's comment debunks cultural feminist generalizations about male power as destructive, competitive and hierarchical.

Jane had been influenced by liberal feminism thought. She said, 'I think intuitively I was a feminist – not consciously, but doing a Gender and Education paper made me think about things that haven't felt right ... things like fairness ... and some awful things have been done to women, myself included.' She described how she had experienced getting back into teaching after being out for three months looking after her brother's children.[12] When she and her friends lobbied politicians about her situation, and she was subsequently offered work, she was appalled by this, saying it was political – the classic 'who you know'. This experience highlighted for her contradictions between the rhetoric of liberal egalitarian discourse and discriminatory state educational employment practices. She realized that there were things about the system that were wrong. Her interest in a liberal feminist focus on identifying discrimination and developing legal remedies fed into her later thinking about women in leadership and finding new and fairer ways of organizing the work of teaching and learning.

Jane's positioning of herself within both professional collaborative and liberal feminist discourses can be read in the second of the proposal's philosophical issues, that 'structural change validates a collaborative school culture'. A liberal feminist interest in finding legal solutions appears in the word 'validates', which suggests that there cannot be a legitimate culture of collaboration in a school without changing the (implied hierarchical bureaucratic and managerial) structure that positions the principal at the head of a pyramid of authority, status and control.

Collective agency as intersubjective discursive negotiations

I have been showing how the women's stories indicate the different ways they were drawing on a range of discourses available to them, as they considered and built some agreements about shared leadership. Their proposal can be read as the result of intersubjective discursive negotiation and meaning-making. Elements of both women's professional values and commitments and slightly different feminist positionings appear in the beginning construction of their new collective identity as the Hillcrest Avenue School co-principalship. For example, Jane's liberal feminist commitment to validating structural change was articulated alongside Liz's radical feminist aim to transform power. As Mouffe (1995) put it, a collectivity can be understood as formed through a convergence of different privately negotiated subject positions around a shared commitment.

As I indicated in my earlier comments on the Picot Report and on Liz's beliefs about women, however, these kinds of discursive negotiations can be uneven and at times, contradictory. In some parts of their proposal Liz and Jane critiqued and deconstructed particular elements of bureaucratic professional discourse, but in others, bureaucratic practices and connotations of hierarchy appear to be uncritically reinscribed. For example, they stated that 'job descriptions, mission statement, goals, administrative tasks' supported their proposal. They said they would give 'priority to establishing systems of communication and decision-making at both high and low levels' and that the shared leadership would 'increase the accountability of all involved'. These statements are all redolent of bureaucratic and managerialist discourse and they could be read as indications that Liz and Jane were complying with the demands of the wider hierarchical system in which the school and their work were, of course, embedded.

These statements could also be read in a Foucauldian sense, however,

as strategic, that is, as Liz and Jane's tactical recognition of the need to acknowledge demands from the state agencies for clear, accountable management systems in schools. Hennessy (1993) has argued that the cultural power
of discursive dis-articulation and re-articulation processes depends on how
successfully the previous ways of understanding and doing things are challenged and then incorporated into a new form of discourse. If these processes
are successful, the new formulation will accrue some legitimacy by acknowledging and taking on board some of the claims of the opposing discourses. Liz and Jane certainly used the language of the prevailing discourses
in parts of their proposal. Liz also told me, however, that at this stage in her
life she was 'working within the structures of education to bring about a
specific change in the hierarchical ways that schools are run, so that there
could be a more power-sharing way of working'. And Jane said, 'it's no good
just saying we'll make it shared. You had to validate it through structural
change. That's the crunch really.'

Extending intersubjective negotiations

During the selection processes, some further significant intersubjective links
were made between Liz and Jane's discursive positionings and understandings
of leadership and collectivity and those held by the board members who
interviewed them. Naomi was a feminist, who spoke through a liberal feminist analysis of the under-representation of women in leadership positions,
and a radical feminist criticism of the male management model in education,
in support of Liz and Jane's proposal. She wanted to change what she described as that whole (male-dominated) approach and was attracted particularly by the idea of a structural change to collectivity. Mary, while not
committed to a feminist analysis, was an educational researcher committed to
a professional discourse that placed the best interests of the children first. She
responded to Liz and Jane's clear commitment to a learning and teaching
focus for the co-principalship. Phil was a union leader who had done academic study in the area of organizational analysis and workplace change. He
was attracted to a collectivist approach that could challenge hierarchy and
narrow views of accountability. These board members were thus very supportive of the co-principal proposal and they wanted it extended to include
Karen, the third teacher in the school.

The agencies the board consulted during the principal selection process
were constructing the co-principalship proposal within different discursive
frameworks that made them critical of its arguments. They were committed,
of course, to an NPM discourse that required a sole principal to ensure accountability. I have explained elsewhere (Court 1998) how the board negotiated an agreement with them that each year: one of the women would be

named as principal. This agreement was kept confidential, however, to protect the co-principals' collaboration as a team of equals sharing leadership.

Karen's positioning of herself within a bureaucratic version of professional team leadership led her to initially turn down the board's invitation to
her to join Liz and Jane in the co-principalship. She was worried that 'things
would slip between the cracks'. After Liz and Jane's appointment though, as a
consequence of observing and becoming involved in Liz and Jane's different
approach to teamwork, she was soon drawn into the co-principalship. How
that happened and the ways that these three women built a very successful
three-way collaboration is another story, however (see Court 2001).

Conclusion

Although some bureaucratic and managerialist discourses may have become
normalized 'regimes of truth' (Foucault 1980a) in the field of educational
leadership, these discourses are not impenetrable or impermeable. My analysis has shown how individual and collective agency can be enacted within
and against dominant discourses. Following Weedon (1997), I have argued
that it was Liz and Jane's recognition of contradictions between co-existing
discourses that opened up for them the possibility of initiating change. They
dis-articulated elements of dominant discourses and re-articulated them
within feminist discourses to build a counter-discourse of co-principalship as
collective educational leadership.

Foucault (1977: 200) commented that 'it is usually the case that a discursive practice assembles a number of diverse disciplines or sciences or
crosses a certain number among them and regroups many of their individual
characteristics into a new and occasionally unexpected unity'. At the level of
their local school, the women's shared leadership proposal and practices can
be seen to be enacting a similar dynamic (Court 2001). As such, this co-
principal initiative shows us how individuals and groups can indeed impact
on dominant discourses and the remaking of cultural understandings, contributing to transformations of practice (Davies 1997; Fraser 1997).

A cultural feminist analysis of women in educational leadership, as ex-
hibiting a set of common characteristics that are essentially different from
men's, cannot enable these insights. Its theoretical tools are not sharp enough
to tease out the multiple motivations and intersubjective negotiations I have
been discussing. In contrast, feminist post-structuralists argue that if we are
alerted to the work being done by the various discourses we are invoking, we
can then more effectively reflect on and change limiting and disempowering
discursive practices, such as those that have marginalized women in the field
of educational leadership.

Notes

1. An earlier version of this chapter was published in *Leading and Managing* (2002) 8(2): 110–122, and is published here with permission.
2. 'Pakeha' means white European or non-Maori.
3. A more detailed discussion of the methodologies and research processes I used can be found in Court (forthcoming).
4. 'Aotearoa' is the aboriginal name of New Zealand.
5. All names of schools and people in this study are pseudonyms.
6. I have described elsewhere what happened during the selection processes (Court 1998). Suffice to say here that the board appointed Liz and Jane as co-principals; Karen worked closely with them and joined the co-principalship at the end of 1993. Although these three women later left the school, their co-principalship model is still working successfully there.
7. *Tomorrow's Schools*, the government's restructuring policy paper, further reduced the principal's leadership role to a middle manager, focused on implementation of state and board policy and completion of tasks such as preparatory work on the charter, allocation of staff duties and performance measurement (Department of Education 1988b: 11).
8. Burns (1978) originally proposed this view in contrast to a transactional view of leadership as involving bargaining negotiations.
9. This was introduced in 1975 as a response to the surplus of bonded teachers. It meant that education boards were required to put to one side the applications of teachers who had not had continuous service.
10. It was argued, for example, that the creation of stars through practices such as a woman becoming spokesperson to the media should be avoided.
11. The market managerial construction of the principal as a chief executive is highly compatible with powerful or hegemonic forms of masculinity (Blackmore 1999). Connell (1987) identified the latter as inflected currently with technical and calculation skills (necessary for balancing the ever tighter budgets) and a confident, competitive toughness (as required for marketing a school's image, or for ensuring that staff measure up).
12. During the 1970s, all those who had had continuous teaching service were given access to vacant positions ahead of those with broken service: the latter were mainly women who had had time out for childcare.

2 Does Size Matter? The Interaction between Principal Gender, Level of Schooling and Institutional Scale in Australian Schools

John Collard

Context

Australian schools are highly feminized workplaces but men hold disproportionate percentages of principalships. In the late 1990s, approximately 69 per cent of teachers in Australia were women, but they constituted only one-third of school principals. This was consistent with broader patterns in the Australian workforce, where 73 per cent of those who classified themselves as managers and administrators were men (Australian Bureau of Statistics 1998). In Victoria, the second most populous state and where this study was conducted, the proportions in principalships adhered to the national pattern: males 67 per cent, females 33 per cent (Curriculum Corporation 1996). It would seem that observations about British and Canadian schools as institutions where 'men manage and women teach' (Ozga 1993; Reynolds 1995) are therefore equally applicable to Australia.

Previous interpretations

Past explanations for the low proportion of women in the principalship in western democracies have argued that it reflects traditional gender roles which sanction teaching as an appropriate sphere for the emotional labour of women but precludes them from school leadership (Blackmore 1993; Reynolds 1995). Conversely, it is claimed that men have been advantaged by patriarchal traditions of public leadership (Hearn 1993; Seidler 1994). Feminists have critiqued educational administration as 'gender blind' and as a 'masculinist enterprise' that consistently marginalizes women (Shakeshaft 1987; Blackmore 1993, 1999; Rusch and Marshall 1995). Multiple role theorists have linked the reluctance of women to apply for principal positions to their other life-roles as wives and nurturers which are incompatible with the demands of public leadership (Antonucci 1980; Acker 1989; Darley and Lomax 1995). Organizational theorists have pointed to the cultures and structures of the workplace as forces which systematically discriminate against and marginalize women from promotional tracks whereas male networks advantage men (Kanter 1977; Connell 1987; Russell 1995). The culture of educational administration itself, especially the limited nature and sexist assumptions that infuse the dominant journals and university coursework, has also been identified as a contributing factor (Rusch and Marshall 1995).

Much preceding leadership discourse has been based upon essentialist assumptions that there are all-pervasive differences between men and women. Unitary stereotypes depict men as 'directive, bureaucratic and instrumental' and women as 'collaborative, relational and organic' (Ferguson 1984; Adler *et al.* 1993). Gilligan's (1982) research into personal decision-making concluded that men operate from a values base of 'abstract principle' and women from a 'relational focus'. This has been generalized to professional contexts. Gray's (1989) gender paradigms in schools are an extreme example of such typologies. He linked a feminine paradigm to primary schools and a masculine paradigm with secondary schools. He characterized the culture of the 'nurturant feminine primary school' as 'caring, regulated, creative, intuitive, aware of individual differences, non-competitive, tolerant and subjective'. Conversely, secondary schools were claimed to conform to a 'masculine aggressive paradigm', which values 'conformity, discipline, group norms, competition evaluation and objectivity' (Gray 1989: 111). However, in typecasting schools according to an essentialist gender framework, he failed to question whether these characteristics might be more directly related to the work, scale and structures of primary and secondary education.

The study upon which this chapter is based moved beyond essentialist naiveté by exploring whether the level of schooling, organizational scale and the cultures had influenced the cognitive frameworks of the men and women leaders. The study therefore parallels developments in the field of gender studies, where more fine-tuned theories have framed studies of gender relations in diverse social contexts. Connell's (1995) concept of 'multiple forms of masculinity and femininity' argues that various socio-economic cultures generate diverse forms of masculinity within Australia. He illustrates this through case studies of working-class, environmental, gay and corporate cultures. He also alerts us to different forms of femininity ranging from compliance with patriarchal cultures to active contestation of them. A logical extension of this perspective is to argue that the characteristics, cultures and histories of particular schools and sectors generate diverse forms of leadership by men and women. Indeed, there is a rich heritage of theory in educational administration, which argues that organizational context is a key influence upon leader behaviour (Greenfield 1975; Avolio and Bass 1988). Recent work from the UK supports such claims. Level of schooling has been identified as a factor, which differentiates the cognitive maps of principals (Hall 1996; Pascal and Ribbins 1998). It is also possible that similar contexts may ameliorate differences between men and women and draw them towards a consensus, which belies oppositional typecasts.

The status of gender typologies in the field of educational leadership is also questionable because they have been based upon limited case studies and narrative accounts (Adler *et al.* 1993; Ozga 1993; Hurty 1995; Hall 1996; Fennell 1999; Limerick and Anderson 1999). The evidence to sustain them is simply inadequate. They cannot be regarded as incontrovertible foundations upon which to build subsequent theory, research and practice and we are well advised to heed recent advice to question such stereotypes (Blackmore 1999; Grogan 2000). This study therefore also attempted to redress the lack of quantitative research in the field by testing the claims of qualitative research across a broad sample of male and female principals.

Research method

In 1996, 76 per cent of Victorian school principals ($n = 2259$) were in primary sites and 24 per cent in secondary schools (Curriculum Corporation 1996). The proportion of females was much higher at primary than at secondary levels (62 per cent compared with 25 per cent). A questionnaire was administered to a stratified sample of principals from both levels of schooling. It drew upon contemporary research findings (Johnson and Holdaway 1991; Ribbins 1999) and direct knowledge of the tasks of Victorian principals. Subjects were asked to respond to items according to a five-point Likert-like scale ranging from strong disagreement to strong agreement. The constellations included perceptions and beliefs about:

- student abilities;
- curriculum goals and pedagogy;
- working with teachers;
- the roles of parent and community members;
- the nature of principalship;
- personal and professional wellbeing.

Each section explored a continuum ranging from hierarchical and bureaucratic to relational and collaborative concepts and, in this respect, sought to test beliefs and values which essentialist theorists have stereotyped as masculine and feminine. The sections on teacher and parent roles, and on the principalship itself, juxtaposed directive and exclusive stances with collaborative and participatory approaches. When it came to personal and professional wellbeing, the items ranged from isolated and aloof stances to collegial modes. A key aspect of this section was the use of metaphors of leadership, which elicited affective responses whereas the rest of the questionnaire relied upon more abstract statements.

A total of 371 questionnaires were returned, establishing a response rate of 73.4 per cent. Of these, 51.1 per cent were male principals and 49.9 per cent female. A method of bivariate analysis was utilized to explore associations between variables. Responses were tabulated according to frequencies and then cross-tabulated according to the variables of gender, school level, sectoral identity, student gender and school size. The cross-tabulations were then analysed using the Pearson Test of Statistical Significance. Associations at the 0.05, 0.01 and 0.001 levels were considered significant and unlikely to be a function of sampling error. This method also enabled analysis of data in the form of paired observations on two variables such as principal gender and school level or school size. The findings indicated the presence or absence of a relationship between the two variables, and also permitted a second level of analysis to determine whether the pattern, according to principal gender as a solitary variable, remained stable when factors such as school level and size were investigated.

Interviews were also conducted with equal proportions of male and female volunteer respondents who had completed the questionnaire. Twenty-four transcripts, twelve from each level of schooling, were selected for analysis. The data were used to confirm, supplement and expand understandings based upon the quantitative data. Passages, which illustrated or provided insights into key findings from the questionnaire, were identified and transcribed. As such it was akin to a validation exercise, in that the knowledge claims, which had emerged from the quantitative research, were tested through a dialogue between researcher and a representative sample of the population who completed the questionnaire (Evers and Lakomski 1996a,b; Kvale 1996). Responses, which contradicted or qualified the questionnaire data and new emergent themes, were also noted. Although six months separated the two processes, there was a high degree of consistency in responses. The combined method was a serious attempt to redress the absence of representative studies in the field and to supplement broad findings with understandings of the meanings and complexities, which characterize principals' beliefs in the lived world.

Key findings according to principal gender

The findings of this study confirm, extend and modify previous claims about differences between male and female leaders (Collard 2001, 2003a,b,c). Claims that women are more responsive to the needs of individuals and groups (Gray 1989) were confirmed. This tendency manifested itself in a stronger commitment to more diverse forms of curriculum provision, whereas men were more likely to be satisfied if generic programmes were in place. As a group, women also had higher expectations of student abilities. Claims that men are more aligned to instrumental and technical curriculum values, and women more orientated towards personal-developmental objectives (Ferguson 1984; Hearn 1993) also received support. However, this apparent conformity to gender stereotypes was qualified by interview responses from both groups. Many argued that a polarization between personal developmental and utilitarian goals was too arbitrary, and that the two were interdependent. A male high school principal from a regional city insisted upon the holistic development of the student, and argued: '... in a school they interrelate, you can't have one without the other. Anytime a school concentrates too much on the academic and not on the personal ... the academic will be unsuccessful. Personal development must co-exist with the academic, it must be of equal value.' Such responses suggest that the more reflective practitioners transcend gender polarities and that more fine-grained theory is required to capture such complexity.

This study only found qualified support for claims that women are more orientated to the ethics of care and service than men (Noddings 1984; Shakeshaft 1987; Hall 1996). While women were more sensitive to individual and group learning needs, there was strong evidence in interviews that many male leaders also subscribe to such values. It could be argued that a stronger nurturant sensibility was reflected in the fact that higher proportions of women identified with the image of 'advocate for children'. However, two-thirds of those who viewed themselves as 'responsible parent figures' were men. This may reflect a patriarchal mindset but it also indicates a strong sense of responsibility and care. The different image preferences suggest that men and women perceive their custodial roles in different ways, but this does not lead to the conclusion that they hold different values. Such findings raise the possibility that differences between male and female leaders may be related more to different perceptual lenses than opposed beliefs.

There was some support for claims that men are more autonomous, rational and analytical than women (Gilligan 1982; Craib 1987; Steinberg 1993; Seidler 1994). Women were markedly more committed to collegiality and teamwork. They were more willing to foster a consultative climate within the school and allow staff to participate in decision-making. They were more receptive to advice and demonstrated a greater tolerance for debate about goals and policies. However, such receptivity did not characterize their beliefs about parent participation. They were less optimistic and responsive in this area than men, who were more willing to consult parents and to engage them as participants in the school community. Such findings contradict an essentialist relational thesis by suggesting that female receptiveness may not extend beyond the schoolyard. This related to another recurrent pattern in the study. Women leaders were less orientated to forces outside the school than were the men. This applied to parents, system activity, and even to consultation with other principals. It suggests that the female principals in Victoria were more internally focused within the organization, the men more sensitive to outside forces. This lends credence to claims that male principals are more politically aware than their female counterparts (Crow and Pounders 1995; Ford 1997).

There was consistent evidence that men perceive their leadership in terms of maintaining authority, status and organizational control (Ferguson 1984; Gray 1989; Hudson and Jacot 1991; Steinberg 1993). They leaned more towards strong, directive approaches than did women, and believed teachers and parents expect such leadership and comply with decisions made in this mode. These beliefs were allied with their tendency to view teachers as agents responsible for fulfilling the policy mandates of authorities, whether they come from an institutional or a systemic level. A logical consequence was their preference for solid structural boundaries for accountability and re-porting within schools. They were also more orientated towards consistent policy and practice. Such tendencies were consistent with their stronger tendency to identify with the image of 'line manager'. Some would view these findings as evidence of a bureaucratic mindset and the polar opposite of the alleged relational modes of women. Men were also more inclined to see themselves as 'initiators', and identify with metaphors of stability such as 'a voice of authority' and 'a rock in stormy waters'. These could be typecast as traditional masculine qualities (Gronn 1995).

Women in this study were more strongly orientated towards consultative and participatory modes of working with staff than were men. They believed teachers want collaborative leadership and favoured collective responsibility rather than frameworks for accountability. The women also held more active conceptions of teachers as 'continuing learners', placed greater value upon teacher autonomy, and were more prepared to grant space for innovation and adaptation of sectorial policies to local realities. They were also more inclined to believe that teachers would question unilateral decisions whereas men were more likely to expect them to implement system mandates without dissent. This was not to say that women lacked strong leadership vision. Indeed, they were more confident that they held an appropriate vision for the school community than were the men. The difference lay more in the way the vision was determined. Men appeared more predisposed to transmit a vision from a position of hierarchical authority, women to engage in more colla-borative processes.

The study also confirmed claims that women are more orientated towards educational leadership than were men (Shakeshaft 1987; Ford 1997). They were more focused on learning issues for both students and staff and held their views with stronger conviction. The fact that they were more likely to view themselves as 'leading learners' was consistent with this trend. Differences between the genders on pedagogical issues were only marginal but women were much more opposed to a competitive ethic, and this lends some support to gender stereotypes. However, they were also more committed to uniform curriculum structures and programme adherence, and this contradicts polarized images of rigid male bureaucrats and flexible women leaders. It suggests that women were actually more definite in their views about curriculum provision. Just as they were more sensitive to the need to cater for individual and group differences, they were also more insistent that the response to such diversity must be structured and systematic. Their sensitivity was more than an ethic of care; it was a strong professional commitment to providing appropriate learning structures for diverse populations of students.

Key findings according to school level

There was consistent evidence that school level was linked to significant differences throughout the sample. At times it reinforced differences between the two genders; at others it united them in shared belief systems. There were also instances where it generated divisions within either gender. However, school size was a less consistent influence upon differences across the six research themes than anticipated. It was most strongly associated with variations in relationships with teachers and beliefs about leadership itself. On issues such as curriculum, pedagogy, attitudes towards parents, and even personal wellbeing, the differences were rarely statistically significant. However, they frequently parallelled trends according to level of schooling, and thereby indicated the interactive nature of these two variables.

The two genders were in much closer alignment in primary schools than they were in secondary sites and this appears to be a consequence of both the nature and the smaller scale of the enterprise. Both men and women at this level tended to share a commitment to collaborative values in their relationships within the school community and in their beliefs about learning and teaching. Secondary school leaders supported more hierarchical and structured forms of leadership. However, this was more so among the men than among the women, and therefore suggests that the nature of secondary schools reinforces tendencies towards formality and authoritarianism in male principals.

Primary school principals were the most committed to fostering student self-esteem (90 per cent) and to meeting the learning needs of diverse individuals and groups. This suggests that the work of laying foundations in the early years of schooling was a strong influence in this regard. Secondary leaders were less orientated towards personal-developmental goals and more focused upon utilitarian ones (80 per cent). This was true for both men and women but with one major exception. Over three-quarters (76 per cent) of female principals from independent secondary schools identified personal-developmental goals as a top curriculum goal, and this was much higher than the proportions from other secondary schools (66 per cent). This suggests that sectoral culture and traditions can also generate differences which ameliorate the influence of gender and school level. In this instance, the origins can be traced to the curriculum legacy of the Victorian era when independent girls' schools placed great emphasis upon 'feminine accomplishments' (Theobald 1996).

The more collaborative values of primary leaders were also evident in their approaches to working with teachers and parents. They were much more inclined to engage staff in consultation and decision-making, and to tolerate debate about goals and policies. They were also more likely to rely upon collective processes to ensure organizational harmony and accountability. In contrast, Victorian secondary principals perceived teachers as more autonomous and territorial beings, and were more reliant upon structures and accountabilities to ensure cohesion. They were less consultative than primary leaders and more inclined to regard the process as time-consuming and inefficient. Such a contrast is understandable when one considers the more segmented structures and larger scale of secondary schools. Secondary leaders were also less inclined to rely upon advice from other principals than were their primary colleagues. This indicates that they were more self-contained within the sites where they provided leadership.

Leaders from primary sites believed that parents had higher expectations about active engagement in the life of the school than those from the secondary level. They were consequently more orientated towards consulting them, to acknowledge that they had a substantial role to play in policy development and to view them as a political force. Secondary leaders were less inclined to believe that parents want active participation and were also less confident about the quality of relationships between parents and schools. However, there were significant variations between secondary leaders according to sector. Government leaders (88 per cent) were the most committed to promoting parent participation whereas those from independent schools were much more exclusive. They were the least likely to believe that they should be consulted or engaged in policy development and did not see them to be substantially involved in decision-making or political agency (58 per cent). Once again we are led to the conclusion that sectorial culture modifies differences according to school level.

The more aloof and authoritarian stance of secondary leaders was reflected in the finding that they were also more isolated and stressed than their primary equivalents (30 per cent compared with 20 per cent). They were also less likely to believe that the role of principal brought out the best in them (70 per cent compared with 81 per cent). This suggests that their morale was lower, and it was consistent that they were less inclined to plan to continue in the role. Primary leaders were more optimistic in both regards. However, they were more likely to experience conflict between personal and professional roles, and this was markedly more so for the females. Men were more likely to experience such tension at the secondary level. It is possible that their more solitary approach to leadership entails a heavy sense of personal responsibility, which generates tension between personal and professional spheres at this level.

Key findings according to school size

The relationship between level of schooling and school size was ambiguous. On matters such as perceptions of students, staff and parents there was clear correspondence between the two variables. On other matters such as industrial relations and professional morale, the pattern was more complicated. Clear distinctions according to school level were less evident in relation to these themes. This implies that on such matters, organizational scale can exert an influence, which is independent of level of schooling, and can also contradict anticipated patterns according to gender stereotypes. The rest of this chapter will explore the impact of organizational scale upon the principals' relationships with teachers and parents, their beliefs about leadership, and their perceptions relating to their professional wellbeing.

Working with teachers

There was a distinct polarization according to school size in how principals in the study perceived teachers. Those from schools with fewer than 300 pupils were the most likely to view them as collaborative beings. In schools with more than 600 pupils, almost half (48 per cent) viewed them as autonomous agents within classroom domains. Men were more likely to hold such a perception in all schools but those between 801 and 1000 pupils. However, there was also a sharp rise in the proportions of women who shared this perception in schools with more than 400 pupils. This suggests that the tendency among female leaders in small schools to perceive teachers as collaborators, is displaced by a view of them as autonomous beings as school size increases. It is likely that when schools reach enrolments above 600 pupils, their organization becomes more segmented and teachers more specialized – especially at the secondary level. This appears to reinforce perceptions of both male and female teachers as territorial.

There was also evidence of increased support for programme conformity as size expanded. Insistence upon adherence to programmes increased

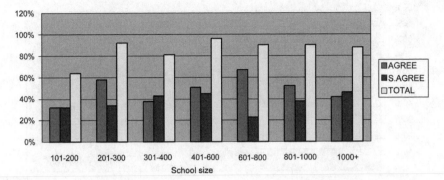

Figure 2.1 Principals' insistence upon adherence to programmes. Proportions of agreement and strong agreement according to school size (statistical significance 0.01, 24df).

markedly in schools with more than 300 pupils, and this trend was consistent for all schools above this benchmark (Figure 2.1).

The lowest support for such adherence came from the smallest primary sites. It is possible that leaders from such sites see little need to insist upon programme conformity because the scale of the schools means they are likely to be working intimately with teachers on classroom matters. It therefore appears that it is the size of the institution, rather than gender or the level of education, which exerts pressure upon leaders to move towards more directive modes of working with teachers. This finding further suggests that a principal's working style with teachers may be as much influenced by practical imperatives as by gender or philosophical beliefs.

Another finding, which was consistent with the preceding ones, was that leaders from the smallest schools were more likely to believe they had harmonious relationships and a shared sense of purpose with teachers. Such confidence declined dramatically in schools with more than 400 pupils (Figure 2.2).

The confidence of women leaders declined more constantly with increases in size than that of men. The only exception to this was women from schools with more than 1000 pupils. With this qualification, it is evident that women become marginally less confident about the quality of their relationships with staff than men in schools of more than 300, and the gap continued to expand after that. Gender theorists may claim that this reflects the greater sensitivity of women to such matters. It is particularly interesting that confidence in teamwork faltered in the middle-sized schools from 300 to 600 pupils. Such a finding was masked by analysis according to level of schooling. It suggests that as organizational size expands and the nature of the institution becomes more complex, less reliance can be placed upon an organic sense of collaboration. This may be true of larger primary schools as

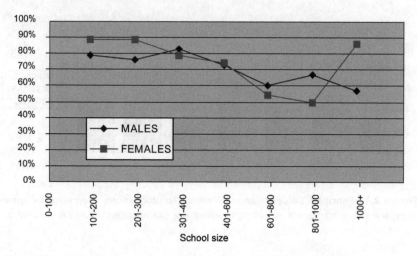

Figure 2.2   Principals' belief of a shared sense of purpose with teachers. Proportions of agreement according to principal gender and school size (statistical significance 0.01, 24df).

well as secondary sites, where the forces for collective and directive leadership styles intersect, conflict and undermine faith in collaboration.

Interview data indicated that women leaders were particularly sensitive to this dynamic. One from a Catholic secondary school complained that in a previous site she was able 'to sit the staff in a circle' but that in the larger school she was currently leading, such dialogue 'was impossible'. Another from one of the rare primary sites with over 800 pupils was struggling to combat the imperative towards more authoritarian structures through the use of teams:

> The whole school is structured into a variety of teams and I guess that occurs even more because of the size of the place ... [E]ach of my grade areas works as a team, ... the curriculum leader of each of those teams is one of my leading teachers. They are responsible for the curriculum management in that area. They are supported by and they have their own team meetings. ... [T]here is an administrative team in the school which of course is my assistant principal and myself, and my most experienced senior teacher who is the Curriculum Co-ordinator ... we work very strongly as a team. There are teams feeding into teams all the way through.

However, the data indicate that women who created innovative structures to combat the impact of expanded size upon staff relationships were the exception rather than the rule. Most women leaders simply accepted the imperatives of scale and lamented its impact upon the quality of their relationships with staff.

School size also had an impact upon how principals perceived staff attitudes to leadership itself. The perception that teachers wanted 'strong leadership from the top' grew stronger with increases in school size. In the smallest schools, the proportion in agreement with this statement ranged from 72 per cent to 75 per cent. In schools with more than 400 pupils it increased to over 87 per cent. Such perceptions in turn influenced leader behaviour and became self-fulfilling prophecies. In schools beyond 600 pupils, over two-thirds of leaders of both genders believed the principal must 'be in charge'; the corresponding proportions in schools under 400 was 37 per cent for women and 45 per cent for men. This finding clearly suggests that increases in school size place pressure upon women leaders to become more authoritarian. One from an urban girl's school felt no need to apologize for the lack of consultation in her regime:

> I think that staff would tend to say ... leave major decisions to the top. ... The way that I operate is, to talk quite openly about what's happening, what's been decided and to give detailed briefings about rationales for this ... and I think by and large it's accepted. In a lot of ways I'm quite autocratic and I think the size of the school makes this even more crucial.

Such a comment clearly indicates a belief that organizational scale determines the shape of the leadership culture. It contrasted sharply with the values of another woman from a small rural primary site who emphasized the importance of being 'open to staff and listening to people ... acknowledging the things that people do, how they do them. ... I have a philosophy that if you treat the staff well you get the best out of them and therefore they get the best out of the children.'

Principals from small primary schools were the most likely to be committed to collaborative values such as fostering teamwork and encouraging staff participation in decision-making (50 per cent). Support for such values was less evident among those from the larger sites (22 per cent). The combined findings provide clear evidence that school size directly influences leader perceptions of teachers, and this in turn shapes their leadership practice and the subsequent administrative cultures of their schools.

Leaders in larger schools, especially those with more than 800 pupils, also indicated greater reliance upon formal channels of advice. Over half (53 per cent) of secondary leaders indicated this, compared with 45 per cent of their primary counterparts. This was true for both genders. There is also a need, however, to distinguish this from a commitment to the collaborative leadership and decision-making evident in smaller primary sites. Seeking advice is not the same as empowering constituents to shape policy. It is highly likely that the finding reflects a more pragmatic reality: that in larger schools the principal is forced to collect information from a wide range of sources because of the complexity of the organization. Such activity may well be undertaken in a collegial mode but this may be more a cultural style than a commitment to participatory practice. This was particularly apparent in the responses of female leaders from independent girls' schools. They were the most committed of all groups in the study to providing 'strong expert leadership from the top' (28 per cent), and to 'keeping the ship running without too much debate' (45 per cent). The corresponding proportions for women from government and Catholic schools were 12 per cent and 21 per cent (government schools), and 35 per cent and 18 per cent (Catholic schools). Such variations produced highly significant differences within the female cohort on both items. In these Independent girls' schools, the collegial culture therefore masked the true nature of the power relationships between principals and teachers.

These findings related to school size carry important implications for school boards and systems. The tendency to increase school size through amalgamations and growth in western nations over the past decade (Caldwell and Haywood 1998) is likely to have a direct effect upon the nature of principal–staff relationships and the subsequent wellbeing of the leaders themselves. In large schools, principals appear to become more remote from their teachers and this carries the danger of less robust relationships and a sense of personal isolation. They are also tempted to foster a more controlling culture for teachers and this may have negative consequences for the quality of their relationships with staff. This in turn raises the question of whether their relationships with parents are also strongly influenced by organizational size.

Working with parents

Findings related to parent participation largely mirrored those according to school level. The more inclusive beliefs of primary leaders were reflected in the fact that those from the smaller schools were more inclined to consult parents and view them as political agents, both within and beyond the school. There was an extraordinarily high level of conviction among men from primary sites (81 per cent) that parents 'expected consultation'. The proportion from secondary schools was significantly lower (61 per cent). This suggests that the nature and culture of primary sites leads male principals in them to view parents in a different light from their counterparts in secondary schools.

A similar trend was evident among the female cohort. It would appear that dealing with young children in the foundational years fosters more direct contact between school and parents than at adolescence. One woman from a primary site stressed:

> [A] principal's role is a people role, the people must come first. The kids have got to come first, then their parents. ... You've got to be dealing with your people and sometimes your people take every minute of your day. And then you turn around and do your papers when they've all gone home because often that's the best way to do it. Basically I'm out there available for the people.

The tone of this utterance is very much a pastoral one; this principal believes her role requires responsiveness to local community above system bureaucracy. It therefore comes as no surprise that primary leaders (64 per cent) were more inclined to 'consult parents' than were secondary leaders (58.4 per cent). By way of contrast, women from secondary sites were more dismissive of parent participation. One commented that while 'the wants of parents are taken into consideration', they are not the determining influence, and cited conflict over the introduction of notebook computers into Year 9 as an instance where parent opinion was overruled. Another insisted: 'Often what parents want is precisely what we don't. ... Obviously every parent wants their child to be special and I respect that ... but I know that there are many parents who want the entire school to change to accommodate their child.'

A more passionate leader from an urban girls' school asserted: 'the idea of a parent-controlled school is absurd and that's what some of them are looking for. They've only got self-interest at heart.' Such a stance is an exclusive one: parents are perceived as demanding clients who need to be kept at bay by vigilant principals armed with a superior knowledge of the common good. Women principals who voiced such utterances clearly contradict the relational stereotypes that characterize cultural feminist typologies (see Court 2002: 110–122). They lead to the conclusion that such typologies radically oversimplify female leadership in schools.

Primary leaders also demonstrated a much stronger commitment to engaging parents than their secondary counterparts. The latter were more likely to believe that parents held relatively low expectations about their involvement in schools. Over two-thirds agreed that 'occasional reports and information sessions' satisfied their needs whereas a third of primary leaders actively disagreed with this assertion. Instead, there was clear evidence that as school size increased, principals were more inclined to believe that parents wanted authoritative control rather than direct consultation. In the largest schools, women were less likely to consult parents than men. This was the reverse of the pattern in small schools and suggests that leadership of large secondary schools tends to diminish the consultative inclinations of women leaders.

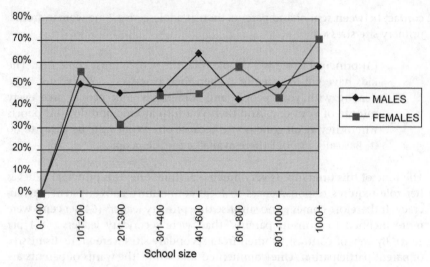

Figure 2.3 Principals' belief that parents wanted strong, authoritative leadership in school. Proportions of strong agreement by level and principal gender.

This trend becomes even more apparent when we note that both genders from large sites were the more likely to believe that parents wanted 'strong, authoritative leadership'. In this respect their perceptions of parents paralleled those they held of teachers (Figure 2.2).

Women from schools with the 1000-plus students recorded the most authoritarian attitudes. They believed that teachers want 'strong leadership from the top', and this suggests that women who are principals in large secondary schools may develop more hierarchical approaches to relationships than those in smaller, primary sites. In other words, organizational scale introduces important variations within the cohort of female leaders. The same happened with the male sample: men from primary sites were more inclusive in their attitudes towards parents than those in secondary establishments. We can conclude that the nature and scale of primary schools encourages more mutual relationships between principals and parents than in secondary sites.

The different perceptions about parents at the two levels also extended to beliefs about the nature of parent activity itself. Primary principals (56 per cent) were more inclined to see them as a pressure group within the school whereas only 42 per cent of secondary leaders viewed them in this way. A further 43 per cent believed that they were 'politically active on behalf of the school', whereas only 25 per cent of secondary leaders believed this. The proportion that disagreed with the statement increased exponentially from 44 per cent at schools with 101 to 300 students, to 62 per cent at the 1000 plus student level. The smaller size of primary schools seems to enable more direct contact between parents and principals, ensuring that leaders at this level are more aware of parent expectations, and some may feel pressured by this. Principals from larger secondary schools tend to be buffered from direct pressure from parents by complex structures and the presence of middle managers.

The findings in this study therefore present evidence of opposed cultures when it comes to encouraging substantial parent participation at primary and secondary levels. It is most likely to be fostered by primary leaders, although those in the smallest schools may not have the resources to support it as well as those from larger primary schools. It is also clear that the interaction of level of schooling and organizational scale operates in such a way that stereotypes about women leaders as 'essentially relational' become discredited. Organizational factors appear to be more powerful determinants than leader gender of the relationships between parents and principals.

Professional wellbeing

Responses on the items related to professional wellbeing indicated that the strongest confidence that 'the role brought out the best in themselves' came from principals in the schools with between 200 and 400 pupils. This was reflected in the relative proportions of agreement with the statement from primary (83 per cent) to secondary leaders (72 per cent). The proportions of men and women at the primary level were almost identical (82 per cent and 83 per cent). However, at the secondary level, women (78 per cent) were markedly more optimistic than the men (69 per cent). Unfortunately, they also had a more pronounced sense of the burdens of office than men from the larger secondary sites. However, the pattern was not consistent across the two genders. In the smaller primary schools, men were more inclined to feel overburdened than were women. This suggests that women leaders in primary schools are more able to marshal the forces of collegiality to support themselves than are their male counterparts (Figure 2.4).

However, in the secondary sites with more than 600 pupils, women felt more overburdened than men, perhaps because of the increased complexity of organizational culture and the diminution of collaborative cultures. It is also interesting to note that the women from the largest secondary schools who had the most exclusive attitudes to both teachers and parents also felt the most overburdened in the study. Their retreat from the collegiality of the small primary school seems to leave them feeling personally vulnerable. Conversely, men in larger sites appear comfortable and protected by the more segmented and bureaucratic structures. The findings can also be related to Kruger's (1996) thesis that gender 'other' cultures are more stressful than heterogeneous ones. Women appear to be less stressed in small, collaborative work environments, which Gray (1989) typecast as 'feminine', whereas men

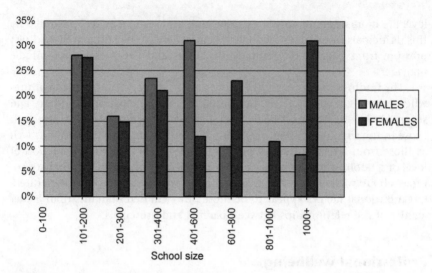

Figure 2.4 Principals holding positive perceptions of their professional wellbeing. Proportions of agreement by school size and principal gender.

are more at ease in larger bureaucràtic contexts, which he characterized as 'masculine'.

Despite the presence of collegial cultures, leaders from the smallest primary schools were the most likely to indicate they felt 'overburdened and stressed'. A woman from a government site commented: 'the job has taken over my life ... the sixty-five or seventy hour week is often a reality'. Her sentiments were shared by a man from a Catholic primary site: 'Number one is just time. I've been here every Sunday in the fifteen years I've been a principal.' Such comments suggest that principals in small schools have to fulfil a multifaceted role and be all things to all people. Those in larger organizations have opportunities to specialize their workloads and delegate many aspects to subordinates. This enables them to have greater control over occupational stress. The lowest indications of stress and exhaustion came from those in schools above 800 pupils. Those in small sites seem to be denied such buffers and this may also explain why principals from sites with fewer than 200 pupils (22 per cent) were also the most likely to say that they would 'not continue in principalship'.

However, the pattern was reversed when it came to industrial relations. Principals from the largest schools experienced the greatest sense of 'frustration' in this area. One explanation for this is that in large sites where there are many teachers, relationships become more complex and potentially problematical. In small or medium-sized schools, the proportions that experienced frustration were below 50 per cent, and differences between the two

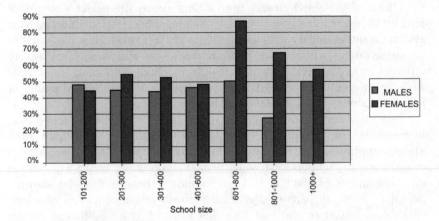

Figure 2.5 Principals' experience of frustration with industrial relations. Proportions of agreement by principal gender and school size (statistical significance 0.05, 24df).

genders were small or irregular. The gap was much more pronounced in schools with more than 600 pupils (Figure 2.5).

It is interesting that women in the larger sites were distinctively more perplexed than men and this can be in turn related to the previous finding that they were more likely to be disconcerted by the decline of collaborative cultures as school size escalated. The findings lend some credence to the claims of gender theorists that the quality of relationships is a more important consideration for women than for men (Tannen 1991; Seidler 1994). The more directive stance of men in large schools, combined with their propensity to use formal administrative structures as vehicles of personal authority, may cushion them from feeling frustration to the same extent. The scale of the institutional setting therefore appears to contribute to differing attitudes and beliefs in each gender among men and women leaders in relation to this area of school life.

Implications

The findings reported in this study clearly indicate that school leadership is a complex matter and that while gender stereotypes have some explanatory power they cannot be regarded as foundational truths that comprehend the phenomena of school leadership. Essentialist typologies are too simplistic. Phenomena such as leadership and organizational culture are multifaceted, and even the typologies of primary and secondary leaders presented by Pascal and Ribbins (1998) tend to oversimplify the reality. We cannot assume that large primary schools embody the same cultural dynamics as small ones, and the efforts of the female leader from a large urban site reflect a strenuous attempt to preserve collaborative values in a big school. Similar complexity is evident in the secondary schools represented in this study. How the leader of a small secondary school of 400 pupils relates to staff and parents may be very different from the style of a principal in a school with more than 1000 students. It seems that essentialism, whether it relates to leader gender or level of schooling, runs the risk of distorting reality.

One clear conclusion from this study, however, is that as school size increases, so the perceptions, beliefs and relationships of principals alter. Their perceptions of teachers alter from seeing them as collaborative partners in small primary schools to viewing them as autonomous agents who require direction and accountability in large secondary sites. In a similar manner, principals' views of parents alter from partners in the education of young children to outsiders who may be either demanding or indifferent. As the perceptions of principals alter, so does the nature of their relationships with teachers and parents. As size increases, they become more insistent upon programme adherence among teachers. Their relationships with teachers appear to become more distant, and more female leaders appear to regret this than their male colleagues. Some women leaders become more reliant upon authoritarian structures to manage their schools, but with a sense of personal loss and increased isolation. Another consequence is that both genders find industrial relations more problematical as they become more remote from the collegial partnerships of small sites.

We should not fall into the trap of eulogizing small schools as relational havens. It appears that the quality of relationships between principals, their staff and the parent communities is more robust than that found in large secondary establishments. However, leaders of both genders in small schools are more likely to experience stress and exhaustion, which is a consequence of the limited human resources of such sites. This in turn leads them to be less optimistic about their long-term commitment to their role.

It is therefore clear that organizational scale can have a major impact upon the leadership of principals, which can be independent of their gender. However, variables such as school level and size, although closely interrelated are not unilateral in their impact. The relationships are complex and ambiguous, and both factors exert an undeniable influence upon the organizational cultures of particular schools. In this regard the study demonstrates that structural variables can have as powerful an influence upon a principal's relationships with teachers and parents as personal ideologies and philosophical stances.

A final implication is that any claim that leader gender determines leadership style ignores the dynamics of organizational culture. Principals do not exist independently of the cultures in which they work. They may attempt to define and articulate them (Lundberg 1988; Sergiovanni 1992), but they may also be constrained by them. Organizational scale helps to shape school culture. It does so through its impact upon how leaders perceive key stakeholders such as teachers and parents. These in turn shape a principal's beliefs about key relationships and how these relationships develop in practice. Organizational culture is a product of all these complex interactions, and leader gender is one variable in the mix. Unfortunately, as evidenced by the collegial gentility of some of the girls' schools in this study, organizational culture can also mask the true nature of power relations in schools. We must learn to discern between the manifestations of organizational cultures and the complex relationships they help to shape.

3 Gender and School Leadership in Sweden

Anna Davis and Olof Johansson

Women are the best school administrators. And, hold on to your hats, because here comes the next deathblow against the male of the species: the best male school administrators are those who use female management techniques most.

(Shakeshaft 1992: 4)

In 1980, an influential study entitled *More Women as School Administrators* appeared in Sweden (SOU 1980: 19). Its purpose was to investigate why women were under-represented among principals in Sweden and what actions could be taken to achieve a more even gender distribution. At that time about 7 per cent of principals were women, whereas 60 per cent of teachers were women. The reason for this, according to the study, was low self-esteem in women and favouritism towards male candidates during the recruitment process. In addition, the School Leader Training Programme was available to candidates only *after* becoming a principal, which put women at a disadvantage at that time (Ullman 1997). The authors of *More Women as School Administrators* clearly stated that they were not expressing any opinions on why differences in leadership style between male and female school administrators should exist. Even so, there was an underlying theme throughout the study that justified the need for more female principals on the basis that women were perceived as especially skilled at handling the more democratic role of school administrator that was emerging.

Suggested solutions included more women substituting during the absence of a principal or assistant principal and using gender as a basis for allocating principal positions. The latter measure encountered hard criticism by the school leader trade union Skolledarna through its publication *The School Leader* in 1980. Quotas, it was believed, would not solve the problems, rather it was suggested that the number of female principals would increase if women dared to claim the right to substitute as principal or assistant principal. There was also concern that increasing the percentage of women in the profession would lower its status. The low number of female principals was therefore not perceived as a problem by the union since it believed women did not dare or want to apply for these positions.

There has been a dramatic change in the proportion of principals that are women (Nygren and Johansson 2000). From a time when males dominated principal positions (in 1989, 93 per cent of all principals were men), the reverse was observed in 2002 with women holding 73 per cent of the principal positions. Three major changes in policy and practice have contributed to this. Firstly, there was a new awareness in school board policy about the lack of women principals. One result of that insight was that school boards started to mention in advertisements that the majority of principals were men and that the school board was striving for a more even distribution of men and women as principals. These advertisements were one measure taken to encourage women to apply for vacant principalships as far back as the early 1980s (SOU 1980: 19). Secondly, in the 1990s, all persons with pedagogical competence, not only schoolteachers, became eligible to become a principal (Nygren and Johansson 2000). Formal administrative certification or previous professional experience as a leader, were no longer requirements for becoming a principal. Thirdly, the number of positions for principals increased due to reorganizations in the school sector allowing more opportunities for women to become principals. This latter point needs some clarification.

In recent years, there have been many changes in the way Swedish municipalities organize themselves and their schools. Nearly all have merged various boards and departments into new units. Superintendents, as well as principals, are no longer responsible only for schools (Regeringens skrivelse 1998/1999: 121). In most cases they are also responsible for day care centres, pre-school for 6-year-olds and after-school activity programmes. Although, principal positions are widely advertised (locally, regionally and in national newspapers and magazines), much of this process has been a charade. When municipalities merged boards and departments into new units, many people with leadership experience in the old system became redundant. These people included those in charge of day care and pre-school centres. The municipalities felt obliged to choose new principals from among their own redundant staff when a post became vacant. Thus, while principal positions were widely advertised, in reality, the positions were filled by people already on staff. It is, however, important to stress that women coming from day care centres were generally well-qualified leaders who have proved to be good school leaders.

Gender and leadership – a glimpse of earlier research

Early research from the 1970s had a gender-neutral approach; sex as a phenomenon was ignored and was not assigned any significance for the study of leadership. There was little research that focused on women as principals (Wingård 1998; Ekholm *et al.* 2000).

Bartol (1978: 806) found in her research and review of the literature on gender differences in leadership few differences between male and female leaders regarding leadership behaviour or style. In most cases, she stated, there are either no differences or relatively minor differences between male and female leaders on leadership style, whether the leaders are describing themselves or being described by their subordinates.

Eagly and Johnson (1990) presented a summary of various surveys about gender and leadership styles. Gender differences were primarily found in laboratory experiments and assessment studies. In these studies men tended to be more task-orientated and women tended to be more interpersonally orientated. However, gender differences were rarely found in natural organization settings. The strongest evidence Eagly and Johnson obtained for a gender difference in leadership style throughout their review was the tendency for women to adopt a more democratic or participative style and for men to adopt a more autocratic or directive style.

Research in the 1990s moved in a direction which displayed gender differences. A form of femininity appeared which emphasized that the experiences of females were different from the experiences of males. In an interview for *The School Leader*, the American researcher Carol Shakeshaft (1992: 4) highlighted the traditional ability of women 'to care about others, to listen and support, encourage and motivate' and to 'get people to cooperate'. She argued that this style suited modern educational administration, which was no longer based on an outdated organizational hierarchy. Shakeshaft's argument complemented the discussions that were occurring in Sweden at that time. By 1995, 53 per cent of Swedish school leaders were women. Because of the shift in numbers, the debate was looking for evidence of effects of gender on principal leadership style.

One theme stressed that women had a more democratic way of handling tasks and a greater focus on school improvement and instructional leadership than did male school leaders (Alvesson 1997). Fagenson (1993) suggested that female managers had a transformational, democratic and networking style rather than a hierarchical leadership style and that they had more satisfied employees than did male managers. Wahl (1997) cautioned and emphasized the need to distinguish between research and popular opinion in the area of female leadership style. She argued that in popular opinion, differences between the sexes are often described as an ideal. This view was also reported by Colwill (1995), who claimed that a dividing line could be drawn between popular leadership books and research literature on gender differences in leadership styles. Popular management books often stress that men and women have very different leadership styles whereas research has generally come to the conclusion that differences between men and women's leadership styles are small or non-existent.

However, Lindvert (1997) developed a slightly different thesis. She maintained that increased numbers of women leaders actually changed organizational culture. The increased numbers of female leaders together with the dismantling of bureaucracy worked for a changed and more equal organizational culture. The increase in numbers of female leaders has led to a new meaning for traditional female competence. Typical so-called female qualities have been upgraded. A reasonable interpretation is that within less bureaucratic organizations these qualities will be more asked for and needed. Yet, it still appears as if those women who have been able to identify with male norms are the ones who have reached the highest leadership positions (Lindvert 1997). Today, initiatives for new forms of leadership are being taken; initiatives unthinkable some years ago, and this new way of thinking may bring change.

The increased number of female leaders and its impact on organizational culture is also confirmed by Pincus (1995). She found evidence that female principals brought with them a more educational than managerial focus. Pincus cited a male superintendent who observed:

> I don't know if it has anything to do with the person or the sex, but it has meant a lot. Women take the job of school administrator a little more seriously than their male counterparts. Let me explain – they bring educational expertise to the job. Previously, discussions focused more on the organization. Now there is more content in the discussion.
>
> (Pincus 1995: 11)

Today there is a growing interest in giving leadership a more participatory, non-hierarchical, flexible and group-orientated style. This places a high value on female qualities. In particular, popular leadership books are shifting the main focus towards an emphasis of women's different leadership skills, which is even argued to be part of a superior leadership style (Due Billing 1997). The spirit of the time and changed definitions of leadership most likely contribute to a more 'pro-feminine' direction (Alvesson 1997).

The debate on gendered differentiation of leadership has progressed further to engage the concept of the androgynous leader. This concept suggests that every influential and successful leader has available to them both sets of characteristics – the empowering and collaborative style of leadership associated with women and the more directive and authoritarian style associated with men – from which they are able to choose the most appropriate for the situation at hand (Cubillo and Brown 2003). All in all, there is no doubt that women have a great deal to contribute to the field of educational management.

Our research on gender and leadership

The pronounced growth in the percentage of female managers in the public sector in Sweden occurred at the same time as great cutbacks were taking place. Earlier research discovered that women are extremely transparent leaders who handled themselves well during this very difficult period when they had to cope with significant budget cuts in their schools (Holmquist 1997; Johansson 2001). It was found that despite the resource reductions they were especially adept at implementing measures that allowed the high ambitions of their schools to be fulfilled. These results are the background to our present research that we report on in this chapter. We report on three different studies.

The first is based on a questionnaire from 2001 that was distributed to a representative sample of Swedish school leaders who were members of the school leader section of the national union for teachers. The return rate for questionnaires was 66 per cent, or 285 school principals, and gave us a robust basis for statistical analysis. From that study we report on attitudes related to gender and leadership among active principals.

In the second study we report on a content analysis of recruitment advertisements for school leaders. Changes were found in the way school boards advertised from 1989 to 2002. We have analysed the text in all the recruitment ads published in the trade union magazine *The School Leader* for the three years 1989, 1998 and 2002.

Our third study is an analysis of how the journalists employed by the trade union, Skolledarna, for school leaders in Sweden report on leadership and school-relevant issues in their union journal *The School Leader*. We have made a content analysis of all articles published in the journal in 2002, looking especially for gender-related material both in text and pictures.

Specific findings

The first study asked about differences between male and female leadership styles. The school leaders were asked to indicate if they agreed with the following statements:

1. There is a difference in leadership style between men and women.
2. It is more difficult for women than for men to get support for their work.
3. Because most teachers are women, it is easier for women than for men to be principals.
4. Female principals are more sensitive to criticism than male principals.

The respondents were given the opportunity to indicate if they disagreed by using 'no', 'sometimes' or 'very seldom' to demonstrate their level of dis-agreement. Two hundred and seventy school leaders answered the questions. The distribution of men and women in our sample was the same as in schools across the country (69 per cent women and 31 per cent men).

We found that men more often than women responded that sometimes there are leadership differences between male and female principals. The fe-male principals did not agree on that point, however, and more women an-swered 'no'. Men indicated that they thought it is more difficult for women principals to get support for their work than for male principals. Women principals did not agree. The same findings are true for statement 3, that it is easier for women to be principals than it is for men.

We also asked our sample: 'Do you think that female principals are considered to be more sensitive to criticism and have more difficulties in coping with an unfriendly working climate than male principals?' On this statement we found that men saw themselves as stronger leaders than women principals. Men answered 'yes' and 'sometimes' much more frequently than woman respondents.

Our survey of active principals illustrates common opinions about gender differences as portrayed in the literature. This is interesting because we found no clear differences between men and women when we asked questions about what it is important to do as school leaders. We found that most women principals argued for more contact with parents and students, and they showed more interest in pedagogical questions. But, overall we found few differences between the way male and female principals understand what is important in their job.

Another common opinion about the working conditions for men and women is that women are restricted in their work life by their care for their families. In our questionnaire we also asked about conference attendance. We found that 54 per cent of women principals never attend national con-ferences. The corresponding figure for male principals was 38 per cent. We also explored the attendance rate at regional conferences. The analysis gave us the same pattern. One-third (33 per cent) of female principals never went to conferences, compared with only 17 per cent of all male principals. However, the pattern changed when we asked whether they had listened to a famous or important school researcher in the past year. Almost 70 per cent of the women principals had done so compared with only 55 per cent of the men. One possible explanation is that the school board had invited famous or important researchers to the municipality, which meant no one had to leave home for that conference. Such findings tend to provide small but important support for the common belief that women are restricted in their work lives by their care for their families.

Another set of questions in our study was about leadership experiences before becoming a principal or assistant principal. Approximately 70 per cent of both genders had participated in leadership teams as a teacher. However, more male teachers (70 per cent) had had the opportunity to work as substitute principals than had female teachers (41 per cent). When we presented the results at a seminar for practitioners, a male superintendent commented that many women teachers indicate that they have difficulty changing their private lives at short notice if they are asked to substitute for a principal. However, a female superintendent at the same seminar only partially agreed with this comment. Instead, she argued that female teachers feel a great responsibility for their students and do not want to let them down by leaving them for a short period. She emphasized another aspect that is subtler and more difficult to prove.

The empirical data we have analysed here indicate that there are differences between male and female principals. As future leaders, they are exposed to literature that asserts that women lead in a special way. Thus, females are expected to lead in a special way that is different from men. The established norm for appropriate behaviour differs between female and male leaders. A dangerous consequence could be that both genders are restricted in terms of acceptable leadership behaviour.

This is interesting because we did not find many clear differences between men and women when we asked questions about what is important in their job. Most respondents believed that a good school leader needs attributes that are both typically male and typically female. This was reflected in comments about what a school leader should be: sensitive and driving, administrative and target-orientated, and educational and administrative.

What do principals need to know when they enter the job?

This section is based on our second study, which is an analysis of job descriptions in recruitment advertisements for principals in the Swedish trade union journal *The School Leader*. We compared the advertisements in 1989 and 1998, to study the differences or similarities in the recruitment pattern for principals before and after 1994, when a new goal and objective-driven curriculum was mandated for all schools in Sweden. The analysis is based on 98 advertisements from 1989, and 85 from 1998. Table 3.1 lists the nine criteria most used for each year according to our analysis.

Only three criteria were the same for both years (italicized in the table). It is also clear that there has been a shift in priorities from strong human management skills to managerial and pedagogical competences. The most important criteria in 1989 were the ability to engage personnel, clarify objectives, cooperate with others, to have good administrative and leadership

Table 3.1 Qualifications for becoming principal specified in recruitment ads in 1989 and 1998

Job descriptions 1989	Frequency (%)	Job descriptions 1998	Frequency (%)
Ability to engage personnel	26.6	Good pedagogical experience	36.5
Clarify objectives	18.4	*Ability to engage personnel*	28.3
Ability to cooperate with others	17.4	Responsible for personnel	22.4
		Responsible for finances	20.0
Good administrative skills	17.4	Clear leadership style	20.0
Good leadership skills	16.4	Good pedagogical training	17.7
Driving force for development work	16.4	*Ability to cooperate with others*	17.7
Positive outlook towards people	12.3	Employer responsibilities	13.0
		Good leadership skills	11.8
Interested in developmental issues	11.3		
Creativity	10.3		

skills, and to be a driving force behind development work. Principals were also expected to demonstrate interest in developmental issues and to be creative.

The most important criterion, according to the 1998 job descriptions, was good pedagogical experience. Ability to engage and motivate personnel seems to have been important in both 1989 (26.6 per cent) and 1998 (28.3 per cent). Ability to cooperate with others, maintained a consistent frequency, but by 1998 was considered less important than personnel and financial management skills.

A comparison between the criteria for 1989 and 1998 shows that the requirements for principals became more stringent. In 1989, a principal needed administrative skills and knowledge of financial considerations, but in 1998, principals needed financial training and had to be responsible for the business side of the school. In the late 1990s, candidates also needed leadership experience from other sectors or industries. Today's principal has to be able to delegate tasks, work independently, support the work of the school, and be a visionary. The changes reflect trends in the broader society during the last decades of the twentieth century.

We also compared the changes between the 85 advertisements analysed in 1998 and the 97 advertisements that were published in 2002 in *The School Leader* (Table 3.2). Only three of the qualifications asked for were the same. Three criteria, 'ability to engage personnel', 'ability to cooperate with others'

Table 3.2 Qualifications for becoming principal specified in recruitment ads in 1998 and 2002

Job descriptions 1998	Frequency (%)	Job descriptions 2002	Frequency (%)
Good pedagogical experience	36.5	Good social competence	92.1
Ability to engage personnel	28.3	Ability to lead school improvement	73.4
Responsible for personnel	22.4		
Responsible for finances	20.0	Goal and results orientated	64.7
Clear leadership	20.0	Ability to cooperate with others	60.0
Good pedagogical training	17.7	Good pedagogical training	55.3
Ability to cooperate with others	17.7	Clear pedagogical leadership	54.6
Employer responsibilities	13.0	Pedagogical insight and experience	46.0
Good leadership skills	11.8	Good leadership skills	41.9
		Ability to engage personnel	41.8

and 'good leadership skills', were qualities which were also thought to be important back in 1989. The criteria employers looked for in 2002 placed stronger emphasis upon social ability and social skills, as well as school improvement and pedagogical skills. In 2002, stereotypical male qualities related to budget, finance and results, had become less important. One other interesting difference is that many of the competences appear in each advertisement. The employers were looking for the complete leader and this demanded many more skills of the applicants than in 1989.

In conclusion, we argue that the qualifications looked for today are more attuned to areas that women in our earlier study said they were most interested in and wanted to work more with in their school. One example of the drift away from stereotypical male descriptions is that 'clear leadership' in 1998 became 'clear pedagogical leadership' by 2002.

Current changes in organizational structures can be interpreted as a development or trend for more democratic school organizations in which equality, understanding and participation in the life of the organization are important. There is a new definition of what constitutes leadership skills. These new skills are more linked to creating understanding of purpose, creative teamwork, creating organizational support, working with organizational learning, and being able to inform and communicate new ideas. One conclusion is that what are considered to be typically female characteristics in Swedish society have become more important. A reasonable interpretation is that the new organizational structures have helped generate greater demand for these leadership skills.

Portrayal of school leaders in *The School Leader* between 2000 and 2002

In this section we analyse what the monthly trade union magazine *The School Leader* chose to write about. Does it reflect that over 70 per cent of Swedish school principals are now women? Has the shift from a male to female principal majority influenced the content of the magazine? We analysed the content of all articles on leadership and school-relevant topics. We have not studied book reviews and official material.

In 2002 we found 42 articles that focused upon male leaders compared with 25 that depicted women leaders. If the magazine reported in a representative way we should have found 47 articles about female leaders and 20 about males. The reality was the reverse. We are forced to ponder whether the magazine considers male leaders much more interesting to write about than their female counterparts. The senior editor of the magazine is a woman.

A second analysis focused upon articles that explicitly reported on school leaders. In all 36 issues of *The School Leader* between 2000 and 2002, the following pattern emerged:

- 2000: 12 articles focused upon men and 7 articles on women principals.
- 2001: 10 articles focused upon men and 14 articles on women principals.
- 2002: 8 articles focused upon men and 6 articles on women principals.

In all, 57 articles focused on school leaders between 2000 and 2002. We found that 30 articles were about male principals and 27 about female principals. Even if the magazine has changed the balance of articles since 2002, it is obvious that the way it reports on school leadership over-represents male principals because 73 per cent of all Swedish principals in 2001 were women and, since 1994, there have been more female than male principals active in Sweden (Forslund Söderberg 2001).

Looking ahead

Sweden will be an interesting case for future research on the effects of the change from male to female principals. For members of the public and even researchers to start referring to the principal as 'she' is a difficult breach with traditions of Swedish language. The analysis of *The School Leader* reflects a culture lag in this respect. So, what kind of changes can we start looking for?

We saw from the empirical data presented, that active principals view the challenges for men and women in the principal's office differently. Men are more inclined to believe there are key differences between male and female principals.

The advertisements for new positions as principals did show a significant shift over the past decade and displayed a greater call for competences that are often viewed as female management techniques. Will this change in how different school boards understand school leadership also influence the way people in schools view their leaders? If so, will there be enough rethinking to change school cultures so that they are more attuned to female leaders?

Here, we would like to introduce the concept of rethinking (Johansson 2000). The learning and reflections of an organization and the leader in relation to goals are extremely important for success. The reflective and learning perspective, along with the structural and cultural perspectives, are central for understanding change.

Our presumption is that the increasing number of female principals represents a new dimension in leadership and a structural challenge and change, which can create a new openness about value structures in the schools and which will reshape school cultures. But, this can only occur if a process of rethinking and abandoning old values and behaviour patterns takes place.

Today, research on female leadership is extensive and varied. At the core is the discussion comparing the leadership styles of men and women. One focus is on how women get and use power as an aspect of leadership. This opens new questions but it also emphasizes the fact that we need to know more about how to study gender differences in relation to leadership and the use of power (Kelly and Duerst-Lathi 1995). For instance, Colwill (1995) defines power at three levels: personal power, interpersonal power and organizational power. By interpersonal power, Colwill refers to 'the ability to influence others'. Leaders exert interpersonal power primarily through the communication of their status. Leaders can influence others verbally by the words they say, paraverbally by the way they talk, and non-verbally with gestures, body posture or the use of personal space. In the realm of interpersonal power, the research suggests that female managers are less effective than their male counterparts – that they are less able than men to influence others. In the area of organizational power, 'the ability to mobilize resources' (the ability to get things done), the latest research indicates that a shift is taking place: that many people consider female managers to be more effective than male managers at mobilizing resources.

Whether men or women are more effective leaders as a consequence of their differing styles is a complex question. Many researchers are unwilling to argue that women's relatively democratic and participative style is either an advantage or a disadvantage. No doubt a relatively democratic style enhances a leader's effectiveness under some circumstances, and a relatively autocratic style enhances it under other circumstances (Eagly and Johnson 1990). Fagenson (1993), on the other hand, refers to research that suggests that women's styles of leadership are more effective and perhaps should be the norm to which men are compared.

To define characteristics of effective managers is not an easy task; at the same time many researchers claim that credibility is more important than anything else. Credibility as a term includes competence, power and the ability to get results. Leaders with credibility were listened to, had room to make more mistakes and could take greater risks because it was believed that they would produce (Kanter 1977).

The great change in the proportion of female principals in Sweden will create a rich source for comparative research on leadership and gender. And there are many research questions left to be asked, analysed and answered. At present the leadership discourse is dominated by stereotypically male values and experiences (budgets, finance and results), but we can see change coming.

4   Gender and School Leadership Discourses: A Swedish Perspective

Karin Franzén

Introduction

As in most western countries, school leadership in Sweden has been an arena created by and for men (Schmuck 1996; Blackmore 1999; Reynolds 2002a). Female leaders have been very rare. Historically they could be found in gen-der-separated 'girl-schools'. It was the male teacher who was promoted to the leader position; female teachers stayed in the classrooms (Söderberg Forslund 2002). Today, I believe Swedish school leadership differs from that of many countries in that the female leaders have increased rapidly in the past decade. Today, more than 70 per cent of the school leaders in comprehensive schools are women (Lindvall and Ekholm 1997). Swedish school leadership also dif-fers in that a school leader could be responsible for several schools whereas in most other countries, each school has its own leader. So, how have all these Swedish women managed their leadership in a context which for so many years has been coded for men? Are they trying to use the male discourses or are they creating new discourses?

Theoretical approach

There are many studies describing female and male leadership in Swedish schools (Franzén 1998; Olofsson 1998; Wingård 1998; Söderberg Forslund 2002), but no one has treated school leadership as a discursive construction. However, my research interest concerns the implications connected to school leadership in different discourses. One important aim is to analyse these meanings in a gender perspective (Kulick 1987; Hirdman 1990). The purpose of my study is to deconstruct what it means to be a school leader, and fem-inist post-structuralist theory is my source of inspiration (Grogan 1996; Scrla 1998; Blackmore 1999; Strachan 1999; Möller 2002). Hopefully, this can help us move beyond simplistic views of the issue of male and female school lea-dership (Blackmore 1999).

Central to post-structural theory are *discourse*, *subjectivity* and *power*.

Meanings of words, for example the term 'school leadership', are determined by discourses, which in turn also govern what is possible to say or do. Researchers also produce scientific discourses determining what school leadership is. These discourses yield 'effects of truths', contributing to the construction of school leadership. They may also affect school leaders' and teachers' views of school leadership. The contradictory results in the field of research concerning school leadership and gender indicate the existence of competing discourses about male and female school leaders (Gilligan 1982; Shakeshaft 1987; Tannen 1991; Eagly *et al.* 1992; Young 1993; Kruger 1996).

Discourse (Foucault 1980b; Laclau and Mouffe 1985; Fairclough 1995; Wetherell *et al.* 2001) is a key concept of my study, but different researchers use it differently, even if everyone would probably agree with Winter Jörgensen and Philips' (2000: 7) rough definition: 'Discourse is a certain way of talking of and understanding the world'. In my view, however, it is not only a matter of language. Firstly, discourse is always contextual: the meanings of words are contextually dependent. What we say depends on what is 'allowed' to be said in a specific situation, where rules and control systems are operating, and where we create our own interpretation and understanding of the world (Fahlgren 1998: 22). Secondly, discourse is not only spoken language: actions are also discursive, as discourses define what is natural, normal and allowed to be done.

From a humanistic point of view, the subject owns sovereignty, and you are personally responsible for what you say and what you do. According to poststructural theories, subjectivity is produced by different discourses within which subjects position themselves (Weedon 1997; Lenztaguchi 2000). Thus, the subject does not precede and determine language: the subject is determined by discourses instead (Butler 1990). Meaning is not created 'inside' the subject but in discursive practices. Thus, post-structural theories reject the traditional dichotomy between *an inner self-assured subject and an outer objective world*: both the lived world and the subject are discursively constructed.

This philosophical standpoint does not necessarily end up in absolute determinism. What to say and think and how to act are not determined in advance. Many competing discourses are always circulating, and to a certain extent you may choose to position yourself. It should also be noted that the notion of the coherent autonomous self is no longer valid. Instead, it is more relevant to talk about *split subjectivities* as subjects move between different discourses.

Method

This chapter is based on data from interviews with eight school leaders, four women and four men. The approach is qualitative because this makes it possible to get a deeper understanding of implications embedded in the concept of school leadership. I have tried to get as much information as possible about school leaders' views of their leadership. What does an ordinary day at work look like? How do they plan the allocation of time for different activities? What activities do they prioritize? Which relations are established with the staff and the students, respectively? How do the leaders define school leadership and how do they regard themselves as leaders? The answers to such questions may all be parts of the discursive construction of school leadership.

It has to be pointed out that interviews are performed in a specific social context. It is a conversation, and as such is mediated through spoken language. The discourses in which the leaders position themselves when talking about their leaderships are probably not always the same as the discourses guiding other leadership activities.

Feminists try to challenge stereotypically taken-for-granted truths about women and men, what is considered as female and male, and what women and men can and are allowed to do. This is also a starting point of my study. Therefore I have interviewed both male and female school leaders. Here the 'school leader' is defined as the person with responsibility for educational and pedagogical aspects of life in school. I have chosen to interview leaders who differ with regard to earlier professional experiences because one hypothesis is that the context in which they worked earlier may affect how they construct themselves as school leaders. Today, the school leaders work in comprehensive schools for children up to 16 years. Earlier, the school leaders in this study had worked in school and military organizations, respectively. One male school leader was an officer responsible for the military training of young men, one man was a pre-school teacher and two men worked as teachers in comprehensive schools. Three women worked in pre-schools for children aged 1–6 years, and one woman worked as a teacher in a youth recreation centre. In my view, pre-school and youth recreation centres are different from compulsory school in that the staff cooperate in teams and with children and parents to a much greater extent than do teachers in school. This study focuses on interviews with leaders but I have also interviewed teachers in the same schools to get their perspective of school leadership.

As mentioned above, I have used interviews for collecting data in order to get a deeper understanding of school leadership. Interviews make it possible to create a personal contact with the respondents, and the opportunities to understand their ways of reasoning increase when they are sitting in front of you. I have used a deep interview technique. An interview guide with a few broad questions about certain themes was written down in advance. I have tried to be flexible, asking more detailed questions depending on what the informants choose to talk about. The interview questions are tools to guide the respondents' narratives in line with the aim of my study, that is, to get an idea of what it means to be a school leader.

Findings

In this study I have found six different discourses that I have called: In Service for Teachers, In Service for Children, In Service for Parents, In Service for Municipality, In Service for Society and In Service for Development. In each of these discourses I have identified two different, but not mutually exclusive, positions for the leaders to use. The most frequently used discourse is In Service for Teachers, and close behind come In Service for Children and In Service for Development. The remaining three are as well used by all leaders but not to the same extent. I concentrate my discussion on how the leaders position themselves within the three dominant discourses.

In Service for Teachers

In the In Service for Teachers discourse, the school leader is responsible for the staff in school. Teachers represent the largest group of the staff, so naturally much of what my respondents speak of concerns their relationship to the teachers. Accordingly one can maintain that their constructions of themselves as school leaders take place in a discourse, which connects meanings in the leadership to that. This discourse is dominant.

I have found two different positions: the Supporter and the Manager, for leaders in this dominant discourse. Both male and female leaders often use these positions, and they use them in similar ways. I found only one small difference. Women used the Supporter position to a greater extent than the men. Men, on the other hand, used the Manager position somewhat more than women. This is interesting since former studies in school leadership and gender describe female leaders as being sensitive and caring and male leaders as being more administrative. My study showed that such differences were relatively small.

The Supporter
The Supporter position indicates that the leader feels that s/he is a supporter for the teachers. S/he stands up for the teachers whenever they need something. Characteristic meanings in this position are *sensitivity to people* and *accessibility*. In this position, leaders must be accessible at all time. To be a supporter is to help the teachers with all sorts of things they cannot manage for themselves. It can also mean substituting and managing a class for the teacher when necessary. The position indicates that the leader must be sensitive to the teachers' needs. The leader must listen carefully to find out: What

do teachers think? What do teachers want? How do teachers feel? It is important for the leader to have a keen ear in the relationship with teachers to get the opportunity to find out their needs:

> I have tried to analyse this several times. ... What do they really think? ... It is their expectations and what they believe that is the most important.
>
> (Female)

> It's important for me to become acquainted with my staff ... to know about the whole person ... why she doesn't feel well today. To meet each other in the hallway and be able to say ... is Johanna well today? ... It is important for me to have this knowledge.
>
> (Male)

In the Supporter position the leaders express that they have to interpret and code the situation before they can act: 'You treat people so differently depending on how you initially read them. What you say and do with one person will be totally different with another one based on your initial interpretation of each person.'

This position indicates the importance for the leader to try to understand the teacher's experiences in different situations. It is important because it increases their opportunities to have meaningful discussions and it opens up the way for reciprocal development. The leader must find out how the teachers think, how they experience their situation in different contexts. S/he has to do that in order to treat people in the best way. The leader tries to understand in what way the teacher thinks even if s/he knows that they have a difference. The leader should listen to the teacher's opinion and at the same time be honest about her/his own. This position indicates that the leader thinks of this management as an opportunity to progress:

> You always start from your own experiences on how you approach something, but then have to question yourself ... can I approach this differently? ... It is not only my co-workers that need to develop their ways of thinking, I need to do that too. ... You have to always question your way of thinking and be generous and listen to others since there is not really a right or wrong here.
>
> (Female)

When leaders position themselves as Supporters they indicate that teachers' welfare is very important for them. They have to know that the teachers are well and are satisfied with their situation. It is about being up to date in what is happening in the organization. The leader must continuously be involved, in order not to fail to observe if anyone does not feel quite well. If a teacher is experiencing a troublesome situation, the leader must observe that, and act:

> After a couple of days I could make new contacts ... and I say ... perhaps ... I just want to check up on you after our last conversation, ... how did you feel today?
>
> (Male)

The Manager

To be a school leader is to have a superior position in relation to other staff in the school. In the discourse In Service for Teachers, my respondents come to the Manager position that connects to their role as head of the organization. Important meanings in this position are *decision-making* and *educational leadership*. The leader's focus is, on the one hand, on their responsibility to make decisions and, on the other, to be an educational leader. The Manager position signals an ambivalent feeling about being responsible for making fiscal decisions and at the same time being responsible for the school's educational issues:

> There is also a side effect; besides being the educational leader you are also the head. You have to make decisions that can negatively affect people and that you might not be that proud of, which can be really hard since you run into each other all the time; during break times, lunch breaks etc. ... Sometimes you wish that someone else could make these decisions.
>
> (Male)

As Manager, the leader feels frustrated about the impact the economic decision-making has on the people of the organization. It seems that the leader very strongly identifies with the teachers' and children's situation. This could connect to the fact that most school leaders have experienced the teachers' situation and have great sympathy for them:

> One can never think ... you can manage. ... You are OK ... one has to stay close and listen to people. ... It was an incident earlier in the spring, they were short staffed and I was contacted by someone who I regard as very competent and capable. She called and said: 'I can't go on any longer, help me!' I said: 'Yes, I will help you but how?' She told me they were too few to handle the class. 'OK!' I said. 'We'll have a temporarily employed person for a couple of months. Will that be of any help?' She answered: 'Oh yes, sure! But what about the budget?' I said: 'I don't care about the budget; I'll take the costs this

> time so you can go on working again. The situation can be hard out there.'
>
> (Female)

In this position, the leader expresses solidarity with the teachers. S/he identifies with them and has great sympathy for their situation. But despite this, the leader is no longer a member of the team. One leader in my study expressed her awareness of being outside the team, and the consequences that follow:

> Well, ... the good leader perceives that she isn't a friend of the teachers team any more. ... That can be sad ... especially when you are picked up from below. ... They are still my friends but not in the same way ... it's very, very important to realize this...
>
> (Female)

The leaders' stories express that they sometimes feel uncomfortable in their role. At the same time, the leaders expressed a strong resolution to successfully tackle issues. The position also indicates that the leader in some way has to defend herself/himself in the role of being the one having to make hard decisions. The leader has a need to get the teachers to understand and even forgive. The leader seeks ways to reduce the consequences of her/his acts. One strategy is to be a democratic leader. This indicates a person who wants everybody to contribute to decision-making; everybody should have the opportunity to make their voice heard. The democratic leader uses discussion and conversations to try to get understanding from the staff:

> I have told my staff ... every time I myself make a decision it's a failure. I can make a decision ... that's not the problem or a failure. The problem is when you want me to make a decision without you having reflected over the issue first ... then the result is not a good decision. ... Everyone has to be involved and reflect. ... To have that as a rule, I believe, describes a good leader. ... It's a lot easier to make up your own mind and then close the door...
>
> (Male)

The other meaning in the Manager position is to be an educational leader. Most leaders in my study expressed feeling comfortable in this role. This could be explained by the fact that this role is not new for the leader. They feel confident. Their own schooling is long and of great influence. Even the leaders who have their roots in pre-school, expressed feelings of great confidence. The leaders know that this field is something they can handle; they have legitimate knowledge in this issue. Leaders do not have to defend themselves in this role:

> To be courageous and stand up and talk to people, show who you are and what you stand for and where you come from. To show that despite my background as a pre-school teacher, I have experience from the school, which made me trustworthy and treated with respect. The credibility for my knowledge increased. I could stand up for the guidelines that exist in our society ... I could stand up for my own conceptions in education even if those don't agree with the others ... to show that you have some theoretical knowledge about this organization.
>
> (Male)

Leaders with backgrounds in both pre-school and ordinary schools expressed their strengths as educational leaders. The study indicates that this could frame conflicts within the organization between the different educational standpoints, on the one hand pre-school and on the other the ordinary school. In comprehensive schools, teachers from several grades, pre-school teachers, and teachers from youth recreation centres work together. These teachers come from different school cultures, with different views of children's education. This could lead to problems in cooperation. In this position the leader indicates that teachers often emphasize the set goals whereas the leader has a wider perspective where the standpoint is the fundamental and democratic values that function as a guideline for our society. This could be explained by the fact that five of my respondents have their roots in pre-school or youth recreation. Traditionally, Swedish colleges for pre-school teachers give more emphasis to psychological education in children's development compared with the training for comprehensive schoolteachers. This could affect how they perceive children and learning. Pre-school teachers and ordinary teachers could have different views about how children learn:

> The Department of Education already talks about having a common curriculum. ... Which I welcome. ... If you should have a complete view of the child you should have a curriculum that covers all levels of the education ... not one for pre-school, one for comprehensive school and so on ... don't separate them. ... I look forward to [getting the] opportunity to influence some parts of the new curriculum for the whole school system ... where they also will focus [on] questions of values. ... We have always talked about this in pre-school. ... I think one can put in the pedagogy from pre-school in a natural way. ... Don't nag about it as today. ... These fundamental values. ... We must concentrate on them, ... work harder with [them] than we do today. ... I think we give more emphasis [to] reaching the set goals and I don't really understand this ... I think the important issue is the values: ... What values should we have? ...

> How should we cooperate? ... This is my view, ... but this is difficult
> and it might depend on the fact that we have different backgrounds
> [from] the teachers in today's school.
>
> (Female)

In Service for Children

In the In Service for Children discourse, the schools exist for the children and,
of course, my respondents talked about their relations with the children.
When they construct themselves as school leaders they sometimes act in a
discourse that connects meanings in their leadership to their role in relation
to the children. It is interesting that males used this discourse to a higher
extent than the females. Maybe this could be explained in that female leaders
were worried about being seen as filling the role of the caring and sensitive
leader, and therefore they disassociated from this role to a higher extent than
male leaders.

In this discourse I found two dominant positions: the Friend and the
Person Responsible. The Friend position expresses a personal relation to the
children; the leader talks in a way that shows s/he cares about the child. The
other position centres the leader as the person responsible for the children's
education. Men and women used these two positions in different ways. The
leaders expressed comfort in this discourse, which could probably be explained by the fact that the leader had worked as a teacher before, this in not a
new experience for her/him.

The Friend

One important meaning in this position is the *personal relation* to the children. The leader should care for the children, recognize them and know their
names. Another meaning is that the leader must be the children's *commissioner*, the one who in every situation looks out for their needs.

The leaders expressed pride in having a personal relationship with the
children. It is important to know most of the children's names. The position
indicates that relationships with the children are a pleasure:

> I'm outdoors with the children a lot. I know almost all their names
> and they know who I am so it is not a problem. It's more fun that
> way...
>
> (Male)

The leaders expressed that they sometimes missed the daily interaction
with the children that they had when working as a teacher:

> [I feel comfortable when] I have been in school and I have met pu-
> pils, discussed and participated in the classroom ... or when I have
> been in pre-school and participated in their activities heard them talk
> and discuss. Well then I feel, wow, this is fun ... I enjoy it ... and I
> feel connected and really understand my role...
>
> (Female)

In this position the leader recovers strength and feels safety; here the
leader may collect energy to manage the hard parts of leadership. The leader
has several years of experience in cooperating with children and the leader
feels confident. The children are a source of satisfaction in the complex role of
being a school leader:

> I can feel really down when I leave the office at three o'clock; then,
> when I enter the youth recreation centre, three children scream at
> me. It's difficult ... I think one must learn to enjoy and find happi-
> ness in small things. ... For me it's very much about relationships
> with people. ... If you have experienced something positive, ...
> that's great. ... You could have great visions for this day ... [and] the
> whole educational union stand up and congratulate you for good
> achievements ... that's not really interesting...
>
> (Male)

The leader should also be the commissioner for the children, the person
who guarantees that the children get as much as possible out of their school
situation. The leaders feel they have a responsibility for the children's welfare.
In relation to the teachers, the leader's task is to bring attention to the children's perspective. Children's needs come first. One leader explained it in this
way:

> To [focus] on the question [of] why we are here: ... we have a
> common mission although the mission differs in relation to the
> different categories in school ... but the mission is the same ... you
> can dislike parts of it ... OK ... but you have to enjoy it. ... We don't
> come here by chance, ... what we do isn't random. ... We are here
> for the sake of the children and our mission is to make it as good for
> them as possible.
>
> (Female)

The Person Responsible
In this position the leader talks about herself/himself as responsible for the
children's education. Meanings found here are *divider of resources* and *con-
troller*. The leader is responsible for her/his school meeting the demands

written in both the national and local curricula. Her/his task is to manage the resources and see that they are divided as fairly as possible. In their position the leader sometimes needs to control. Occasionally the leader has to visit the classroom in order to be informed. The leaders feel a responsibility for the quality of the education in school since they are responsible for ensuring that the school meets the children's needs. Sometimes it can be hard to manage the demands that are set by society:

> Then it's the issue of resources. ... Do I have the competence that the pupils need to make the next step? That is your main responsibility really ... to make sure that the competence level among the staff is there. The hardest task is to make sure that the resources are placed where most needed. Unfortunately you have to prioritize. We have the curriculum, which clearly states that the main goal is to make sure that all pupils pass, but sometimes that is not the case, and that is hard.
>
> (Male)

The position indicates that the leader should divide resources but also be responsible for the learning in school. The children must get the 'right' knowledge. The leader must be up to date in education research. In this position, the leader has to be involved in these issues. S/he absorbs what happens in research and transforms the knowledge into her/his own attitudes of education and learning:

> The view of children's education is very much anchored in theoretical knowledge not in a wider perspective of children's learning. I feel that sometimes one is too faithful to the book. Is it important that Lisa does three pages of maths or does she have to do these specific three pages in the book? ... Much has changed but not enough ... [laughing].
>
> (Male)

In this position, the leader expresses a need to control teachers in order to mediate the right knowledge:

> I am the one responsible that my children are met by adults who follow the set goals. ... In a way I am their commissioner. I am the one responsible for making sure that we follow the demands set by our society.
>
> (Female)

Sometimes there is a demand for the leader to participate in the classroom. The leader participates in activities in school in order to experience how the teachers manage their missions. From these visits, the leaders have an opportunity to start discussions with the teachers:

> I try to participate out in the school since you see so much ... regardless of whether you have lunch with them or are participating in a PE class or any other outdoor activity. ... You see the relationships between the adult and the children and you have more to discuss when you have participated in these activities.
>
> (Female)

In Service for Development

The In Service for Development discourse focuses on the leaders' relation to school development. Even in this discourse, female and male leaders position themselves in different ways. Two positions have been identified in this discourse: the Guide and the Evaluator. In the Guide position the leader talks about her/his role of being a challenger and a pioneer working for the school's development. This position is used to a higher extent by male leaders. The other position, the Evaluator, concerns the leader as somebody who evaluates the activities in school. It is here one finds the females.

The Guide

In this position, the leader talks about her/his role to challenge prevailing patterns that do not fit with her/his own views. The leader is responsible for the school's development and the important meanings are *to question* and *to inspire*. The leader's tasks are not only to question prevailing patterns but also to inspire and encourage teachers to new ideas and ways to think. The position indicates that the leader must be brave and dare to challenge the teachers' activities. One leader in this position says:

> Sometimes I say to people that come to see me, and are very stressed by not having enough time ... 'Who do you need time for? Is it for you, the children or the parents? What is it you don't have time for?' I believe that sometimes it is easy to get into an evil circle and just run around and believe that you should manage everything that you have in the past. ... Teachers' work situation has changed dramatically in the past years.
>
> (Male)

In this position the leaders' background could give rise to questions. Perhaps the leader has her/his roots in other parts of the school organization or even in another area. This could lead to disagreements between the leader and the teachers regarding education management:

> I can see how the work teams look at learning differently depending on their background. As a teacher in a youth recreation centre I have a broader view of children compared with a teacher. ... Generally, though, I think the teachers try to get a broader comprehensive view. ... But what is a comprehensive view now? ... That's a view covering the child's whole day in school – both school and after-school activities.
>
> (Male)

The position indicates the leader has a role to inspire. The following leader expressed that she encouraged good initiatives and she also tried to come up with ideas:

> When you are sitting with a team, where you know that someone has special competence ... and you know this person does not have the courage to use it ... and when she suddenly stands up ... you know that you have encouraged her, you feel great. It is very rewarding to see people grow.
>
> (Female)

Another leader indicates from this position that he is responsible for improving competences in the teacher team:

> To be able to give challenging questions ... that guide to new processes for people ... dare to challenge ... not lead ... not show them but challenge the teachers to get the knowledge about learning themselves.
>
> (Male)

The Evaluator

Female leaders mostly use the position of evaluator. Females talked to a higher extent than males about how their acts affected the organization. In this position the leader gives much emphasis to self-restraint and to looking back and learning from experiences. The leader in this position expresses a humble attitude towards her role as a leader:

> Reflect upon your actions. ... Why do I do the things I do? What do I have to develop? How did I do this? From my perspective I have been supervised all the time since I started this work and I don't think I would have survived without it.
>
> (Female)

The leader positioned as an Evaluator tries to understand the teacher. The leader pays attention to the teachers' opinion and then relates them to her/his own. S/he knows that it is important not to stagnate. The leader has a responsibility for the school's development and has to get discussions moving. The school does not benefit by stranded discussions:

> It's important to listen and try to understand. ... How did he/she think and what is the reality of her/his experience? Try to understand their way of thinking and from that try to meet and move on and develop perhaps a deeper understanding. The meeting is important ... you must listen but also question your own opinion in order to develop...
>
> (Female)

The leader in this position talks about the importance of paying attention to the way they express themselves. What words they use in a situation could decide how other people react to what they have to say:

> I often reflect on my job and meditate upon words and the words' value. 2001 was an awful year ... it was very hard. ... It was really crazy. ... You had to face desperate parents ... angry parents ... heartbroken staff. ... It was very hard. ... How do you treat them with respect? At this time I worked a lot with myself. ... How should I be able to? How could I speak to these parents about this? And then I found a sentence ... 'Your child gets as much help as we are able to give.' ... That could be very provoking, I thought. ... What kind of nonsense is that? ... But none of the families I told that to reacted in this way. To say 'we have no money for this' is the same, but I said it in a different way...
>
> (Female)

From the teacher's perspective

From the teacher's point of view, the most important thing is to have a leader who is listening to what they have to say. The leader should show interest in their situation in the classroom and be involved in the kinds of problems they struggle with in their everyday work. The leader should be there whenever the teacher needs her/him:

> The good leader from my perspective is a leader that listens ... is interested in listening and discussing ideas. ... Suddenly it might be possible to realize this idea you had once that did not work then,

> but might now. To be able to listen ... to understand. The leader's door should be open and you should have access to her/him, be able to talk about problems etc. and she/he needs to listen and make you feel important.

Teachers have a need to be noticed. From the teacher's perspective it is important that the leader knows what s/he is doing in the classroom: 'A leader is someone who tries to understand what I do and visits in the classroom ... gives comments on our work and gives support.'

Today, many teachers work in a team; several teachers cooperate with one class. But still many teachers are quite alone in the classroom and also alone with all the problems. My findings indicate that teachers need a leader who supports them. Someone to share their experiences with, '... that we can discuss together ... so I don't have to bear all the burdens myself'.

Teachers indicate that the position Supporter is important and this investigation shows that leaders have understood that it is valuable for them to position themselves in a discourse that focuses on the relation with the teachers. In the discourse In Service for Teachers, two positions were identified, the Supporter and the Manager. The study shows that teachers also emphasize the position Manager. A leader must, from the teachers' perspective, be able to make decisions. Leaders' and teachers' opinions differ in that leaders want teachers to be involved in decision-making to a higher extent than teachers really want. Teachers think that the leader should be responsible for some decisions. In their opinion they did not need to share all the decisions the leader makes. The teachers indicate that their confidence in the leader does not increase because the leader shares all decisions with them. They want the leader to take responsibility for determining which decisions they have to involve teachers in, and which should be made by the leader alone:

> This filter I was talking about is missing in this school since one has to participate in all decision-making although sometimes you feel that you should not really be involved. One has a tendency to be too nice in a way. A leader has to share and let people take part but instead of having filtered issues they often let the teams be involved in too much of the decision-making and one can feel, 'Why should we discuss this? This is really the leader's responsibility.'

The teachers in the study state that this does not mean that they are not interested in what is decided in school. They assert that other solutions could be used to get people involved in such cases:

> Really, I don't mean that everyone must be involved in the decisions since that would be too inefficient, but there should be a forum where we could all talk about it before, and give you the feeling of being a part of, the decision.

The teachers indicate that the leader should not be afraid of being the manager. The leaders, on the other hand, feel that they must get the teachers' forgiveness for their need to make uncomfortable decisions. According to teachers' experiences expressed in this study, leaders should not be concerned since teachers indicate great understanding for the leaders' situation and problems:

> I think what's most difficult are situations when they have orders from above. When they have to make a decision that they might not fully agree with but it is their responsibility to establish the decision with the staff. ... The role of being the middleman, I believe, can be very hard for them.

> When it comes to decisions that have to be managed from a higher level ... which do not benefit the staff ... and takes a step back, ... I think she feels bad about that. ... When she has to decide something we don't like ...

> I think the leader has a very tough role. ... On one hand he should be a supporter for the staff and inspire, and on the other hand he should ensure that the school does not exceed the economic frames.

The teachers in the study indicate that they do not want to have a leader who is able to manage all kinds of issues without any mistakes. From their perspective the leader should show her/his limitations and be able to make mistakes:

> It's necessary for a leader to be brave and to dare to get involved in challenging issues that can be really chaotic ... but we don't see many of them do that. ... To dare this free-fall and see where you land ... and at the same time be prepared to fail.

Another tendency in the teachers' reports indicates that teachers want the leader to challenge them. They want the leader to question their activities in the classroom and discuss educational issues with them. This result is interesting because there are studies (Berg 1995) concerning the relation between teachers and leaders that assert that teachers are comfortable when they are left alone and could take care of education themselves:

> Yes, some feedback but also ... perhaps some suggestions. ... Maybe you should try this; get a dialogue started on how you work in the classroom.

Perhaps to challenge could in some way be to show interest in the teachers' work. A leader that challenges what the teachers do shows interest in educational issues, and this increase from the teachers' perspective gives the leaders legitimacy.

Gender shows its face

Stereotypes and taken-for-granted 'truths' that flourish in society and in some research assert that female leadership is characterized by more humbleness and greater awareness of the staff members and their needs. On the other hand, a stereotypical view of male leadership is characterized as more directed to administrative issues. According to this study, both female and male leaders use positions that connect to humbleness, the needs of the staff attention to administrative issues. Results from this study show only small differences between how female and male school leaders related to such stereotypes. Maybe the great number of female school leaders today has affected the leadership discourses. Results from this study suggest that meanings connected to female leadership and meanings connected to male leadership affect the construction of school leadership. We could conclude that stereotypes did not work, but elements in this study indicate that they still work. Both leaders and teachers talk about the importance of listening to the teachers and their needs. In the study both female and male leaders use the Supporter position quite often. The two most used positions in the study are the Supporter and the Manager, and there are very small differences in the way female and male leaders use them. The leaders are both supporter and manager.

Teachers express that they are very comfortable with a female leader who uses the Supporter position quite often. They praise their leaders' qualities and express that they are satisfied with the leadership:

> I think it works very well here. ... I don't have any extra help in the class but I have her back-up and support ... and she participates in my conversations ... with other authorities.
>
> (Female)

> I think it's amazingly good really. ... I feel I can defend this school. ... Our leader is really trying to run a learning organization.
>
> (Male)

An interesting result in this study is that when teachers who have a male leader who is mostly positioned as a Supporter, talk about how they experience their leader, the result indicates that there is something that does not fit. Something in this leadership is experienced as uncomfortable. When asked to describe a good school leader from her perspective, one teacher says:

> It's a question of communication ... open dialogues and open discussions. ... It's hard to be a leader if you're not sensitive to your staff. ... It's important to understand the staff and in a way understand how they think, how they operate, and how the organization operates ... also to try to understand the thoughts and ideas of the staff, since they are the experts.
>
> (Female)

This is her view of the ultimate school leader. Her leader describes good school leadership in this way:

> You are a part of the organization ... you have a dialogue with the staff ... to understand what they are doing and be able to discuss with them at team meetings ... and then it's very important to support the staff when they have an idea so they could proceed with things...
>
> (Female)

From my perspective these two explanations of what characterizes a good leader are very similar. The teachers and the leaders emphasize the same meanings. Why, then, is the teacher not comfortable with her leader:

> In some way ... too kind [laughing]. ... He wants everyone to be happy ... and he wants to share a lot with the staff ... but finally it's too much.
>
> (Female)

One explanation could be that this leader does not fit the stereotypical picture of what a male leader is like. Similar tendencies could be viewed when male leaders use the Manager position only seldom. This leadership is also experienced as slightly uncomfortable. Two teachers with a leader who does not often position himself as a Manager say:

> He does not dare to stand up for himself. ... In a way he's a bit cowardly ... a bit unstable. Here ... one has to dare...

> Maybe he's a bit obscure ... he didn't guide very forcefully. ... You
> have to dare to be clear enough.

These two teachers express that they miss the strong leader who is able to
show his power and put his foot down when necessary. This could be an
example of how gender shows its face and indicates that stereotypes still exist.

Female leaders in this study used the Manager position quite often but
this is not something that disturbs the teachers. It seems that male leaders
who use the Supporter position are received more uncomfortably than female
leaders using the same position. It seems that male leaders who use discourse
stereotypically coded as female meet more resistance than female leaders
using male-coded discourse. Female leaders who are humble in relation to the
staff and show sensitivity for their needs match the stereotypical view of
female school leadership. A male leader who often positions himself as a
Supporter and shows all these qualities does not fit into the stereotypical view
of a male leader. A male leader should be very much a Manager and he should
show that he is able to put his foot down. When a male leader does not show
much of this, his leadership is experienced as uncomfortable. It seems that it
is harder for a male leader to cross discourses than for a woman. Perhaps this
is not so strange. Swedish society signals in its curriculum and in the labour
market that girls and women should chose education and jobs that are male-
dominant. But there is very little emphasis on boys and men choosing a
female-dominant education and work. This tells us that it is more normal for
women to cross gender barriers than it is for men.

Conclusion

What could we learn then from these results? It is important to keep in mind
that this study is based on how teachers and school leaders talk about school
leadership. We know that what we say is not always the same as how we act.
However, my purpose was to find how school leaders construct themselves
discursively. I think these constructions say something about Swedish school
leadership today. According to this study, the most used discourse is In Service for Teachers. In this discourse there were two frequently used positions:
the Supporter and the Manager. The Supporter position could be linked to
stereotypes in society that are female-coded. The Manager position could be
linked to what stereotypically is coded as male-directed leadership. The result
in this study indicates that both male and female leaders use these positions.
Tendencies in this study indicate that in Sweden today the leadership discourses are coded by both men and women. Perhaps this could be a result of
the high number of female school leaders in Sweden today.

Another marked tendency in this study is that male leaders can meet resistance when they cross between discourses and use what we stereo-typically see as female-coded discourses. This is very interesting because most discussions concerning gender relations talk about women's oppression and assert that women meet more resistance in leadership positions than do men. This study does not indicate that. The results indicate that it could be harder for male leaders who use positions connected to humility and sensitivity than it is for female leaders who use positions connected to administrative skills. This result suggests a shift in leadership discourses.

Does gender matter when school leaders construct themselves as leaders? This study indicates that there is very little difference in how female and male school leaders construct themselves as leaders. They meet the school's demand to be both supporters and managers. They take good care of staff and have no problem with the role of manager. It seems that gender matters most at the present time in the ways teachers react to leadership by men and by women.

PART II

LEADERSHIP PRACTICES AMIDST GLOBAL AND LOCAL CHANGE

5   Steel Magnolias in Velvet Ghettoes: Female Leaders in Australian Girls' Schools

John Collard

Introduction

The second wave of feminism, which swept through western democracies after the 1960s, has had a profound influence upon assumptions about gender, social roles and leadership. It also promoted critiques of patriarchal inheritances in both private and public realms (Ferguson 1984; Hearn 1993; Reiger 1993). In the 1990s it also sparked a belated interest in concepts of masculinity. The field of gender studies in education has become increasingly important in this context. Enormous attention has been paid to the intersections between gender and student development (Kenway 1990). Less has been paid to the role of gender in school leadership and this prompted Marshall and Rusch (1995) to lament that the field of educational administration is gender blind.

As far back as 1962, American trait theorists argued that the leadership styles of men and women were 'fundamentally different' (Hemphill 1961). In the 1980s, feminists began to insist that women wanted to lead in opposed ways to men. Ferguson (1984) typecast the latter as fundamentally 'authoritarian, bureaucratic, functionalist and utilitarian'. Gilligan's (1982) research into male and female decision-making was adopted as a foundational plank to argue that women were more 'compassionate, co-operative, communal and relational'. Noddings (1984) built upon this with her popular 'ethic of care'. Another dimension of early theory built upon Harstock's (1983) argument that women leaders valued 'organic relationships' over 'hierarchical accountabilities'. By the 1990s, this logic had led Hegelson (1991) to define 'feminine principles', which she contrasted with a masculine style she ridiculed as 'dominant and dysfunctional'. Eisler (1995) followed by arguing that women sought to be more 'inclusive' and work through 'weblike structures of networks, partnerships and relationships'.

The development of masculinist theories in the 1990s tended to duplicate the stereotypes of preceding feminist discourses. Seidler (1994) and Steinberg (1993) both critiqued modern masculinity for its instrumental bias, which scripts males to value rationality, authority and task-orientation over more affective and nurturant possibilities. Hearn (1993) argued that public patri-archs who held these values had displaced feminine values from domains such education, childcare and social work under a bureaucratic British state. Subsequent theorists such as Biddulph (1994), Edgar (1997) and Tacey (1997) have tended to accept authoritarian and utilitarian definitions of male leadership.

However, the field has developed more sophisticated and nuanced un-derstandings of the interaction between gender and social contexts in recent years. The most important is the work of Connell (1995) who argued against unitary typecasting and in favour of a theory of multiple femininities and masculinities. By this he meant that interactions with social variables such as class, ethnicity, professional life, rurality or sexuality, produce variations which belie simplistic stereotypes. MacInnes (1998) has argued that the concepts of femininity and masculinity have become generic terms which mask other key social variables such as class and ethnicity. Stereotypes of male and female leadership therefore have less credibility in gender discourse today than they had a decade ago.

Educational leadership discourse

It is possible to trace a growing awareness of the role of gender in school leadership since 1980. This was fostered by feminists who sought to combat and explain the low representation of women leaders in a profession where they represent approximately 70 per cent of employees in many western democracies (Ozga 1993; Collard 2001). A consistent feature of the writings was its excessive and uncritical dependence upon essentialist typologies of male and female leadership styles.

In the USA, Biklen argued that women possessed a stronger natural pre-disposition towards collaborative modes than men (Biklen and Brannigan 1980). Shakeshaft (1987) completed the first major study into women in school leadership in the USA. She identified five key differences between men and women. One was a claim that women were more focused upon instruc-tional leadership than men, who had a more managerial focus. Another was that women were more consultative, inclusive and participatory than men. A decade later she was arguing that women were more likely to use a collegial style, to focus on personal and relational issues and to provide environments which empower women (as cited in Collard 1996). In Britain, Gray (1989) developed gender paradigms. His feminine paradigm stressed care, creativity, intuition, sensitivity to diversity, tolerance, subjectivity, informality and non-competitiveness. Conversely, his masculine paradigm stressed high regula-tion, conformity, competition, evaluation, discipline, objectivity and formality.

This essentialism had gained almost mythic authority by the 1990s. An extreme example was the feminist polemic of Adler and her colleagues (1993), who argued for the existence of a feminist leadership style which drew upon organic structures from the women's movement and displaced the pyramidical and linear models preferred by men. It also informed burgeoning consultancies and development programmes about women's ways of leading in many countries.

However, feminists who held more complex understandings of social processes began to conduct grounded research and complain about the naivety of typecasts. Evetts (1994) found that some female leaders were authoritative and hierarchical and some men collegial and participatory. Kruger (1996) studied 49 matched pairs of female and male leaders in the Netherlands and disputed that women are more relationship orientated than men. In New Zealand, Court (1998) studied co-principalships and concluded that there was little substance to Hegelson's (1991) claim of a distinctive female leadership style. In Britain, Coleman (1998) argued that the female heads she studied exhibited both feminine and masculine qualities.

Critical feminists also drew upon Connell's (1987, 1990) insights into the role of power in gender relations. Reiger (1993) agreed that educational leadership was a masculinist enterprise and that women carried a disproportionate amount of the emotional labour in schools. Others began to acknowledge that some women lead like men (Marshall and Rusch 1995; Sinclair 1998; Wajcman 1998).

Grounded studies in educational leadership continued to undermine the credibility of the stereotypes as the decade proceeded. In Hong Kong, a study of 77 female principals disputed the stereotypes advanced by Gray and Shakeshaft (Shum and Chen 1997). British researches demonstrated increasingly complex understandings on the impact of institutional cultures on leader behaviour and beliefs. Hall (1996) indicated that level of schooling tended to undermine differences between male and female leaders. Others pointed to the influence of institutional cultures and social variables such as ethnicity and class on leaders (Ribbins 1996, 1999; Pascal and Ribbins 1998). In Canada, Reynolds (2002b) stressed generational changes and the impact of historical contexts on the leadership work of men and women in schools. In Australia, Gronn (1995) pointed to how conveyer belt systems comprising a handful of expensive and selective schools, academies and universities, transported the well-educated and well-connected male progeny of wealthy established families to positions of public power. Detailed analysis by Teese (2000) supported his contention.

A discrete silence in feminist accounts of school leadership was also punctured towards the end of the decade. In 1997, Tacey called for the recognition of traditions of maternal domination. Mertz and McNeely (1998) alerted us to traditions of matriarchal control in Afro-American settings.

Sperandio's (2003) accounts of girls' schools in Norwich, England, in the Victorian era clearly indicated that headmistresses tended to wield considerable power and to dictate to parents. Those who are familiar with the histories of non-government girls' schools in Australia did not find this surprising. Historical and fictional accounts of such schools had portrayed powerful matriarchs who brooked little interference with their regimes (Lindsay 1967; Richardson 1970; Gardiner 1977; Burren 1984). Such examples contradicted the claims of earlier theorists such as Gray and Shakeshaft.

By the late 1990s a variety of influences had therefore converged to question typecasts of leadership and gender in schools, which had become popular in the preceding decades. The understandings of researchers in both gender studies and educational leadership were becoming increasingly sophisticated and unlikely to accept single-factor explanations of complex social phenomena. There was an emerging challenge to explore whether specific contexts and traditions helped to differentiate leadership approaches both between and within genders. One area of neglect was the leadership of women in girls' schools, a domain where we could expect to see feminine leadership styles flourish. It was in such a context that this study sought to explore leadership in girls' schools in Victoria, the second most populous state in Australia. Many of these were located in the independent sector and have served socially mobile middle classes throughout their history. We need to ask if they too operated as conveyor belts to privilege in the manner described by Gronn. What attitudes and values did their leaders hold? How did these shape the leadership culture within the schools? Conversely, did leaders from government and Catholic sites, which have traditionally served broader publics, differ from their counterparts in independent schools? Some understanding of the history of girls' schools in Australia is essential before we proceed further.

Historical context

The genesis of single-sex girls' schools in Australia can be traced to a number of origins and traditions. The first stems from the domain of home schooling on the frontier. This resembles similar traditions in other immigrant communities in the nineteenth century. Family members, who were predominately mothers and older sisters, took responsibility for the basic education of young siblings in locations where schools simply did not exist. Fathers and older brothers oversaw craft and vocational learning. In rare cases, wealthy families were able to provide governesses for their children (Austin 1977; Barcan 1980; Theobald 1996).

The second tradition related to the rise of small primary schools conducted by religious communities. These tended to combine basic education with religious instruction and only serviced a small proportion of children in the Australian colonies. After the Gold Rush in the 1850s brought new affluence to some families, some of these expanded to develop secondary classes. The foundation of the Academy of Mary Immaculate in Fitzroy in 1853 by the Sisters of Mercy is one such school and continues to the present day (Martin 1986). Others such as Methodist Ladies' College and Presbyterian Ladies' College were founded by other denominations. Such schools, if led by women, were responsible to religious authorities for their conduct. In all cases they were initially under the aegis of clerical patriarchs (Fogarty 1957; Fitzpatrick 1975; Zainu'ddin 1982; Martin 1986; Donaldson 1993; Leonard 1995). There are instances in the histories, especially in Catholic congregations, where this yoke was a source of conflict between female principals and priests. However, it is also possible that the women leaders in some congregations duplicated the authoritarian traditions of male control in the absence of competing leadership discourses or models.

These denominational schools were clearly a manifestation of a separation of powers between church and state. When colonial governments moved towards creating a system of universal public schooling in the 1870s, church authorities that administered these schools mounted strong opposition. Fuelled by fear that a secular heathenism would corrupt their young, they defended, consolidated and expanded their provision. The most extensive manifestation was the creation of a system of Catholic parochial schools. Bishops recruited religious congregations from Ireland to conduct these schools, and the last decades of the nineteenth century also saw expanded secondary schools. By the end of the nineteenth century, congregations had built extensive networks of convent schools for girls throughout Victoria and other colonies. This was paralleled by a series of boys' schools operated by male religious congregations (Martin 1986).

A third tradition stems from cottage schools conducted by independent women and their family members. Theobald (1996) has documented a striking pattern of matrilineal control in these establishments as mothers supervised daughters and other female subordinates at Rhyton, the Kyneton Academy or Clyde Girls' School. These were small, private academies geared towards servicing the educational aspirations of an emerging colonial middle class. They frequently believed their primary task was to teach the accomplishments young ladies would need to become wives and mothers. Their schools were private enterprises and they ran them with authoritative rigour. Theobald defined them as matriarchs accustomed to wielding power.

The cottage and church-based schools for girls remained the dominant providers of girls' secondary education until the expansion of state secondary schools in Victoria after the 1920s. Even then, the state created only a few specialist academies for girls. However, technical education was provided in segregated sites for boys and girls who were deemed unsuited for academic education. The boys' techs placed a strong emphasis upon manual and vocational skills; the girls sites concentrated upon domestic science or secretarial skills, which were considered appropriate for working-class women. These never really competed with the middle-class academies and were generally phased out in Victoria in the 1970s. The non-government sites have therefore retained pre-eminence as appropriate sites for daughters of an upwardly mobile middle class to this day. They have become large, prestigious establishments. By 1990, Methodist Ladies' College had over 2000 students and the sites investigated in the following study had enrolments ranging from 700 to 1100 pupils.

Much of our evidence about female leadership of Australian girls' schools in the colonial era is drawn from fictionalized accounts. Henry Handel Richardson's portrait, first published in 1912, of her days at Presbyterian Ladies' College in East Melbourne reveals stern female leadership preoccupied with conformity, order and social status (Richardson 1970). The portrait betrays little compassion or sympathy for the personal struggles of female students or staff. The Annie Johns episode, where a wayward petty thief is cast from the temple of middle-class respectability by a brimstone cleric, leaves an impression of a harsh matriarch enforcing Victorian codes of morality.

Joan Lindsay (1967) attended Clyde Girls' School in the same era, and her *Picnic at Hanging Rock* is believed to be her memories of her days there (Theobald 1996). Appleyard College is an example of a cottage industry and its principal a beleaguered matriarch who is more concerned about financial balance sheets than the welfare of her charges. It too portrays the female principal as a harsh, authoritarian leader. She and Mrs Gurley from Richardson's account are the very antithesis of the relational typologies developed by cultural feminists as they sought to define a distinctive female leadership style a century later.

Official histories of independent and Catholic girls' schools or religious congregations did not begin to emerge until the 1970s as female historians sought to assess the legacy of the past. They tend to provide broader insights than the fictional cameos by documenting decision-making and conflicts. However, we need to distinguish between critical histories and laudatory accounts commissioned by some schools and congregations. The latter are likely to have censored some of the more colourful episodes from the archives and to represent history as a heroic narrative of achievement (Gronn 1995). Critical historians provide more searching analyses. They highlight the struggles many female leaders had with local, church and state authorities, their strengths, weaknesses and idiosyncrasies. Nevertheless they help to build a composite portrait of leadership in such sites. Theobald (1978) does not flinch from naming the fierce territorial stance of the founder of Rhyton. Gardiner's (1977) account of Tintern celebrates the benevolent family atmosphere of its early years but also chronicles how Miss Ball (principal

1918–1928) 'kept her distance', held 'an essentially hierarchical view of the school' and 'would not admit mistakes'. Zain'uddin (1982) documents the exclusion of women from power for much of the history of Methodist Ladies' College and the struggle to reverse this tradition in the 1960s. Burren (1984) does not camouflage authoritarian leadership at Mentone Girls' Grammar. Indeed, her portrayal of Jeanie McCowan (principal 1938–1955) is one of an unapproachable matriarch besieged by disgruntled parents who considered her leadership style inappropriate.

The fictional and historical accounts of girls' schools in Victoria provide insights into female leadership which are absent from the theory developed by cultural feminists in the last decades of the twentieth century. They have overlooked the considerable strength demonstrated by women in establishing schools or in working with marginalized communities. The theory also suffers from a form of historical amnesia by ignoring authoritarian uses of power, which are the antithesis of claims about sensitive, inclusive and relational styles. This constitutes an unacceptable silence in the discourse about leadership and gender which must be redressed.

Research method

The findings reported here are based upon a questionnaire and interviews which explored the perceptions and beliefs of a balanced gender sample of 370 Victorian school principals. This constituted over 10 per cent of the total in the state and a return rate of 73 per cent of 500 mailed questionnaires. The sample also reflected the relative proportions of primary and secondary sites and the three sectors in the state at the time (Curriculum Corporation 1996). In addition, 28 of the respondents to the questionnaire also participated in subsequent structured interviews.

The questionnaire sample included principals from 38 girls' schools. Of these, 32 were women. One came from the government sector, the remaining 31 from Catholic and independent sites. All but two of these schools had enrolments in excess of 600 pupils. Six of the female leaders were also interviewed: one from a government site, two from Catholic sites and three from independent schools. None of the six male principals from girls' schools were interviewed but their questionnaire responses revealed them to be in close harmony with their female counterparts on many issues.

The study drew upon coherentist epistemology, which argues that diverse methodologies can be harnessed to generate more comprehensive explanations than singular approaches (Evers and Lakomski 1991, 1996a,b,c). Knowledge claims from the quantitative data were validated through dialogue between the researcher and a representative sample of the questionnaire respondents. It was also influenced by Kvale's (1996) insistence that contemporary researchers need to move beyond confirmatory validations to explore deeper understandings of the meanings and complexities which characterize human beliefs. Interview data were therefore used to confirm, explore, expand and qualify the quantitative findings. Contradictions and tensions were also noted and explored in interviews that questionnaire instruments could not render.

The questionnaire was structured to reflect gender polarities that dominated the current leadership and gender discourses. Items were organized around the themes of curriculum goals, pedagogy, working with teachers, and relationships with parent and community members. If the claims of theorists such as Gilligan (1982), Ferguson (1984), Shakeshaft (1987), Gray (1989), Adler *et al.* (1993) and Hearn (1993) are sound, we could expect women leaders to favour personal-developmental curriculum goals, support collaborative pedagogies and endorse participatory modes of working with teachers, parents and community representatives. Such values would counterpoint with items that reflected assumed masculine priorities, such as utilitarian goals, competitive pedagogies, authoritarian and bureaucratic relations with teachers, and exclusive stances towards parents and community groups.

Questionnaire responses were tabulated according to frequencies and then cross-tabulated according to the variables of gender, school level, sectoral identity, student gender and school size. The Pearson Test of Statistical Significance was used to determine statistical significance at the 0.05, 0.01 and 0.001 levels, which were unlikely to be a function of sampling error. This method enabled analysis of data in the form of paired observations on two variables such as principal gender and school sector. The findings indicated the presence or absence of a relationship between the two.

The interviews provided opportunities for principals to elaborate, qualify or refine the responses they had provided to the questionnaire. For instance, they were asked whether they favoured collaborative or competitive pedagogies, consultation over executive command, collegial or bureaucratic approaches to staff management, and inclusive as opposed to exclusive relationships with parents.

Interview responses were transcribed, coded and cross-referenced to questionnaire data. A subsequent stage drew the two data sets into an interpretative pattern. This was aided by reference to school and sectorial histories. At times the emergent patterns from the questionnaire and interview data became comprehensible only when linked to these historical accounts. In this sense, qualitative, quantitative and historical findings contributed to the construction of triangulated interpretations.

Findings

These findings are presented in relation to how respondents perceived and reacted to three key stakeholder groups: students, teachers and parents in their schools. There were significant differences between those from independent and other sectors. While there was some consistency between the findings related to students and teachers, parents were perceived and treated in surprisingly different ways.

Students

Victorian secondary schools do not all serve the same types of student communities. There is diversity in the landscape, which ranges from highly privileged enclaves of families with considerable financial and cultural capital, to concentrations of learners with social backgrounds and specific disabilities which impede their educational progress (Teese 2000). In Victoria, there is a common perception that the majority of government and Catholic schools provide forms of public education. This diversity was reflected in responses to the questionnaire. Over two-thirds of female principals across all types and levels of schooling (68 per cent) believed their sites contained high proportions of students who find learning difficult. However, only 15 per cent of women from the independent sector (15 per cent) believed this. Indeed, almost 80 per cent believed the reverse, that their schools contained many high achievers.

This positive perception of the student population appeared to influence the curriculum philosophies of women leaders in such sites. They were much more aligned with liberal traditions of education as individual development (Stefkovich and Shapiro 2003) than those from government sites who stressed more instrumental, skill-orientated agendas. Almost 80 per cent of female leaders from the independent sector agreed that learning in their schools was a search for personal meaning. The comparative levels of agreement among women from Catholic (61 per cent) and government sites (48 per cent) were significantly lower ($p = 0.01$, 6df). Interview responses confirmed this. One argued: 'I want to claim that personal meaning is the most important thing. The fact that we are an independent school means, however, that we are interpreted as being an academic school.' Another viewed her role as a curriculum leader as 'working at creating an environment that will be a personally meaningful experience. That's really fundamental to our philosophy.' Over one-third (38 per cent) of her colleagues were in strong agreement on this matter. This was almost five times the proportion of women from the government sector (8 per cent) and over double that from women in Catholic schools (17 per cent). Such goals may be partly attributable to past legacies where these schools provided a curriculum for girls in the accomplishments and humanities to prepare them for future family and social roles (Theobald 1996). There was evidence of the persistence of this rationale in the interviews: '. . . who else is going to introduce them to Mozart and Beethoven, who else is going to introduce them to the classics?'

Women leaders from government and Catholic girls' schools shared this commitment to personal-developmental curriculum goals. However, their utterances had a different flavour. It was much more strongly orientated towards philosophies of pastoral care. One argued: 'Anytime a school concentrates too much upon the academic and not the personal pastoral care role, I think the academic will be unsuccessful. Personal development must co-exist with the academic; it must be of equal value.' A leader from a Catholic girls' school demonstrated an interventionist approach to students at risk: 'I said to them last year, when Gina comes in and whether her hair is purple or green and she's got ninety-five earrings, nobody is to say anything about that to her. It's my priority to get her out of the drug scene and into school. So don't blow it on me over those things.' She continued to articulate a philosophy of care which echoes of the human potential precepts (Maslow 1968) and Nodding's (1984) feminist ethic: 'You are not teaching mathematics, you are teaching people. . . . I say to parents so often "unless your child is happy, she can't learn! So we've got to work on this part first. Let's not worry whether she is doing her homework. Let's work on how we can make her happy and then she can learn." It's that belief in the person . . .'.

The different concepts reflect the different contexts in which these leaders of girls' schools work. The government and Catholic leaders appear focused upon a student needs hierarchy. Emotional wellbeing is perceived as a precondition for learning for struggling students. Those from the independent schools seem more committed to a tradition which sanctions individual development as a curriculum goal for relatively privileged communities. It is possible that traditional liberal ideals can continue to flourish for their clientele even at the end of the twentieth century, when Australia was experiencing unprecedented levels of youth unemployment and social dislocation (Woden 1998).

The three sources – the questionnaire, the interview transcripts and the historical accounts – all provide consistent evidence of a strong commitment to personal-developmental goals in non-government girls' schools in Victoria. However, the evidence also calls for a refinement of Shakeshaft's claim that women are more instructionally focused than men. It suggests that their focus is actively shaped by the institutional cultures and social contexts in which they work. They appear to be working in a common site, girls' schools, but we need a nuanced understanding and explanations for the differences between them. Differences within a gender group can be important, a fact that much past theory on leadership and gender has overlooked.

Women from independent girls' schools also differed from other groups in the study when it came to pedagogy. They were significantly less supportive of individual responsibility for learning (82 per cent) than women from government (92 per cent) and Catholic (88 per cent) sites ($p = 0.04$, 6df). It appears that women from these sites favoured more supportive pedagogical approaches. This is somewhat surprising when one recalls the strong emphasis upon individualism in liberal traditions of education. Several argued that collaborative learning was the most highly valued in their schools. One explanation is that many girls' sites have operated as protected worlds or 'velvet ghettoes' in the past. Those with cottage origins deliberately fostered an atmosphere of strong familial care. Gardiner's history of Tintern stresses its caring environment in the Victorian era: 'Many a shy youngster was reassured by a warm cuddle on her headmistress's knee; older ones were certain always of her abiding sense of justice, of her idealism, and of her deep sincerity' (Gardiner 1977: 55).

Women from Catholic and government sites placed stronger emphasis upon individual responsibility for learning. This pattern may reflect the higher proportion of co-educational and primary sites in these sectors. However, the interview responses from those in girls-only sites expressed reservations that too many teachers spoon-feed students.

The sole interviewee from a government girls' school suggested that she was more influenced by contemporary research than inherited traditions:

> I've done quite a bit of research on this. Girls do much better at team learning than independent learning. ... [G]irls learn when they have good relationships. The better the relationships the higher the success rates. ... Because it is a girls' school, we ... emphasized co-operation.

Such comments suggest that the cultures of girls' schools provide more supportive pedagogical environments than other schools, but how their leaders view this may differ. Catholic and government leaders may well value independent learning highly because their schools have often been gateways for poor and immigrant groups who cannot rely on established cultural capital and must succeed through their own efforts (Gamble 1982; Vlahogiannis 1989; McConville 1993). Conversely, the independent sites appear to allow greater dependence in pleasant enclaves where curriculum is geared to a genteel femininity for the established middle class. Such a finding qualifies generic claims that all women leaders are orientated to catering for individual differences. It appears that the characteristics of specific schools, especially their different clienteles, institutional histories and cultures, work to introduce important differences between them.

Teachers

Both male and female leaders from girls' schools (95 per cent) were characterized by strong faith in the collaborative abilities of teachers, whereas three-quarters of those from boys' schools viewed them as territorial individuals. Historical accounts confirm the existence of a collaborative worldview which values teamwork and relational modes of work for staff as well as students in girls' schools. Miss Neilson's period at Presbyterian Ladies' College from 1938 to 1956 was characterized by her efforts

> to cultivate a relationship with her colleagues other than that of command. She instituted regular and frequent staff meetings, and she took up a personally democratic attitude towards her teachers several of whom have testified to her accessibility, her lack of self-importance and the desire to dominate.
>
> (Fitzpatrick 1975: 190)

Commenting upon Rhyton in the 1970s, Theobald (1978) noted the atmosphere of professional freedom and equality which pervaded the staffroom. One interviewee commented: 'I respect the classroom teacher, when he or she is there with their particular group. . . . However, reality does mean in a school like this, that you may have your class for half a day but they are going to go off to others, so being on your own island is not on.' Her Catholic counterpart was more emphatic: 'I value the initiative of individual teachers and the ability to deal with their own class . . . but they can still work as a team to plan it. . . . I don't value the person who doesn't even know what others are doing and is so independent that they are eccentric or insular.' This valuing of collaboration over individualism tends to support the claims of Gilligan (1982) and Eisler (1995). However, it is really the articulation of a collegial work ethic and should not be confused with a commitment to empowerment and participatory decision-making.

Nevertheless, there was also acknowledgement of the value of staff participation in decision-making. A leader from an independent site stressed how curriculum reviews provided opportunities for a teacher voice in her school:

> I encourage bottom-up initiatives. I believe that teachers, your regular teacher in a classroom, may not have any position of responsibility but will have a brain, and will be a good manager and has enormous capacity to be responsible and has very important ideas . . .

However, such comments do not clarify whether structures exist which facilitate teacher voices in broader policy levels as advocated by recent leadership theorists. If this is not so, the collaborative ethos may be a genteel surface culture rather than a deep participatory infrastructure in such schools. One spoke of consultation as a struggle as she attempted to transform the residual culture of the school where a previous woman was autocratic and would have the staff do as they were told. However, her desire to sit the staff in one circle at a staff meeting was frustrated by the size of the school (1100 students). Such comments suggest that even if individual leaders are committed to participatory ideals, organizational forces may still work against them (see page 28).

Further analysis revealed considerable ambivalence among female leaders on this issue. One described staff involvement in terms of delegated responsibility within an administrative hierarchy: 'I think it depends on what the task is if you are going to delegate responsibility. If we are really going to have staff working in collaborative teams then we equally need a director of studies who would have heads of departments reporting and to whom she could refer things.' Such a concept seems more akin to traditions of bureaucratic line management than the organic webs advocated by Adler *et al.* (1993). Another embodied the tension between authoritarian and democratic approaches to staff management in her description of her practice:

> In a lot of ways I am quite autocratic, but in the process of being autocratic, I'm consultative. I will consult but I will decide. . . . I'd say I was directive and consultative. . . . I think I'm more consultative at the upper level so I would tend to consult with the directors. . . . [O]ther consultation takes place at the lower levels and everyone on the staff would recognize, I think, that they do have a place in consultation.

The comments indicate that these women continue to be locked into hierarchical mindsets about organizations, which Ferguson (1984) caricatured as a male trait. They have little understanding of organic models or empowering structures advocated by some feminists. The collaboration is bounded by power structures which constrain teaching staff to 'lower levels'. We cannot equate the practice of collaboration in such schools with the democratic ideals of communitarian and democratic theorists who argue for authentic participation in decision-making (Lieberman *et al.* 1990; Bottery 1992, 1993).

Parents

The collegial dispositions of leaders from independent girls' schools appear to dissolve and even turn to hostility when it comes to parents. Their beliefs were rooted in a perception that their parents prefer strong leadership from an administrative hierarchy to active participation. An even higher proportion of these women (90 per cent) also believed that 'lack of parent participation' was not a constraint upon the operation of their schools. Indeed, many actually voiced hostility towards extensive parent involvement. One asserted: 'the idea of a parent-controlled school is absurd and that's what some of them are looking for. They've only got self-interest at heart.' Another insisted: 'Often what parents want is precisely what we don't. ... Obviously every parent wants their child to be special and I respect that ... but I know that there are many parents who want the entire school to change to accommodate their child.' The comments suggest that parents are more likely to be perceived as a threat and potential source of conflict, especially if they become demanding clients in the education marketplace.

Historical accounts suggest these attitudes have been inherited from matriarchal traditions, which viewed the school as a fortress where outside interference was not tolerated. The histories of Tintern, Rhyton and Mentone Girls' Grammar, which all developed from cottage origins, recall colourful incidents when female principals asserted authority over parents who dared to question it (Gardiner 1977; Theobald 1978; Burren 1984). The headmistress at Mentone from 1937 to 1955:

> tended to have firm ideas on many matters and put them into effect without reference to anyone. ... She owned the school, most of the land and most of the buildings. ... The headmistress seemed concerned to run the school in the way she wanted and was apprehensive of any challenge to her position.
>
> (Burren 1984: 101)

In this respect, Australian girls' schools appear to have shared similar administrative cultures to their English counterparts. Sperandio (2003) has observed that headmistresses in Norwich in the latter part of the nineteenth century exercised 'considerable power' and were inclined to 'dictate to parents' and insist upon their 'independence' from their influence.

Histories of independent girls' schools also indicate the absence of parent participation in governance. At times there were bitter struggles between the female principals and governing boards composed primarily of male church elders. However, parents were rarely members of such bodies and patriarchal governance remained uncontested for decades. Indeed, it was not until the 1960s that a challenge was mounted at Methodist Ladies' College, and the 1970s before the parents' association was successfully integrated into the life of Presbyterian Ladies' College (Zainu'ddin 1982). This study therefore clearly suggests that women from independent girls' schools have inherited and continue to hold more exclusive attitudes towards parent participation than those from the government and Catholic sectors. Their practices appear to contradict the inclusive feminist discourses from the last decades of the twentieth century.

Leaders from girls' schools were significantly more inclined than other groups in this study to admit they did not consult parents. The single-sex schools tended to generate more exclusive practices towards parents by both male and female leaders. It seems likely that an interaction between sectorial traditions and student segregation generates a more exclusive professional attitude in women principals in such locations than found in co-educational sites. Even in the Catholic sector, consultation was strictly limited: 'We do consult with parents from time to time on some issues but we're pretty careful with whom we consult and what the issues are.' Only one interviewee indicated any attempt to respond to parent expectations: 'I've set up an Education Committee within the Parents and Friends structure and we've had two Education Forums for parents to be involved in planning.' Male leaders from other Catholic secondary sites discussed similar strategies, and this suggests the developments may have been influenced by inclusive philosophies at the sectoral level in the 1990s. This leader's attitude was also consistent with her inclusive approaches to at-risk students and staff engagement, which have been cited previously in this chapter.

The quantitative and qualitative data and the historical accounts therefore yield a consistent picture, which clearly qualifies universal claims (Gilligan 1982) that women are, in essence, more relational than men. In particular, leaders of non-government girls' schools who may be quite pastoral and collegial in their relationships with students and staff, treat parents differently. We may question whether this is because they are outside the institutional hearth and are perceived as a threat to the matriarchal power within it. If so, it appears a 'territorial imperative' overrides inclusive impulses. Many women who demonstrated relational dispositions within their schools demonstrated exclusive attitudes towards parents.

Conclusions and implications

This study clearly renders a complex picture of female leadership in schools. It demonstrates that there is no one, distinctive, female leadership style in schools but multiple forms, which appear to be dependant upon a variety of contextual and historical factors. Differences between women principals are significant, and theory and research into school leadership must now recognize this. In this respect the study aligns itself with the more nuanced theories which have developed in the field of educational leadership in the 1990s.

This study provides some support for claims advanced by feminist theorists in the past two decades. Women leaders do appear to be more instructionally focused than men. They also appear to be more predisposed to develop relational cultures with students and staff in their schools. However, there is also a need for awareness that collegial atmospheres are not synonymous with democratic empowerment and have the potential to mask hierarchical power relationships. Conversely, the findings about attitudes to parents among female leaders from single-sex sites discredit relational typologies and suggest that 'territorial power' is still a reality.

When it comes to female leadership in girls' schools, the picture is complicated. In Australia, some of the complexities can be traced to the fact that independent girls' secondary schools serve different clienteles from those of their counterparts in the government and Catholic sectors. They traditionally have been attuned to the values and expectations of the middle class and may well have become bastions of a privileged minority in the broader society. Women in such schools tended to operate from different cognitive frameworks compared with those of their counterparts in government and Catholic sites. Pastoral issues were less at the forefront and this appears to be a result of their more privileged realms. Curriculum provision was more likely to be conceptualized as developing personal potential than as redressing social disadvantage. Their curriculum and pedagogical philosophies may therefore be an artefact of privilege, a more genteel educational provision than required for the children of immigrant and working-class parents. Have things changed all that radically from the late nineteenth century when Ethel Florence Lindsay learnt 'accomplishments' in the parlour at Presbyterian Ladies' College, while less privileged girls struggled with basic literacies in large classes in government and Catholic sites?

The collegial surface culture in many independent girls' schools appears to mask the real power relations that exist within them. Hierarchical organizational assumptions appear to remain unchallenged. Teacher autonomy is bounded to the classrooms and consultative processes are not necessarily linked to decision-making. Power still remains firmly in the hands of principals and school boards as it did in the reign of Thomas Finchiner at Methodist Ladies' College in the 1890s. However, a key difference is that women in such sites have now replaced male incumbents. We need to ask whether women have simply assumed the patriarchal mantle of the past without questioning the power relationships that informed it. There is also some evidence that the leaders of Catholic girls' sites have continued matriarchal legacies in the same manner. They appear oblivious to the theories of contemporary cultural feminists (Court 2002) and have not renegotiated power relationships within their institutions but continue to rely on authoritarian and bureaucratic traditions. These findings clearly suggest that much contemporary theory about women in leadership suffers from a form of historical amnesia, which also operates to obscure clear-sighted analysis of present realities.

A leader from an independent site argued that girls' schools develop 'motivation in young women' and provide 'role modelling' which prepares them for leadership roles after they complete their schooling. The role modelling revealed by this study is alarmingly conservative. It was not an authentic effort to empower staff within the schools and was deliberately exclusive of parents. In this regard, these women leaders continue to disempower other women. The role modelling may be seriously out of step with contemporary feminism and democracy. It may replicate the same traditions that Gronn (1995) complained about in selective boys' schools. We need to ask whether such provision adequately equips young women to become future public leaders in western democracies where past gender orders have been displaced.

6 Influences of the Discourse of Globalization on Mentoring for Gender Equity and Social Justice in Educational Leadership[1]

Margaret Grogan

This chapter considers the process of mentoring women into educational leadership in the context of current globalizing trends in education. Mentoring is presented as a paradox: on the one hand eminently desirable and necessary; yet, on the other hand, associated with the detrimental side effects of assisting to maintain the status quo of unequal gender relations and socially unjust educational practices and policies. In advocating for a more equitable distribution of women in elementary, secondary and post-secondary educational leadership, I am interested in both increasing the numbers from an equal rights perspective, and in the potential of changing leadership discourses to better serve those who have not benefited from traditional leadership discourses. Blackmore (1999: 5) makes the point that since 'leadership is treated ... increasingly ... as a set of generic competencies rather than holistically, the social, ethical and political dimensions of leadership are leached out'.

It becomes imperative to situate leadership in the widest sense possible, as embracing opportunities for fundamental educational reform. Thus, *access* to leadership is a prerequisite for those whose moral vision extends beyond individual self-interest to a desire for a more inclusive, democratic society. It is not argued that women are more likely than men to have such principles. Rather, the issue is that fewer women than men serve in the educational leadership positions that are currently maintaining the status quo. Any disruption of the status quo to bring about equity, equality and diversity is desirable. Therefore, we must consider how access to leadership is gained and, once gained, how leadership for greater social justice emerges. At the outset, we must strive for equity in leadership positions themselves.

The first section of the chapter deals with the process of mentoring women into educational administration. As a power relation, mentoring is inextricably linked to access. This section also establishes the dark or hidden side of mentoring, as its essential function appears to be to reproduce the status quo. The second section provides a current context for the final discussion of the potential of mentoring practices and philosophies in the third section. From the literature, we know how the mentoring of women into leadership has proceeded in the past (see Bolton 1980; Edson 1988; Johnsrud 1991; Ehrich 1995; Gupton and Slick 1996; Gardiner *et al.* 2000), but little attention has been paid to the opportunities or deterrents for women to be mentored into educational leadership in today's shifting world. To explain this shift, the second section outlines the ways in which globalization appears now to be shaping the dominant discourse of education. And the third section brings together the two earlier discussions. The power of mentoring is affirmed and considered necessary for any real change in the discourse of educational leadership, which is seen as particularly critical within the context of globalization.

The process of mentoring women into educational administration

'What is interesting about women being mentored into educational administration is that the activity offers women access to a different kind of subject position in the discourse' (Gardiner *et al.* 2000: 192). It is understood that 'different' implies more desirable in terms of career advancement and the consequent power to influence educational policy and practice, at least at the local level. Mentoring is seen as especially important for women who are still greatly under-represented in the higher ranks of both elementary and secondary and higher education. The figures for women in the superintendency, the top executive educational leadership position in the USA, have risen over the past ten years from 6.6 per cent in 1992 to 13.2 per cent in 2000 (Glass *et al.* 2000: 15). However, considering that the majority of teachers are women and that over half the graduates in administrator preparation programmes are women (Shakeshaft 1999), these figures are abysmal. Similarly, women account for only 31 per cent of full-time faculty in higher education today (Cooper and Stevens 2002). The national tenure rate for women has remained under 50 per cent whereas the rate for men is 70 per cent (Trautvetter 1999, in Cooper and Stevens 2002). Further, women who reach the position of dean or president of a university are also rare. Quoting El-Khawas in Eggins (1997), Luke (2001: 4) states that women hold only 16 per cent of chief executive positions in US colleges and universities.

The literature on mentoring focuses, in the large part, on mentoring as one of the most important means by which individuals move up the hierarchical ladders of success in the corporate world and education. Those who have written about experiences of women have either advocated the time-honoured male model of grooming the next generation of leader (see Bizzari

1995; Didion 1995; Ehrich 1995; Pence 1995) or provided critical reflections on traditional mentoring practices (see Swoboda and Millar 1986; Johnsrud 1991; Stalker 1994; Sandler 1995; Darwin 2000; Gardiner *et al.* 2000; Schramm 2000; Sherman 2002). Both approaches acknowledge that mentoring is fundamentally a transmission of knowledge, beliefs and values from the mentor or mentors to the protégé. Along with helping the protégé gain confidence, the primary purpose of mentoring is to provide opportunities for protégés to grow and develop, although many good mentors certainly learn from their protégés as well.

For mentoring to be described as good or worthwhile, the desires of the protégé must be at the forefront of the relationship. One definition of quality mentoring states: 'mentoring is characterized as an active, engaged and intentional relationship between two individuals (mentor and protégé) based on mutual understanding to serve primarily the professional needs of the protégé' (Gardiner *et al.* 2000: 52). This implies that important element is the deliberate attention given to the success of the protégé – echoing the original notion of the Greek Mentor (the goddess Athene in disguise) guiding Telemachus along his journey. Few question that the means by which this is accomplished is through the close connection of the more experienced mentor to the novice or aspirant. In educational leadership terms at the elementary and secondary levels, this usually involves principals mentoring teachers and assistant principals, and central office administrators mentoring principals. In academe, tenured professors mentor assistant professors up the ranks, and administrators sometimes work with faculty members who aspire to leadership positions in higher education.

The best mentoring process is often a haphazard one sparked by some chemistry between two individuals that encourages a relationship. But it is also frequently a supervisory relationship. Sometimes these are formal arrangements set up by external agents such as universities who place individuals in internships. In academe, it is often assumed that the role of the department chair includes mentoring junior faculty. McDonough (2002: 136) argues: 'A crucial role for academic department chairs in supporting the work of untenured faculty is mentoring ... [to] ensure that pre-tenure faculty receive structured, systematic feedback on all aspects of their performance.'

Individuals who aspire to leadership positions or who simply want to be successful in their organizations, benefit from mentoring in multiple ways. There is access to the unwritten rules, the 'way we do things around here', which are only made explicit within the mentoring relationship. Then there is the power of knowing someone of influence. Few can manage without the support of an individual or individuals who will speak on their behalf, sponsor or promote them when it counts. Mentoring leads to networking, which is an activity limited to certain individuals in certain situations. Even the gaining of confidence that is so important to many protégés is contextualized within a particular organization enhanced by the perception of the mentor. 'For centuries, mentoring has been used as a vehicle for handing down knowledge, maintaining culture, supporting talent, and securing future leadership' (Darwin 2000: 197). Indeed, Darwin argues that the mentor's 'primary role was to maintain culture' (p. 198), so that while the protégé herself is growing professionally and often personally, the organization too is benefiting from the reproduction and continuation of approved behaviours, ideas and values. Unfortunately, if neither mentor nor protégé approaches the process from a critical perspective of how leadership policies and practices need to change to provide more equitable educational experiences to all students, mentoring maintains the status quo.

To call this function of mentoring the dark side of mentoring is to draw attention to the fact that not only has the status quo not served all students well, but it has also not served women aspirants to leadership well in the past and is not likely to serve them well in the future. The same must be said for individuals of colour, both women and men. In focusing on leadership, despite claims to the contrary, very little has changed over the years: 'the benchmark of leadership remains white, middle-class, heterosexual and male' (Blackmore 1999: 6). More importantly, the dominant leadership discourses have made very little difference in the lives of the poor, of children of colour, and those marginalized in any other way. Thus, one can equate maintenance of the status quo with inequities and injustices on many levels.

The tension is clear. Mentoring is identified as vital if women are to gain entry into the ranks of leaders who are best positioned to act upon the injustices in the system at both micro and macro levels. Because the realization of aspirations is usually a time-consuming process, and because it depends on being approved of by those who wield the power, successful protégés grow to think and act like those who mentor them – even if they had differing philosophies initially. An assistant principal describes the process this way:

> Before I accepted the job as assistant principal, Sylvia explained to me that she would be a hands-on supervisor. She would monitor my work closely, and I was to inform her about everything I was doing. She did not want me to be offended or feel that I did not know what I was doing; she just needed this time to train me. ... It was months before Sylvia started letting me do things on my own. It seemed to me to take extra time to run everything past her. She had suggestions, revisions, and other ideas. ... She always seemed to find something she could improve on. ... She ran meetings I set up. She told me how I should conduct business. ... Eventually she stopped managing me.
>
> (Hibert 2000: 18)

Actually, despite giving the impression of having been micro-managed, Hibert presents the experience of being mentored by her principal in a very positive light. She likes learning to think and act like her supervisor because she values the same things as Sylvia does. 'Passion and a sense of urgency about improving schools for students are contagious. Sylvia has infected me with the desire to make things right for all students every day' (Hibert: 2000: 18). So let us suppose, in this instance, that maintaining the status quo in Sylvia's building helped to advance those who have not fared well under traditional leadership. That would put a positive spin on the story. Unfortunately, though, it would be a rare building where no improvement was needed. Because many mentors lack a critical perspective or the desire to change the status quo, mentoring may really cement undesirable practices. In every instance, the mentoring process is a powerful one as the example shows – one that offers little room for manoeuvring if the protégé *does* want to operate differently from her mentor.

Thus, by the time the protégé has matured into whatever position she is seeking, she has been, to some extent, co-opted by the system. 'Traditional mentoring may have been [women's] only means to enter the ranks of administration, but once they are within the network, how do they keep themselves from succumbing to the same attitudes and beliefs that discriminate against so many others like them?' (Gardiner *et al.* 2000: 188). One line of defence is for the protégé to develop and retain a strong sense of self throughout the process. This allows for a critical awareness of what is happening and positions the individual as one who understands the need for engaging in the process of mentoring while being wary of its effects. However, this is often easier said than done. Although faculty members of colour in higher education, for instance, receive less mentoring than white faculty members, when they do receive it, mentors often recommend serving on committees as a high priority. Because of their low numbers at any one institution, faculty of colour often have to serve on more committees than their white counterparts, and are sometimes expected to deal with minority affairs single-handedly.

> People in college or university administrative positions are commonly expected to speak using the institutional 'we'. [Faculty of colour] describe the dilemma of being called on to do so within a predominantly white campus. No matter what faculty members of colour decide to do in these instances, they are placed in uncomfortable positions.
>
> (Turner and Myers 2000: 95)

Indeed, it has been suggested that being mentored is like assuming a disguise. In order to fit into a gendered and/or racially acceptable notion of leader, the protégé sometimes has to pretend to be someone other than herself. Women of colour, in particular, 'must in some ways disguise themselves, acting as dominant White men in leadership roles' (Enomoto *et al.* 2000: 568).

Another, more promising strategy to prevent a protégé's total assimilation into an undesirable organizational culture, is for the protégé to seek out multiple mentors. Curry (2002: 125) advises women to 'have as many [mentors] as you can manage without allowing the diversity of opinions that come with them to be confusing and cloud your own judgment. ... [I]t is better to have the wisdom of several people rather than a single individual.' This is particularly true for those being mentored across gender, race or class, since one's opportunities and disappointments are shaped so powerfully by such social structures. However, despite maintaining a critical awareness of the process and/or accepting guidance from more than one mentor, it is difficult to think entirely 'out of the box'. This is because of the power of the discourse of leadership itself and the homogeneity of available subject positions based on gender, race, sexuality, disability and other marginalizing factors.

One response that some women make is to avoid mentoring, or networking activities, altogether. There is a disdain for the process because of its privileging and exclusivity. '[T]raditionally, the mentoring relationship has been framed in a language of paternalism and dependency and stems from a power-dependent, hierarchical relationship ...' (Darwin 2000: 198). Some women like to distance themselves from such practices and to do things or achieve things on their own. Andrea, a superintendent aspirant, explains this sentiment:

> I don't like people to help me, I like to do it on my own, and I don't want to have to be grateful to anybody for anything. I just want to do it ... I want to get it on my own merits ... the whole concept of networking bothers me. I don't have any desire to be part of that, none at all ...
>
> (Grogan 1996: 79)

However, this is not a very practical response given the reality of how individuals gain entry into educational leadership positions, though it does illustrate the fears of cooptation and loss of integrity associated with the notion of 'old boys' clubs' that can accompany success. At the same time it is undesirable for women to create 'old girls' networks, for their equally homogenizing effects (Reynolds 2002b).

Other women choose not to participate in mentoring and sponsorship out of ignorance. In a study of women in a formal mentoring programme to identify and develop the next generation of leaders in a school district, Sherman (2002) found that some participants did not understand the purpose or value of networking as a means of gaining entry into administration. '[They] conveyed the misconception that networking means getting along with and working collaboratively with their teacher colleagues. Therefore, they believed they did not need any help with networking because they already knew how to get along with others' (Sherman 2002: 121). In viewing networking simply as social behaviour, these women missed the power of sponsorship that mentors can offer. No matter how much potential an aspirant has, if it is not brought to the attention of those with clout, it is likely to go unrecognized.

It is tempting to think that the dark side of mentoring is fading as more women do gain administrative positions and as educational reform movements attempt to address the serious inequities at least at the elementary and secondary levels across the USA. However, although the discourses of educational administration and educational policy have changed over the years, there are still disproportionately few women administrators, and there is no sign of a widespread socially just education on the horizon as yet. On the contrary, the discourse of globalization, perhaps the most often cited 'new' trend in education, appears to reinforce, in some respects, the status quo of much of the twentieth century. In the following section, I consider the possible effects of globalization on the discourses of education and of educational leadership before turning back to the phenomenon of mentoring. The next section helps to situate the promises and pitfalls of mentoring women into educational leadership in an increasingly global twenty-first century.

How globalization, the new educational trend, appears to be shaping the dominant discourses

In the context of a discussion about women accessing the power and privileges reserved for those in leadership positions in education, it is imperative to notice what is happening to the dominant discourse of education. Blackmore (1999: 5), argues that 'the capacity for feminism, and feminists in leadership, to work for social justice generally in public school education, and gender equity for women in particular, is currently at risk.' She attributes this loss of confidence to the nature of the educational restructuring that is taking place in most western nations. Gender equity reform has suffered with the spread of neo-conservative politics and market liberalism. Instead of intervention, the state appears only to mediate market relations embracing various forms of corporatization and privatization. 'The trend is towards education labour markets, globally and locally, to become more feminized, casualized, and deprofessionalized' (Blackmore 1999: 5).

Writing of the gains women have made over the past twenty or thirty years, Luke (2001) acknowledges that gender equity has been a priority for many governments, and much research and scholarship, mostly conducted by women, has deconstructed the myths of meritocracy as masculinist fictions. She believes that 'concepts of career have been subtly altered to include women's different life and career trajectories' (Luke 2001: 9). But she warns of the 'stubborn persistence of shifting glass ceilings and chilly climates in the academy' (Luke 2001: 9). The new market values sweeping all levels of education have particularly affected women, as work becomes increasingly part-time, contractual, and masculinist definitions of quality, productivity, and performance become reinstated (Luke 2001).

Some are calling this a 'new work order' characterized by the notions of global markets, new knowledge economies, the use of converging communication and information technologies, increased cultural diversity and population mobility (Blackmore 2002c). For some, globalized education means the rise of supranational institutions shaping policy options for particular nation-states; for others, it is the impact of global economic processes on education policy; and, for still others, it refers to the rise of neo-liberalism as a hegemonic policy discourse (Burbules and Torres 2000). Burbules and Torres go on to say that the term can also be used to describe

> a perceived set of changes, a construction used by state policymakers to inspire support for and suppress opposition to changes because 'greater forces' (global competition, responses to IMF or World Bank demands, obligations to regional alliances, and so on) leave the nation-state 'no choice' but to play by a set of global rules not of its own making.
>
> (Burbules and Torres 2000: 2)

Whatever the specific definition, notions of globalization have shaped the dominant discourse of education in a variety of ways, all of which seem to be embedded in requirements to change policy and practice in response to the idea of a new world order and the demands of immediacy.

One might conclude that a positive effect of globalization on educational leadership is a greater appreciation of diversity of cultures, ideologies and perspectives. The potential for it is surely enhanced by the technologies of communication and free flow of ideas transnationally. Electronic networking has certainly enabled conversations, exchange of ideas and knowledge between academics and practitioners across the globe. It is not uncommon for educators now to reference policies and practices outside the country in support of or as deterrents to proposed local legislation. However, there is also a tendency towards homogenization of practices and policies with the seemingly ubiquitous enthusiasm for accountability mechanisms and testing at the elementary and secondary levels and, in higher education, increased standardization of qualifications, credentials and expertise.

Perhaps most dangerous at both levels are the effects of marketization, competition and entrepreneurial forms of financing education. Pusser (2002: 111) argues that '[f]aith in the market and its potential role in reforming the provision of higher education is based in a fundamental tenet of market ideology, that competition creates efficiencies, productivity gains, and cost savings.' Elementary and secondary policy-makers cite similar reasons for the emergence of charter schools and voucher programmes across the USA. Apple (2000) asserts that the neo-liberal agenda in the USA is based on the idea that what is private is good and what is public is bad. There is a stubborn belief that '[p]ublic institutions such as schools are "black holes" into which money is poured – and then seemingly disappears – but which do not provide anywhere near adequate results' (Apple 2000: 59). Instead of being motivated in the interests of the public good, however, this agenda is advanced in the belief that people should act to increase personal gain. Apple goes on to argue that neo-liberals see the world as a vast supermarket. ' "Consumer choice" is the guarantor of democracy. ... [E]ducation is seen as simply one more product like bread, cars, and television' (Apple 2000: 60). When state governments collude with business and industry to reform education, it is inevitable that existing social and cultural inequalities will remain unchallenged.

A particularly disturbing example of the above is the emergence of what Castells, in Morrow and Torres (2000), calls the Fourth World. He attributes it to the forces of globalization. Characterized by social exclusion, 'the Fourth World comprises large areas of the globe ... but it is also present in literally every country, and every city ... populated by millions of homeless, incarcerated, prostituted, criminalized, stigmatized, sick and illiterate persons' (Morrow and Torres 2000: 49). Morrow and Torres argue that, in the context of globalization, a weakened state embracing neo-liberal strategies of economic and social policy authorizes few interventions to assist such communities. At the same time, the removal of decision-making from the local lessens the capacity of marginalized groups to understand the structural processes that determine their fate. This polarization of poverty stemming from increased academic achievement gaps, the technology-rich versus the technology-poor, and gender gaps in earnings, is evident in most western post-industrial nations and to a greater extent in developing nation-states (Blackmore 1999). Despite rhetoric to the contrary, hardly any educational restructuring efforts have made significant, sustained inroads in reducing the effects of poverty on the lives of children. The Fourth World has become as much a taken-for-granted part of the social landscape as the privileged middle class. Few people question the sources of the privilege or concern themselves with the structural reasons for marginalization.

But this is not new. It would be hard to argue that globalization is totally responsible for the current manifestations of social injustice. Conservative trends associated with globalization can be said to exacerbate existing inequalities, however, and to mask new ones. In the name of responding to global forces, many educational policies and practices simply promote an agenda of personal benefit as opposed to collective benefit. Strong leadership is necessary to reverse those trends. The dominant leadership discourses influenced by globalization advocate more individual initiative and less trust in the community. Reform is constant. Because most of the reforms are imposed externally, educational leaders are using less discretion and relying more on universalizing narratives that encourage 'global' rather than local perspectives. In schools and colleges, at the moment, everything appears to be in flux. Indeed, globalization is associated with change for the sake of change as much as anything else, and leaders are expected to be change agents. *Responsible* leadership, however, asks who most benefits from each change. Otherwise, change becomes another way to reinforce the status quo.

Do critical thinkers become educational leaders? Or more to the point, do educators who adopt critical perspectives, once in leadership positions, retain their critical perspectives? The last section of this chapter examines why the likelihood of maintaining a critical stance in leadership is diminished because of the dark side of the mentoring process, which is instrumental in deciding who assumes leadership in education and in approving which values and beliefs leaders should hold. Yet, finally, it is suggested that the opportunities are there for non-traditional mentoring to meet the challenges posed.

The influence of globalizing trends on the process and effects of mentoring in the developing of educational leaders

As outlined in the first section, the dark side of mentoring refers to its exclusive, privileging process that serves to reinforce recognized behaviours and ideologies. Often unintentionally, protégés become imbued with the ideals and philosophies of their mentors who represent, for the most part, the dominant discourse. Women who aspire to leadership positions in education are particularly vulnerable since they are still under-represented in most administrative positions elementary, secondary and post-secondary, and in positions of power and influence such as professorships in academe.

Although conditions for women in education have been researched in the recent past and many of the factors influencing women's career possibilities have been identified, the results have not been very encouraging. Looking cross-generationally, Reynolds (2002b: 46) found that 'dominant scripts changed for women and men in school leadership over [a] thirty-year span, [though] it is less clear whether these changes represented improvements in gender relations or in the overall political leverage of women in school organizations'.

Nevertheless, as a means of gaining entry into leadership circles, and of enhancing women's success in organizations, the practice of mentoring is still often regarded as the key. It could be said that over the past few years, mentoring in education has gained popularity and legitimacy. In the USA, for instance, many states have mandated mentors for beginning teachers. This is an effort to retain teachers in a time of teacher shortage. It is somewhat ironic that this practice can actually increase the workload for women, who comprise the majority of teachers especially at the elementary level, although the major beneficiaries of the regulation are also often novice women teachers. And in the elementary and secondary leadership literature, mentoring is advocated as a way for school districts to develop their own leaders. However, it is important to note the paternalistic, surveillance approach that some take. 'Mentoring has become a popular concept in school administration ... a mentor is one who helps an aspiring or relatively inexperienced professional to develop and advance a career by improving his or her productivity and effectiveness' (Kowalski 1999: 391).

There are many examples of women educators especially benefiting from other women mentoring them and providing them with alternative role models (Edson 1988; Shakeshaft 1989; Regan and Brooks 1995; Schmuck 1995; Grogan 1996; Blount 1998; Brunner 1999; Gardiner *et al.* 2000; Young and McLeod 2001). However, much of that research points to the fact that such alternative leadership approaches have made little headway in changing the dominant leadership discourse. Especially today, in the globalized context explained above, 'entrepreneurial leadership is still modelled on particular hegemonic masculinist images of being strong, able to make the hard decisions, independent and taking unilateral action' (Blackmore 2002c: 210). Leaders, who must respond to market forces and the push for accountability, have to rely on image-making and conformity. Women who wish to lead differently and who wish to make different educational decisions are at the mercy of a current discourse that discourages innovation and creativity. A tension is created by strong state oversight of curriculum and testing for students and teachers, and raising standards for elementary and secondary education, on the one hand, and deregulation of credentialing for teachers and administrators, reduction in state funding, and a general state encouragement of competition and privatization in education on the other. More than ever before, in the name of stability, mentors are choosing protégés who are committed to implementing change in the context of top-down reform. And whether they like it or not, 'successful' leaders, those who move into more powerful positions, have to be good at following state mandates and toeing the line.

One must sympathize with aspirants and leaders who fight to retain or embrace an activist stance in the face of globalization trends. The more an individual remains in a system, the more she reflects the values of that system. If one system resembles another as much as the homogenizing forces of today suggest, the opportunities for redefining leadership appear limited. Yet, there are those who rise to the challenge (see Duke *et al.* 2003). They are leaders who take hope from exactly the same global trends that oppress their peers. With the emphasis on raising standards and meeting benchmarks, and the public reporting associated with accountability measures, leaders have access to more accurate data than ever before. Handled wisely, these data can be used to attract increased funding to assist teachers in designing more authentic assessments and helping students reach their full potential, for instance. Market forces can be harnessed to better educate disadvantaged populations even if only in the name of increasing their potential as consumers. The emphasis on preparing future workers for an unpredictable labour market requires attention to critical thinking to prevent a labour force incapable of participating in the democratic process. I see possibilities in practices of deliberately mentoring individuals whose ethnic, racial or religious backgrounds differ from the dominant or whose sexual orientation marginalizes them in the interest of meeting the needs of those who have not been well served in the past. From the foregoing discussion it is clear that mentoring is instrumental in grooming future educational leaders in all settings. Albeit a slow process, I take heart from the idea that mentoring could be just as powerful in producing a new collective of critical thinkers devoted to addressing issues of equity and injustice, as it has been in reproducing a damaging status quo.

Iris Marion Young (2000: 45) believes that '[t]ransportation, communication, and economic interdependence have made it unlikely that we could reverse the process of globalization of society'. If this is so, then it is most important for us to mine the experience for those aspects that can help to counteract the culture of indifference that has characterized education in the twentieth century. As homogenizing as globalization can be, it can also be diversifying. The transnational border-crossings becoming so much a feature of our lives today can lead to new associations and relationships. Hybrid identities emerge from our mobile populations, breaking down many of the inhibiting notions of gender, race and ethnicity. The real challenge is how to capture those ideas and put them to work in redefining a leadership discourse that serves all our people equally well. For those of us who have been mentored into organizational cultures that do not embrace those values, we must not succumb to a comfortable acquiescence. On the contrary, if we have any power at all, we must be committed to deliberately mentoring or recruiting women into leadership and to identifying those men and women who are prepared to engage in the struggle against social injustice. And if we are without the power we need to make significant change, we must actively seek those who can mentor us into such leadership roles.

Note

1. An earlier version of this chapter was published in *Leading and Managing* (2002) 8(2): 123–134, and is published here with permission.

7 Gender, Leadership and Change in Faculties of Education in Three Countries

Sandra Acker

This chapter draws from a small, qualitative, comparative study of women leaders in university faculties[1] of education in Australia, Britain and Canada. The research examines how the women meet two major challenges: (1) being part of the first generation of women to be involved in university manage-ment in any significant numbers, and (2) operating within a context of global trends that have made the work of academics and academic managers more difficult than in the past. This work follows an earlier comparison of women in university management in Australia and Canada based on interviews in the mid-1990s (see Wyn *et al.* 2000). The current phase, which is ongoing, more explicitly targets questions about restructuring and change. Interviews with six women from each country, conducted between 1999 and 2002, provide the data for this chapter. Participants include women who are deans, associate or assistant deans, chairs or heads of department or school, associate or deputy chairs/heads, programme coordinators or research centre directors.[2]

Women are no longer a rarity among academics. Representation is similar in the three countries discussed here. In Canada, women account for slightly over one-third of new appointments, consistent with their representation among doctoral recipients in the past decade (AUCC 2002: 26), and they are about 30 per cent of all full-time academics. In Britain, figures from the Equal Opportunities Commission (2001) indicate that women constituted 32 per cent of full-time academic staff in higher education institutions in 1998/1999. Similarly, in Australia, a full-time-equivalent (FTE) count of full-time and fractional full-time academic staff shows women academics were 37.8 per cent of the total FTE in 2003 (DEST 2003).

In all three countries, men dominate higher ranks and managerial posi-tions, but women's representation at that level is also gradually increasing (Wyn *et al.* 2000). In 1999/2000, women comprised 12 per cent of professors in the UK (*Times Higher Education Supplement* 2003). In Australia in 2003, women were 19.2 per cent of categories D and E ('above senior lecturer') (DEST 2003). Women made up 16 per cent of full professors in Canada in 2001 (AUCC 2002: 21). It is difficult and often misleading to compare countries using such statistics because of different definitions of rank and different conventions in compiling the data. Even within a country, statistics from alternative sources are not always consistent. Moreover, figures on the proportions of women holding administrative or management responsibilities do not seem to be readily available. As we shall see later in this chapter, some of these positions are 'lower' or middle level. Furthermore, academics frequently move in and out of leadership positions, rather than making them a career.

After several decades of research on women academics, we now have a body of knowledge about their situation (see Acker and Armenti (forthcoming), for a review). A smaller number of publications have addressed more directly questions of gender and university managerial roles (for example Heward 1994; Doyle Walton 1996; Deem and Ozga 1997; Eggins 1997; David and Woodward 1998; Kolodny 1998; Blackmore and Sachs 2000, 2001; Eveline 2000; Wyn et al. 2000; Currie and Thiele 2001; Hearn 2001; Luke 2001; Currie *et al.* 2002). Some of these writings are explorations of individual narratives of career struggles or experience in managerial roles, whereas others detail gendered institutional cultures. Increasingly popular in recent writing is a framework that evokes globalization. Here what happens to women within universities is seen as shaped, at least in part, by the practices derived from neo-liberal economic policies that have impacted upon universities across the globe in significant and similar ways, for example by heightening emphasis on entrepreneurialism, managerialism and performativity.

This chapter uses narratives but sees them as placed in both contexts: the micro-political, gendered university and departmental cultures; and the rapidly changing, globalized university sector.[3] However, while striking similarities across nations can be observed, notable local variations also obtain (Vidovich 2002). Thus in the narratives of women leaders from Australia, Britain and Canada, there are both commonalities and divergences.

One challenge is to understand the dialectical relationship between public higher education policy changes at the macro level and the responses of those placed in management positions at the micro level. Another is to comprehend the extent to which gender may structure the contemporary, as it did the traditional, university. The particular concern in this chapter is to explore the ways in which the new generation of women in management cope with the turbulence of the present-day university. The new-style universities have been characterized as 'cultures which focus on short-term targets, see people as costs rather than assets, and have a "macho cowboy regime"'(Deem and Ozga 1997). Morley (1999) notes that equity issues have been marginalized under these conditions while a particular style of tough management has been encouraged. At the same time, there is a competing rhetoric about 'women's ways of management' (see Acker 1999) that would suggest that as more women make their way into senior ranks, alternative values such as collegiality, democracy, participation and caring might surface. It is in these contradictory circumstances that the women in our study struggle to define what leadership means to them.

Below I first summarize the general trends reported in the interviews when the participants talked about their work. Then I focus in greater depth on underlying issues of identity and control.

Working hard in hard new times

In all three countries, three major themes related to changing university conditions were apparent in the interviews: financial cutbacks, work intensification, and scrutiny. All the women spoke about declining funding often coupled with increased numbers of students and fewer staff. Canadian participants were particularly preoccupied with financial constraints and inadequate resources, referring to being 'in a crisis' (Hester)[4] and 'under siege' (Anna). Terry, in Australia, explains how funding changes altered the working situation:

> I think, basically, ten, fifteen years ago, Australian universities were funded through government funds. Basically, we assumed that all the monies would come through government. Basically we assumed that we needed to be both teachers and researchers. Some people would do more teaching, some would do more research, but the notion that your value to the organization was related to your income generating activities was totally alien. ... It wasn't seen as fundamental that you had to go out and get funding.

Participants in Britain gave very clear descriptions of 'doing more with less'. Verity explained that an 'efficiency gain' meant that 'every year you get less money, and you have to teach more students for less money ... so it means that universities have very few resources, but more students, more expectations, more kind of audit culture'.

'Doing more with less' translates into work intensification. Like women academics interviewed by Currie *et al.* (2002: 11), one of whom likened university management to 'working in a deli that is open seven days a week, 24 hours a day', participants in my project gave accounts of working for many hours but never finishing. As Olivia (Australia) comments: 'You could work 24 hours a day and you'd still not get everything done.' Hester (Canada) laments: 'My throat is sore on some days when I go home, and, you know, you've had 50 emails and dealt with those and meetings and this and that, and yet, it doesn't matter that you've worked for 12 hours or whatever. It doesn't matter because there are 200 things that you didn't do.' The Canadians, in particular, spoke of fatigue related to work intensification as well as conflict management and trying to keep up high standards of research productivity. Technology appeared to make the job more intense. In Australia, where participants might work on several campuses, some kept their mobile phones going through car journeys between sites. Women in all three countries mentioned the demands of email.

The 'audit culture' that Verity mentioned was becoming pervasive. The interviews in Britain were replete with references to various forms of external judgements. For example: 'There's been a stronger government hold over the numbers of students you can recruit. ... You're set a number of students you can get funding for, and if you under-recruit you don't get the funding, obviously, and if you over-recruit you're positively penalized' (Portia). As Henkel (1999) notes, the scrutiny involved in the Research Assessment Exercise has had a dramatic effect on British academic culture:

> The Research Assessment Exercise, where every research-active academic in every subject area [submits] every four to five years with details of what they've published, of research money, of students they've supervised, the research culture of the unit that they're in, all that has to be submitted to peer panels of academics who then award grades to departments on the basis of these submissions, and moneys attached to it, so it's not just a kind of symbolic thing. The difference between the top grade, which is a five star, and the bottom grade, is massive.
>
> (Verity, Britain)

External scrutiny of teaching had also been introduced. Results of these exercises are made public, often in the form of 'league tables'. Participants saw these changes as part of a business orientation: 'We're now in a highly entrepreneurial situation and we have to be a very, up-together, focused, targeted corporate enterprise and we are, you know, the biggest business in [city], basically' (Susan). Rebecca refers to a 'kind of very, very close management control sort of culture'. Participants commented that they felt these exercises conveyed a lack of trust.

Australians were also concerned about performativity or scrutiny (Blackmore and Sachs 2001). Various forms of performance review were widespread:

> Certain senior people in the faculty get designated as performance enhancement reviewers and they get trained to do that, and then academic staff have a planning meeting and a review meeting and write a report.
>
> (Christine)

> Heads of School really are, are responsible for ... our performance management sort of process.
>
> (Vera)

> There has also been, I think, a move, really apparent at this university but I think it's fairly common, for a lot more corporate procedures and that form of performativity where you have to be seen to be filling in paper and doing things.
>
> (Miranda)

Research performance was also assessed and a component of departmental funding depended on the outcome, although it was not as extreme as in the British case. As in Britain, there were statements about 'the business-type management system that goes on' (Lorna).

Assessment was a major issue in Canada, but it took a different form. Concern related to evaluations of *individuals*, not departments. The tenure system, whereby academics needed to undergo a major evaluation of all of their work in order to keep their jobs after a probationary period, was thought to create inordinate stress. Most universities also had annual merit evaluations, which could affect salaries. The participants sometimes had to implement these various reviews but were also subject to them. Notable in Canada was the lack of central government direction, compared with the other two countries. Canada is unusual in its system of provincially controlled education; there is no federal ministry of education that could dictate the kinds of changes imposed elsewhere. On the whole, the Canadian respondents were less likely to speak of system-wide changes and more likely to talk about the policies of their particular institution and its management.

Clearly, features of the 'global' university were impacting on the participants, with both similarities and variations from country to country. In the next two sections, I focus on the ways in which the women tried to make sense of what seemed to many of them both a threat to their identity and an impossible job.

Questions of identity

Blackmore and Sachs (2001) argue that the enormous changes in universities have impacted upon and reshaped the 'academic self'. Certainly, identity-related tensions were widespread in the interviews. What we have here is the new generation of women in teacher education, now reaching leadership positions. These women, especially those in the 'younger' generation, have always understood research to be an essential part of their position as academics. They may have fought for recognition as scholars and teachers in a male-dominated university. Now that they are moving into leadership posi-tions, they find their previous identities hard to maintain. There are many references to the job being 'just too big'; the workloads simply do not allow sufficient time for anything else. Ironically, the conflict is stronger because of the performativity culture: the women find themselves with responsibilities for promoting the research of others, with hardly any time to do their own.

The discussions carry tones of *yearning* (sometimes shading into *regret*) and *sacrifice*. Yearning is there because research is a forgone pleasure, some-thing that is important for the women's self-image, and something that would give them credibility with colleagues. Yearning comes across very strongly in this quotation from Britain:

> What I would dearly like to be able to do now is to ... re-con-ceptualize for myself what my role is in relation to the development of other people's research. ... There are alternative models which would leave me more time to get on with my research, and what I feel at this moment is I certainly do not yearn to become an ad-ministrator or a manager. ... [W]hat my ambitions are for the rest of my working life are to return to being the good researcher that I know I can be, and to prioritize research activities above all other.
>
> (Portia)

In Canada, Hester's comment expresses the sense of diminution of self:

> I had lost myself as a writer. I had lost the Hester who could work with complex ideas and see them through sustained argument over the course of 30 or 40 pages. I've lost touch with that person a little bit because the job makes you lose touch with that person. It's just, it's like you're under this constant shellfire, rat-a-tat, a-tat, a-tat, and, you know, I can't even talk in full sentences at the end of the day sometimes.
>
> (Hester)

Hester also talks about the loss of a teaching identity during her term as a programme director. She is looking forward to being a member of the teaching faculty again:

> Next year, I will be back as a professor in the programme. I am so ecstatic about that I can hardly wait. I can hardly wait to teach. This has given me a whole new level of desire in relation to my teaching. I didn't realize that I enjoyed it as much as I do. I didn't realize that it succours me and nurtures me the way that it does, and energizes me the way that it does ... and what I've really missed this year is being

able to write and do research. I haven't done any significant new writing since June of last year.

(Hester)

Lorna, in Australia, repeatedly refers to 'the pressure of not having a strong research record', which she says makes her feel 'uncomfortable'. Here is a case where there is a note of regret. Like some of the others, she says that she could not do the management job well and keep up a research profile. 'It's really hard. ... I've had projects, but ... the amount of time you give to them, it's pretty sketchy.' She adds, 'I suppose I find as I've got older and [given] some of the issues you face, I'm drained by the end of the day.' Olivia, also in Australia, responds similarly: 'Certainly if I wasn't [in a management position] I'd probably, uh-m, write a lot more than I do. The writing that I do tends to be either just conference papers or reports.' But she adds, 'Uh-m, but that doesn't unsettle me.' She believes that what she is accomplishing is more important.

What comes across in most of the interviews is a sense that there is a choice between being a manager and being a scholar, expressed well in this quotation from Britain: 'I was very torn [about taking a senior management position] because I realized it would mean soft pedalling, if not completely closing down on my academic activity. ... [I]t's a necessary decision to go down the management route or the academic route' (Susan).

Basically, the 'choice' entailed the prospect of sacrifice of one's prior identity. Some fought to continue their research. Claire, in Canada, says: 'On the other hand, research was one of the few things that kept me sane, as little as I was able to do, and the writing was a very great pleasure. ... So I didn't want to give it up, and so it was a source of frustration because I could get to so little of it.'

Country and career stage influenced how the women experienced and dealt with the issue. Some of the women in Australia and Britain had been promoted to the position of professor or had applied for a professorship advertised in an institution. These designations carried very high prestige, especially in Australia, and recognized scholarly accomplishments. While frequently carrying management responsibilities, these were not inevitable, and sometimes were relatively minor, with the expectation more likely to be that the person would serve as a leader and role model. People in this position tended to want even more time for research than they already had.

In Canada, a full professorship is highly respected, but is something many academics aspire to rather than being reserved only for a few stars. There are no formal quotas on how many people can get to that rank, nor are there restrictions based on money available in the system. There was a rough correlation between rank and responsibility in all the countries, but it was notable in Canada that one could find full professors with relatively minor management responsibilities (without necessarily operating as role models) and, conversely, people somewhat lower in rank filling managerial positions. The difficulty for these individuals is that many of them still aspire to promotion, and for that, they need to be concentrating on research and publication. In the individualized accountability ethos in Canadian universities, they are very aware that they are being evaluated, often yearly in a merit system.

The positions the women in the Canadian sample held were more likely to be in 'lower middle management' roles, such as associate department chair or programme director, than they were to be chair or dean. From one perspective, those positions could be seen as training for management or tasters of the management experience. The jobs seemed to expand beyond anyone's capacity to do them, and the compensation by way of teaching reductions or other supports were minimal. Many of the Canadian women appeared to fall victim to what might be called 'the myth of the part-time administrator'. Deans do not usually teach; associate deans sometimes do so; and chairs usually have some teaching responsibilities. The women in the 'lower middle management' positions (Hester, Claire, Anna, Victoria, Faith) are all teaching either two or three half-courses – a 50 per cent or larger load – a not inconsiderable contributor to their sense of being overwhelmed by work.

One way to 'solve' the problem was to leave the field: 'At this stage for me, it's not really what I want so I'm going to be among those women who, I think, gets to this level, could continue in administration but doesn't, you know, because, because there's still other things I want to do' (Anna, Canada). At the time of interview, Claire had left her position and Hester was about to do the same. In Britain, Rebecca reduced her perception of conflict by moving from a high-level management position to take up a research-orientated post.

Several of the Canadians believe that their institutions are doing very little to give people incentives to take up leadership positions. Faith, for example, says: 'Administration is a service job, and yet, within the structures of the university, service is not rewarded.' Her concern is that she is being evaluated (on merit reviews, for example) in terms of research productivity, yet her job makes it impossible to spend enough time on research. Before she took the job, she says that she was warned 'administration would take over all of your time and that is, in fact, the case'. She works in a team with two men and they are all in the office from early in the morning to late at night, with open doors. She notes that academic jobs in her university are meant to be 40 per cent teaching, 40 per cent research, and 20 per cent service, while in fact 'it's become 100 per cent teaching, 100 per cent research and 150 per cent service'. When asked about changes she would like to see, she says: 'I would give more credit to service within the kind of assessment that we're doing. ... one of the major challenges that I, as an administrator, face is the fact that people don't take service seriously.' Faith has also noticed a paradox in the academic/administrative career path:

> For the next stage in my career ... if I choose administration, one of
> the things that I have learned in this position is you cannot keep up an
> active research profile if I'm doing the job the way that I think the job
> needs to be done and be a full-time administrator, but, unless you have
> active research and publishing as a part of your profile, then you're
> not going to get the opportunity to have an administrative career
> because you will be hired for what research direction ... how your
> programme of research can enhance the reputation of this institu-
> tion that you're going to lead. ... Read how our administrators here
> at the university announce the appointment of [senior] people. They
> are announced from their research profiles – and how can you give
> 100 per cent to a research profile when you're doing administration?
> (Faith)

Certainly, these accounts raise questions about what is being expected of
this new generation of administrators. They have been raised in the new
research culture within teacher education and have already received grants,
written books and accomplished much along those lines. Whatever they have
tried to accomplish in their management roles, it appears that what is being
asked of them is to *sacrifice* this key component of their identity and their
satisfaction in academic life.

Questions of control

Also evident in most of the interviews was a struggle to maintain a level of
agency and control. The word 'control' is used repeatedly. This sense of
struggle may be somewhat unexpected, given the belief widely held that
administrators or managers revel in power and control over others' fates and
fortunes. In some cases, especially in Australia, participants talked about the
challenges all academics faced in trying to survive the increased demands
made on their time. They speak of moving from a situation where academics
'did their own thing' to one where they are 'employees'. Vera describes what
she calls a 'fundamental change' in the conditions of employment:

> I call it the corporatization of universities ... the change from uni-
> versities being a collection of individuals, you know, doing their
> own, generating their own work, you know, teaching out of their
> own experience and expertise, doing their research, you know, from
> their own things – you know, the collection of individuals organized
> in departments and collegially managed – to an organization of a
> university which has a mission and is doing things and everybody is
> actually employed to do that.

Terry, also in Australia, seems to be talking about both herself and her colleagues in these thoughtful extracts:

> The amount of work that you have to do is one of the problems, but I think it's a problem because you no longer control your own labour. That there are so many things that you have to do, that even if you would have been working as many hours ten years ago or fifteen years ago, it was discretionary – it was discretionary in the sense that you got to control it.
>
> ...
>
> You might have been one of these people who were driven so that you sat up all night, or you overdid your teaching, so everything was perfect, but you felt much more control over it. I think much more now, that the work is controlled and partly it's controlled because there is so much. You might have been working an 80-hour week, but before, 30 hours of that you had to do and the rest you chose to do, and it tended to be things that you felt some control over. Now you may be working 60 hours a week, but you don't control any of it, and you feel as if you don't control any of it.

There is sometimes a hint that the new conditions carry some element of improvement over the old. Researchers are given more credit, Rebecca (in Britain) notes. She gives a humorous description of the recent past:

> When I was at [name of university], it was very amusing because people, a group of men in particular, used to troop down the corridor at 10.00 in the morning for coffees, to the coffee lounge. They'd have a coffee break, which went on until 11, then they'd come back and then they'd go down again at 12.30 for their lunch. It was like the crocodile [a line of people walking two by two], you know, and then they'd all knock off at 4.30 and go home.

In many accounts, there is a strong sense that the jobs themselves are on the verge of being 'out of control'. Allusions to stress and health are common. The prime culprit seems to be intensification, although it is likely to be the combination of factors rather than any single one at fault. For example:

> I'm working much longer hours than I have ever worked in my life, and I do feel, I do have times when it feels like it's out of control, and I do feel stressed.
>
> (Miranda, Australia)

> Yes, it's [the job] huge and it didn't take long before it began to take a toll not only on my physical health through things like [lists several illnesses] but even more, perhaps, worry. I was even more worried about the toll that it was taking on my psychological health because it just made me so sad because who can get it all done?
>
> (Hester, Canada)

Specific points made included the necessity to be in the office for long hours and the incessant demands of email:

> One of the biggest changes of my life is that my whole schedule's changed. I'm in the building from eight in the morning till seven at night every night. . . . As an academic, if I didn't get to my email, you know, over two or three days, it wasn't a big deal, right, and I don't have that kind of freedom. So I do have less control over my own time and space than I ever did before and it was just easier to have a presence every day.
>
> (Victoria, Canada)

> Information technology . . . adds another level of kind of burden in a way, so that as well as your post you get 100 emails a day, all of which need to be answered immediately because you got them immediately, didn't you, unlike a letter which, you know, someone sends you a letter, you read it, you think I'll reply to that tomorrow, you send it back and it all takes two weeks. But with email it's instant.
>
> (Verity, Britain)

> I suppose at the moment, it's, what, 200 emails a day, and they range from the absolutely ridiculous to something that could affect the future of this faculty for ever.
>
> (Elise, Britain)

Various strategies were used to take back some measure of control. I have mentioned that some of the women gave up the management position. Other decisions involved changing universities, quitting the job, taking time off or modifying the responsibility. Apparent in these quotations is the search for a sense of control:

> Then I got sick in the fall after this review and after these hours, and just age, I think . . . I decided I really couldn't even face going quite till the end of June before my sabbatical . . . so I asked if I could go on leave and take a couple of months without pay at the end of April. You see I'm buying myself out.
>
> (Anna, Canada)

> The fact that I moved to [city], and that I changed my lifestyle, I have more freedom than I had before. Because it's a bigger faculty I have more people working under me, I actually can control my own work much more. Although it is a very, very busy job, I work long hours I actually can – I control the labour much more than I was able to before.
>
> (Terry, Australia)

> [Having changed jobs] I feel much happier now because I feel more control ... I've freedom to control my own diary ... I sort of feel that I do have more control over my life and I also have control about who I work with.
>
> (Rebecca, Britain)

Other responses involved, in Vera's words, 'finding the spaces'. Vera, in Australia, gave an example of turning a university requirement to achieve research targets from an oppressive requirement to a source of pride for her colleagues. In Canada, Victoria told of being proactive, and taking pride in accomplishments on behalf of students, something, which gave her 'joy'. Elise (Britain) manages to save one day a week for research by 'being very firm and in control of my diary' as well as setting up highly organized systems for keeping track of her work. Terry (Australia) described her 'constructive' stance:

> I am actually the kind of person who finds the cracks in things. My strength is making a good thing out of something that looked like it might have been a bad thing. I mean, if I was a house builder, I would be renovating houses, I wouldn't be building a new one. ... I can take things that look like disparate ideas and policies that are actually a bit off, and turn them into something that is OK.
>
> (Terry)

A strong sense of positive thinking comes across in some of these Australian interviews, something less frequent in the other two countries. Australians Olivia and Vera, in the extracts below, sound more fulfilled than depleted:

> I was eager to have a go at it [the position]. I love this place, and I love the work, there are no parts of different jobs that I haven't enjoyed. I tend to like whatever I do ... and I had clear ideas about how I want to reorganize things.
>
> (Olivia)

This university has such wonderful possibilities ... I think that if we're really talking about providing equity, if we're looking at education as something that can make a difference, this university is so well placed to do that.

(Olivia)

Ah well, I mean, I love it. I mean ... although, you know, sometimes I think, what did I do today? I talked to this person ... but I love the staff.

(Vera)

Conclusion

As the new waves of women academics 'come of age' (Martin 2000), attention is turning to their practice and potential as leaders in the academy. In the next few decades, we are likely to see a rising proportion of women academics and women managers, as the generation of mostly white men who have run the universities begins to retire in large numbers. Questions have been raised as to whether we can expect major alterations in university ethos if women become the majority (Acker 2003). Currently, however, what we see is a transitional generation, a group of women who themselves may have been marginalized in their careers and often have strong commitments to change (Wyn *et al.* 2000), now appearing in increasing numbers in important university roles. Currie *et al.* (2003) point out that the problem is not that women never get to the top – in fact in the 'corporatized university' a select few are actively sought out – but that those who are there face strong pressures to conform to a generally masculinized and inhospitable culture.

The women interviewed for my project have progressed at least part way up the academic management career ladder and are strong and assertive. Yet sympathetic, in-depth interviewing elicits ample evidence of conflicted emotions (see also Acker and Feuerverger 2003). The unhappiest people tend to be those in stressful lower middle management roles, where few adjustments have been made in their workloads or promotion requirements while they take on huge responsibilities, often with little support and under conditions of financial stringency. Some who may have hoped for managerial careers find themselves relieved to return to teaching, a situation rather problematical for future recruitment to leadership positions. Others have developed strategies that allow them to swim rather than sink. A certain kind of optimism and buoyancy serves them well. The quotations above from Olivia and Vera exemplify this positive thinking. Pearl (Canada), too, says, 'I love administration', while Elise (Britain), referring to the familiar contrast between seeing a glass as half full versus half empty, describes herself as 'very much a half-full person'.

The positive thinkers, those who have 'found the spaces', are likely to be more experienced and to be at the level of head of school or dean, although there is not a perfect correlation. It is hard to know whether there is a certain amount of self-selection going on, or whether those with better experiences stay in management. Even the most optimistic people, however, must contend with the increasing pressures of insufficient finances, government reforms, workload intensification and growing scrutiny. Few can maintain a stellar level of research and scholarship along with a punishing administrative workload. These women are indeed pioneers. Perhaps they spoke so freely and emotionally to the researchers because they rarely are able to share their experiences with other sympathetic peers. A few universities had institutionalized forums where managers could share and discuss problems and issues, but most had not. Similarly, some institutions had extensive managerial training programmes, but these too were rare. Most of the women were learning what to do as they went along. Struggle and stress seemed endemic and occasionally extreme. Governments and institutions are eager to set targets and measure performance, but who is caring about what happens to the individuals who are sacrificing many aspects of their hard-won careers to manage the madness?

Acknowledgements

Several people assisted me in important ways in conducting this research. In particular, I would like to thank Michelle Webber for help with data analysis and Johanna Wyn and Mary Fuller for facilitating the data collection in Australia and Britain, respectively. Johanna first noticed the frequent use of the word 'control' in the transcripts. I would also like to thank Jo-Anne Dillabough for inspiring conversations and insights on gender and globalization.

Notes

1. This term is meant to subsume other similar units, such as colleges, departments, schools or institutes of education.
2. There are many variations in terminology across the countries. Positions referred to as management in Australia and Britain are often described as administration (sometimes academic administration) in Canada. Similarly, faculty members in Canada are likely to be called staff or academic staff in the other two countries. Heads of department in Australia and Britain will usually be termed chairs in Canada. Quotations from participants reflect their local usage.

3. On institutional or workplace cultures in educational settings, see Acker 1999; Blackmore 1999; Fogelberg *et al.* 1999; Morley 1999; Currie and Thiele 2001; Hearn 2001. On the intersection of globalization and university work, see Slaughter and Leslie 1997; Currie and Newson 1998; Inayatullah and Gidley 2000; Marginson 2000; Marginson and Considine 2000; Stromquist and Monkman 2000; Brooks and Mackinnon 2001; Dillabough and Acker 2002; Stromquist 2002.
4. All names of participants are pseudonyms.

PART III

DISRUPTING THE NORMATIVE
DISCOURSE OF LEADERSHIP

8 Women Performing the Superintendency: Problematizing the Normative Alignment of Conceptions of Power and Constructions of Gender

Cryss Brunner

> We suggest that ... theory should identify the kinds of people who view power in social production (rather than social control) terms and whose life experiences have engendered the habit of acting as collaborative (rather than controlling) power agents. While many types of people may have such power orientations, feminists suggest that the life experiences of women have made women especially likely to think and act as collaborative leaders, suggesting that the presence of women in central leadership roles ... may increase their effectiveness.
>
> (Brunner and Schumaker 1998: 32)

The purpose of this empirically grounded chapter is to draw attention to the notion that modern conceptions of power align, in large part, with particular constructions of gender, and further, that social norms that expect a congruence of power and gender have strong potential to limit access, for some groups of people, to roles that have been masculinized, specifically the position of superintendent of schools – a role that has come into being within the context of western modernism.

To begin, the chapter discusses the construction of gender by disaggregating the meanings of sex, sexual orientation and gender. The chapter then reviews how gender is socially constructed and serves as a social organizer. Next, through literature and the findings of several research studies, power is shown to be a gendered concept, that is, power as a masculine and/or feminine performance. Finally, the chapter closes with an assertion that social norms governing power/gender alignment has the unfortunate yet strong effect of restricting women's access to the superintendency.

The social construction of gender

The notion of gender is complex and constantly evolving, and its full discussion is beyond the scope of this chapter. What follows is a brief highlighting of some of the more critical points.

Disaggregating meanings: sex, sexual orientation and gender

To begin, I offer my understanding of what the term 'gender' does not mean. The term 'gender' is not to be confused with the terms 'sex' or 'sexual orientation'. As Lugg (2003: 98) states: 'Gender is an ongoing, lifelong series of evolving performances. Sex is chromosomal.' Yet Lugg does not intend to imply that sex is dichotomous – a view currently held in the US legal understanding (Case 1995; Franke 1995; Valdes 1995; Nye 1998; Greenberg 1999, 2000; cited in Lugg 2003: 98). She continues:

> According to medical research, there are common variations between XX (female) and XY (male), including XXX, XXY, XXXY, XYY, XYYY, XYYYY, and XO (Greenberg 1999). Additionally, some individuals who are legally male (XY) and female (XX) are born with ambiguous genitalia – that is, one cannot distinguish whether the infant is a boy or a girl by visual inspection. Other individuals develop ambiguities as they mature (Greenberg 1999; Potter and Summers 2001). The collective term for such individuals is *intersexed*. ... Additionally, there are individuals who are transgendered, meaning that they do not identify with their sex or sex characteristics. ... A transgendered person who was born a male will identify as a female throughout most of, if not her entire, life. Likewise, a transgendered person who was born female will identify as male. Those who elect to pursue sexual reassignment surgery are known as transsexual (Nye 1998).
>
> (Lugg 2003: 98–99)

Thus, the term 'sex' has to do with a person's chromosomal make-up and cannot necessarily be determined through visual examination alone. Building on this understanding of the term 'sex', Lugg (2003: 100) and others define 'sexual orientation' as the sex of the person with whom one can most easily establish emotional connections – or sexual object of choice (Somerville 2000). In other words, with whom does the person 'fall in love'? This capacity or proclivity for love (Valdes 1995) may or may not have much to do with actual sexual behaviour. Even celibate individuals have a basic sexual orientation although they do not engage in sexual acts (Valdes 1995; Terry

1999). Terms that describe sexual orientation include 'heterosexual', 'homosexual' and 'bisexual'. Thus, 'sex' has one meaning and 'sexual orientation' has another.

To be sure, there is much confusion about how, when and where the terms 'sex', 'sexual orientation' and 'gender' should be used. For example, US politics and the judicial system still consider 'sex' a binary term, that is, that there are only two sexes. Further confusion occurs because the term 'gender' has been conflated with the terms 'sex' and 'sexual orientation' in research studies. Lugg (2003: 99) points out that '[i]n much of the politics of education and educational leadership research, gender has tended to mean research focused on biological women and girls (for example, Foster 1999) who are all assumed to be non-queer'. To say it another way, the term 'gender' as used in this particular research provides no explicit indication of sex or sexual orientation and therefore, in its default mode, implies that the participants are non-queer women and girls and pays 'less attention to how individuals, who are considered females and males, and are queer and non-queer, perform according to their respective (and constructed) gender roles or social scripts within school settings (Blount 1996, 1998; Clifford 1989)' (Lugg 2003: 100). Conflating 'sex' and 'gender' creates many problems, in particular legalistic ones, for school administrators and others.[1]

One of the clearest explanations of the differences between the notions of gender and sexual orientation can be found in discussions of 'straightenizing' (Seidman 1996). The term 'straightenizing' is used to describe lesbian, gay, bisexual and transgendered (LGBT) people when their behaviours and mannerisms are like those of a 'typical' male or female of their own gender (Fraynd and Capper 2003: 99). In other words, a lesbian (sexual orientation) may behave as a 'typical' female, and a gay (sexual orientation) may behave as a 'typical' male. According to several researchers (Seidman 1996; Fraynd and Capper 2003), behaving 'straight' or 'normally' for one's sex – adhering to gender role stereotypes – is certainly no guarantee, but may have the potential to position LGBT people for greater acceptance or tolerance because they are an exception to what is considered the stereotypical LGBT behaviour. As stated by Fraynd and Capper (2003: 110–111), when discussing the views of their sexual minority, administrator participants:

> When these [sexual minority] school leaders adhered to gender role stereotypes, positioned themselves away from gay/lesbian stereotypes, and concealed their identity by passing, covering, separation, or reputation, these actions all contributed to reinforcing heteronormativity in the school. In a few cases, the administrators became agents of the heteronormative process by encouraging some of their minority students and staff to develop better internal discipline and external suppression of things lesbian or gay.

As noted by the most 'out' participant in Fraynd and Capper's (2003: 99) study, '[M]aybe if I were single, this would be different. Because I have a stable family, I'm married we have kids. And I think if I were single or if my partner were 21 instead of 46 it may be different. Everyone loves Dante, so if they had any problems with my being gay, it didn't last long because of my connection to Dante.'

The social construction of gender

How and when, then, is the term 'gender' to be used? For the purposes of this chapter, I have chosen to adopt the definitions laid out by Lugg (2003). As Lugg (2003) stated it:

> Gendered behaviours may have little to do with a given individual's biological sex or sexual orientation. ... [S]exual orientation is about emotional attachment, gender is about the performance of identity, and sex is about biology – the legal definition. Although these three categories may well interact at times and are legal constructions, they should not be considered predictive regarding an individual's behaviour or identity (Case 1995; Chauncey 1994; Franke 1995; Miller 1995; Valdes 1995; Somerville 2000; Yoshino 2002).
>
> (Lugg 2003: 101)

Gender, therefore, is socially constructed – a construction that begins with birth when a sex category is assigned based on how the genitalia look (in countries with modern medicine, when genitalia are ambiguous, surgery is often performed to make a category obvious).

Babies are dressed or adorned to indicate one sex category. Once a sex category is explicit, it becomes a gender status through gender markers – names, clothing – and others treat the baby in ways that society has decided are gender-appropriate. In spite of the fact that gendered roles change and continue to change over time, by the onset of puberty, sexual feelings and practices have been shaped by gendered norms and expectations – whatever those norms and expectations are at the time. Later:

> Parenting is gendered, with different expectations for mothers and for fathers, and people of different genders work at different kinds of jobs. The work adults do as mothers and fathers and as low-level workers and high-level bosses, shapes women's and men's life experiences, and these experiences produce different feelings, consciousness, relationships, skills – ways of performing that we call feminine or masculine.
>
> (Lorber 1994: 14)

All of these events create the socially constructed statuses of gender.

Thus, '[a]s a social institution, gender is one of the major ways that human beings organize their lives' (Lorber 1994: 18). For example, one way to organize people is to categorize them by their talents and skills, other ways to organize them include gender, race and ethnicity. And while some societies use talents and skills as organizers, all societies use gender and age, and, by constructing similarities and differences within and among the categories, roles, status and responsibilities are established for each group. Each group is further shaped, gendered by their respective assigned roles and responsibilities (Lorber 1994). In contrast to humans, Lorber (1994: 15) states: 'animals group on sex and age, relational categories that are physiologically, not socially, different'. Humans create gender and age-group categories that are socially, and not necessarily physiologically, different.

All one has to do to realize the importance of humanity's organization of human life by gender is to be faced with a human who is not quickly identifiable as male or female. Androgyny is not comfortable for us. We study androgynous people closely for any indication of their sex. We insist, to ourselves, that they must be gendered, so we continue to seek gender markers or gender appropriate behaviours that render their sex explicit.[2]

Some societies have three genders, but western societies have only two: 'man' and 'woman' (Lorber 1994). However, western societies do recognize a category of 'transgendered' people. 'Transgendered' means one who has crossed gender lines in some way.

> Modern Western societies' *transsexuals* and *transvestites* are the nearest equivalent of these cross over genders, but they are not institutionalized as third genders. Transsexuals are biological males and females who have sex-change operations to alter their genitalia. ... They do not become a third gender; they change genders. Transvestites are males who live as women and females who live as men but do not intend to have sex-change surgery. Their dress, appearance, and mannerism fall within the range of what is expected from members of the opposite gender, so that they 'pass'. ... Genders, therefore, are not attached to a biological substratum. ... These odd or deviant or third genders show us what we ordinarily take for granted – that people have to learn to be women and men. Men who cross-dress for performances or for pleasure often learn from women's magazines how to 'do femininity' convincingly (Garber 1992: 41–51). Because transvestism is direct evidence of how gender is constructed, Marjorie Garber claims it has 'extraordinary power ... to disrupt, expose, and challenge, putting in question the very notion of the "original" and of stable identity' (Garber 1992: 16).
>
> (Lorber 1994: 17–18)

To restate, males and females have to learn to be men and women. A person's sex does not necessarily determine their gender. We as modern westerners categorize people at birth – even construct our legal system and laws (see Lugg 2003, for example) – into only two sexes and thereby construct gender as two categories that, through social norms, spell out the appropriate behaviours, clothing, styles and mannerisms. All a person has to do, to be viewed as one gender or the other, is to carefully adhere to the appropriate gender markers for the category of her/his choice. This polarization of gender operates in at least two ways: (1) it defines 'mutually exclusive scripts for being male and female' (Bem 1993: 81),[3] and (2), it defines

> any person or behaviour that deviates from these scripts as problematic – as unnatural or immoral from a religious perspective or as biologically anomalous or psychologically pathological from a scientific perspective. Taken together, the effect of these two processes is to construct and to naturalize a gender-polarizing link between the sex of one's body and the character of one's psyche and one's sexuality.
>
> (Bem 1993: 81)[4]

The next section focuses on the gendering of power conceptions.

Modern conceptions of power: a competing and gendered discussion

Modern western philosophy and political science hold two major discussions on the concept of power.[5] The larger portion of this literature focuses on power conceptualized as dominance, control, authority and influence over others and things – where some have it and others do not (see Weber 1924; Russell 1938; Lasswell and Kaplan 1950; Hunter 1953; Simon 1953; Dahl 1961; Bachrach and Baratz 1962; Lukes 1974; Trounstine and Christensen 1982). This conception of 'power over'[6] holds within it the notion of powerlessness. The smaller of the two discussions conceptualizes 'power with' as a synergistic, co-active, collective melding of common being or action – where all have a part of the collective energetic whole, and where actions, taken with others, are grounded in a democratic ideal (see Follett 1924; Emmett 1954; Arendt 1969, 1972; Parsons 1969; Pitkin 1972: 276–277; Kanter 1977, 1979, 1989; Harstock 1981, 1987; Ferguson 1984; Habermas 1986; Clegg 1989: 21–38; Stone 1989: 277; Albrecht and Brewer 1990; Wartenberg 1990: 9–50; Cantor and Bernay 1992; Isaac 1993; Jones 1993; Miller 1993). Both modern conceptions of power have been critiqued in post-structuralist and postmodern literature, and both, each grounded in competing worldviews, appear to be heavily woven into the social fabric of the USA – certainly into the social fabric of the public school system. Indeed, as Shapiro (1984: 37) asserted, schools are unlike any other social institution in that 'notions of hierarchy and equality and democracy and authoritarian control forced [are] forced to co-exist in ... the same proximity'. The existence of competing, polarized views is one of the hallmarks of modernism.

The next two subsections contain a discussion – supported by examples from research studies (Brunner 1995, 1998; Brunner and Schumaker 1998) – of the relationship between conceptions of power and constructions of gender.

Masculine performances of power: power-over

Without a doubt, the more heavily researched and discussed modern conception of power – power-over – forms the foundation for most processes, including decision-making, within public school systems. In addition, political science research and other studies of power most often define power as power-over for purposes of observation and analysis. In addition, most literature focused on administration has detailed various types of power-over while ignoring the possibility that power-with exists. For example, Etzioni (1961) advanced the proposition that there are three general kinds of power: coercive power (for example, negatively evaluating an employee), remunerative power (control over resources), and normative power (control over prestige). Parsons (1963) proposed four types of power or what he also referred to as influence: persuasion, inducement, activation of commitment (for example, use of negative sanctions to influence another person's intentions) and deterrence (negative sanctions to control a situation). Going further, French and Raven (1979) identified five types of power: reward power (for example, capacity to provide rewards), coercive power, legitimate power (power conferred on individual by law and/or position), referent power (power gained through connections with others who have power) and expert power (knowing more than others in an area). Clearly all of these varieties of power fall under the larger umbrella of conceptions of power-over – all of them imply that one person has more of something than others do.

Moreover, while it is well-known that women perform acts of power-over, several theorists argue that thinking about power in social-control/domination terms – as power-over – has been a male preoccupation (Harstock 1987). To be sure, Weber (1924) believed that 'domination by authorities and obedience by subordinates were important requisites to social action and bureaucratic performance' and thus, 'defined power as the imposition of one's will upon the behaviour of others' (Brunner and Schumaker 1998: 30–31). Other male theorists Bertrand Russell (1938), Harold Lasswell and Abraham Kaplan (1950), Herbert Simon (1953) and Robert Dahl (1961) 'contributed to a social control paradigm of power that has dominated political science' (Brunner and Schumaker 1998: 31).

While the argument that power-over is primarily a male conception – that is, one conceived of and advanced by the male sex – exists in the literature, I suggest that the conception of power-over should more accurately be referred to as a masculine one – that is, it falls within the gender construction of man. During interviews in one ethnographic research study focused on power, I found that 17 of the 18 participants who performed as men (I did not verify that they were male) and were identified by others (through the use of Hunter's (1953) reputational method) as the most powerful members of a community, conceptualized power as dominance, authority, influence or as power-over (Brunner 1995; Brunner and Schumaker 1998). Some of them acknowledged uses of consensus-building, but with the exception of one, all strongly stated that ultimately their ideas or wishes would dominate all others and determine future actions. As recorded in Brunner and Schumaker (1998: 38): 'In short, men tended to view the democratic use of power as using such legitimate resources to achieve their *own* conception of the common good rather than using their leadership position to facilitate others defining and pursuing the common good collectively.'

In the same study, when describing their performances of power, men power-wielders' comments about power included:

> On the council, I am a consensus builder until it gets to the point of being intolerable – then I move on it.

> It's the ability to establish something you want to accomplish – then you work with people to help you get there. It could be me dictating what I want to have done, but that would not be successful power. People must want to do what *you* want accomplished (emphasis in original).

> I try not to dominate. I bring people together and do the right thing. ... I run with something until I get what I want. I go back, and I go back until it happens.

> I am the one who brings an idea to the group and then attempts to get consensus. I wait for a while, then, when results are not forthcoming, I take off running.

> I must work with others to get things done ... things are not completely in my control. But I push in that direction. I don't accept 'no'.

Another man asserted that if you cannot persuade people to follow your orders, then you must use the chain-of-command and make them do it. He

believed that use of the chain-of-command should occur only when abso-
lutely necessary. In brief, all but one of the identified men power-wielders
believed that

> [h]aving power enables people to secure their personal preferences
> when decisions are made, to banish from the agenda those issues
> that threaten their interests, and to control the preferences of other
> actors, enticing them to want what those with power want, often
> instilling in them 'false consciousness' about their real needs.
> (Brunner and Schumaker 1998: 32)

Even the one man, who talked about collaboration, regarded the need for
collaboration as somewhat negative because he believed it undermined one's
power. In other words, he did not believe that collaboration was another form
of power – rather collaboration created weakness.

Some of the men also distinguished between what they considered positive power and negative power. Both forms allowed that one person dominate
and make the final decisions, but positive power meant that the leader or one
in control made decisions that were good for other people (study participants
did not question the assumption that 'any decision made by a leader was
good for others'). Negative power occurred when power 'went to someone's
head' and caused her/him to act only for selfish interests. Power was not
conceptualized as collaboration, consensus-building or power-with by any of
the powerful community men (leaders in politics, business or education, or
moneyed) in this study.

In a second qualitative study (Brunner 1998) of superintendents ($n = 47$) –
women ($n = 22$) and men ($n = 25$) selected for their excellent performance in
the position – I again asked participants about their conceptions of power.
This sample differed from the sample in the first study in that the participants
in the first study were named by a broad base of community members who
identified them as the most powerful people in the community – I had to ask
that they also include names of women because women's names were not
volunteered. In the second study, the superintendents were named by a large
panel of experts who identified them as the most exceptional superintendents
in the nation – I also had to ask for names of women in this study in order to
get a balanced sample. I speculate that the findings of both studies would
have been almost identical if I had asked for the most powerful superintendents in the nation. To be sure, however, in the case of the second study,
the superintendents were assumed to be the most powerful employees in their
districts by virtue of their positions.

After interviewing superintendents about their conceptions of power
in the second study, the superintendents' answers were then triangulated
with multiple interviews of community members.[7] Most of the men

superintendents (n = 15) in the second study conceptualized power as power-over, in much the same way as those in the first study discussed earlier. Not surprisingly, because of the current rhetoric about collaboration in schools, four of the men talked about power-over and power-with, in other words they had mixed conceptions of power (at times these conceptions were grounded in understandings of power-over and at times of power-with). And finally, six of the men conceptualized power as with others. In summary, the men's conceptions of power in the second study fell out as follows: power-over 15; mixed power 4; power-with 6. Clearly in this study of powerful school leaders (identified as exceptional by others), gender was a strong indicator but not a determinate or an absolute predictor of the men superintendents' conceptions of power.

Adding the findings of the second study (15 out of 25 men superintendents held power-over conceptions) to the findings of the first study (17 out of 18 powerful community men held distinctly power-over conceptions), one can say that of the 43 powerful men interviewed, 32 held power-over conceptions. As a result of these two studies, I concluded that power-over is a masculine conception of power, that is, power-over is gendered as masculine/ man. Further, although power-over is gendered as masculine, it is *not* the conception that every male (sex), perceived as powerful, holds.

Feminine performances of power: power-with

The less researched power-with finds its home, at least implicitly, in modern discussions of topics such as collaborative decision-making, site-based management, authentic participation, and other conversations of inter- and intra-agency arrangements and is less analysed and appreciated. And while these topical discussions of power-with can be found – in education broadly, in educational publications, in philosophy, and in political and feminist theory (see Follett 1924; Emmett 1954; Arendt 1969, 1972; Parsons 1969; Pitkin 1972: 276–277; Kanter 1977, 1979, 1989; Harstock 1981, 1987; Ferguson 1984; Habermas 1986; Clegg 1989: 21–38; Stone 1989: 277; Albrecht and Brewer 1990; Wartenberg 1990: 9–50; Cantor and Bernay 1992; Isaac 1993; Jones 1993; Miller 1993) – the concept of power-with (as the unit of analysis) is rarely studied empirically. This is not to say that research is non-existent or that practical models and applications of shared power do not exist. In fact, beyond education literature (see Schmuck and Schmuck 1990; Dunlap and Goldman 1991; Beck 1994; Hurty 1995; Regan 1995) and practice, some relevant research literature on collaborative models and conceptions of management and decision-making can also be found in the fields of business (see Cohen 1989; Senge 1990, 1994; Helgeson 1991; Brunetti 1993; Juran 1995; Scholtes 1996) and psychology (see Cavalier 2000).

While not exclusively a feminist idea (see, for example, Parsons 1969;

Habermas 1986; Isaac 1993), the alternative conception of power, power-with, has perhaps been discussed most prominently by modern philosopher Hannah Arendt (1972). For Arendt:

> [p]olitics is more than a matter of domination; it is (or at least could be) a process by which free and equal agents create collective power, the capacity to act in concert to achieve collectively those common goals that individuals cannot achieve for themselves. Politics thus involves acts of communication and cooperation that establish collaborative relationships among people and that enable transformations of problematic social conditions. Power, then, is a capacity that a community of people attains when their acts of communication, cooperation, and collaboration have been successful (Brunner and Schumaker 1998: 31).
>
> (Arendt 1972)

A follower of Arendt, Nancy Harstock (1987), asserted that such understandings of power could also be found in most of the writings by women power theorists. Continuing this tradition currently are theorists such as Kathleen Jones (1993) and Cantor and Bernay (1992), all who view power as collective and consider such a conception of power as a feminine one.

Other studies focused on gender differences related to power have found that women use their power differently from men. Miller (1993), drawing on Ruddick (1989), argued that women most often experience their power by creating change and by empowering others through their roles as mothers and teachers. When discussing Miller (1993), Brunner and Schumaker (1998) reminded readers that Miller believed that women use their power for the benefit of others. In studies of women in state legislatures, Kirkpatrick (1974) found that women are less likely than men to view the legislature as an arena where people compete to advance their own interests and more likely to consider the legislative process as a search for solutions for public problems and to serve the common good. Thomas's (1994: 6) ideas aligned with Kirkpatrick's in that she advanced the notion that women legislators' backgrounds socialized women to focus 'on solving problems for constituents rather than on legislative battles'. Kirkpatrick's and Thomas's research found that women in positions of power are more likely than men to ground their actions in power conceptualized as power-with rather than as power-over.

I agree with Kirkpatrick, Harstock, Thomas and others when they assert that power-with is primarily a feminine conception, that is, it falls within the gender construction of 'woman'. During interviews in the same first ethnographic research study discussed earlier, I found that all of the identified powerful community participants ($n = 13$, one was the superintendent of schools in the community) who performed as women (I did not verify that they were female) conceptualized power as the ability to get things done with others, or as power-over (Brunner 1995; Brunner and Schumaker 1998). Indeed, in interviews, they stated that their

> accomplishment[s] involved consensus building, empowering others, enlisting the help of others, motivating others, and being a servant. Compared to men, women did not view power as a quality of particular persons – especially themselves. Rather, they considered it collective action taken as a result of collaboratively made decisions.
>
> (Brunner and Schumaker 1998: 38)

When describing their conceptions of power, women power-wielders' comments included:

> Power doesn't reside within a person, but needs others.

> You don't get it, someone gives it to you.

> It's teamwork.

> It's letting people know that they are important. What we are talking about here is interaction.

> ... empowerment.

> I like to include people in the decision process even when the decision doesn't go my way.

Interestingly, two community women were identified as powerful and then *deleted* from the list by the same community members who named them. Therefore, both were not part of the actual study. These women were referred to as 'bitches' and were not allowed the label of 'powerful' because they did not 'deserve' it. Even though they were not participants in the actual study because they were taken off the lists, I interviewed them using the same protocol. Both women conceptualized power as over others. In short, they espoused and performed power as masculine.

The community women participants in the first study, like the men, discussed negative power. In contrast to the men in the first study who were comfortable with power understood as dominance and control, the women in the study stated clearly that they did not want to experience 'control over' or 'power-over' or 'violence' to intimidate others. Representative comments about negative power were:

Some people do it all themselves, keeping more of the action to themselves.

Some people want you to do everything through them.

In other words, they agreed with the men when reflecting that negative power was self-serving actions that ignored the common good, but their notions of common good were articulated as empowering other people and including them in activities and/or processes. Further, it was clear that power enacted over others – advancing their own ideas over others' – was an uncomfortable notion for the women. The women did not conceptualize power as power-over. Instead they conceptualized it as with others.

Returning to the second qualitative study (Brunner 1998) of superintendents – women ($n = 22$) and men ($n = 25$) – most of the women superintendents[8] ($n = 17$) conceptualized power as power-with, in much the same way as the women in the first study discussed earlier. Three of the women talked about power-over and power-with, in other words, they had mixed conceptions of power. And finally, two of the women conceptualized power as over others. In summary, the women's conceptions of power in the second study fell out as follows: power-over 2, mixed power 3, power-with 17.

Adding the findings of the second study (17 out of 22 women superintendents held power-with conceptions) to the findings of the first study (13 out of 13 powerful community women held distinctly power-with conceptions), one can say that of the 35 powerful women interviewed, 30 held power-with conceptions. As a result of these two studies, I concluded that power-with is a feminine conception of power, that is power-with is strongly gendered as feminine/woman. Further, although power-with is gendered as feminine, it is *not* the conception that every female (sex), perceived as powerful, holds.

Conclusion: the limitations of power and gender alignment

In brief, because of studies like the two examples above and the preponderance of similar views and findings in the literature, I have come to believe that for community and school leaders, power-with is gendered feminine/woman – and power-over is gendered masculine/man. However, although power-with is gendered feminine, it is *not* the conception that every female (sex) leader holds. In addition, although power-over is gendered masculine, it is *not* the conception that every male holds. To be sure, this conclusion includes the notion that some females (sex) leaders conceptualize power as power-over and that some males (sex) leaders conceptualize power

134 LEADERSHIP, GENDER AND CULTURE IN EDUCATION

as power-with. Clearly, in these two studies of powerful community leaders (identified as power elites by others) and powerful school leaders (identified as exceptional by others), gender was a strong indicator of the conception of power that a male or female leader held, and yet gender did not determine or predict the conception a person held – both female and male leaders conceptualized power as power-over, as mixed or as power-with. In addition, participants' conceptualizations of power more closely aligned with their performances of power than did their genders. To restate, conceptions of power proved to be a stronger predictor of enactments of power than did constructions of gender.

What is most interesting in these studies, however, are the complex negotiations required of the women who seek, attain and keep heavily masculinized roles such as the superintendency. On one hand, women who were considered successful were gender-appropriate even in their use of power. Like the sexual minority administrators in the Fraynd and Capper (2003) study, during interviews the *successful* women in these studies suggested heteronormativity when they advised women to act like a 'lady' as the way to success.

On the other hand, women superintendents who had a majority of appropriate gender markers in place but who did *not* adhere to conceptions of power that are considered feminine, were (a) viewed as unsuccessful (not well liked), (b) disallowed the label 'powerful' by community members, and (c) called 'bitches' by many participants during triangulation interviews. One interpretation of this phenomenon is that these women were gender bending – something extremely uncomfortable for others around them. They were enacting their masculine conceptions of power – which was appropriate for the role – but not for the gender they explicitly displayed through other markers and looked dangerously transgendered.

Strikingly, neither participant group was able to identify its own conceptions of power as gender markers. Such insight is rarely explicit in the literature. Neither group articulated or reflected consciously that power-with is the socially acceptable, gender-appropriate behaviour for women. While still off the mark, the strongest realization came from successful women superintendents when they expressed that enacting power-with allowed them to value relationships and people (including children) – values that were very important to them.

Ironically, much like the sexual minority administrators in the Fraynd and Capper (2003) study who at once reproduced and disrupted heteronormativity, the successful women superintendents in my studies at once reproduced and disrupted sexism and the bias created by gender constructions. Women superintendents, who acted 'like men' and disrupted gender constructions, flew in the face of strong social norms and suffered consequences – diminished access, poor support, personal attacks, unfair criticism and short tenures – that all superintendents experience from time to time, but in exaggerated and extreme forms. There is no doubt that the gendered nature of the concept of power – the social norm of power and gender alignment – creates difficulty and limitations for females who wish, first, to be superintendents, and second, to be viewed as successful when in the role.

Notes

1. For a full discussion of this phenomenon see Case 1995; Franke 1995; Valdes 1995; Terry 1999; Siegel 2002; Lugg 2003.
2. For a full discussion of the differences between human action and animal behaviour, see Lorber 1994.
3. See also Bourdieu 1990; Lorber 1994.
4. See also, Lorber 1994: 23.
5. For full discussions of the distinctions between the two, see Clegg 1989; Stone 1989; Wartenberg 1990.
6. Mary Parker Follett (1924) was one of the first to use the terms 'power over' and 'power with'. Her exploration of the qualitative distinction between these two concepts was the foundation for her work on co-active power. And while Follett did not hyphenate the terms, for purposes of readability, I have hyphenated the terms here.
7. For a description of the full study see Brunner 1998.
8. I purposely use the term 'women' to modify the noun 'superintendents'. The use of the term 'women' moves the study to one of people who adhered to gender-appropriate behaviour, that is, behaviour that matched how they 'marked' themselves (with dress or other explicit markers). To use the term 'female' to modify the noun 'superintendents', can imply that the study was one of people of the same sex when in fact there was no effort to prove that all the women participants were female (sex).

9 Leadership, Embodiment and Gender Scripts: Prom Queens and Chief Executives

Cecilia Reynolds

Introduction

In my writing and research in the area of school/university leadership and administration (for example, Reynolds and Young 1995, Reynolds 2002a), I have come to recognize that three dualisms prevail. There is much written about good/effective leaders, as opposed to poor/ineffective leaders. There also is literature describing the differences between male and female leaders, particularly their leadership styles. Across most of this work, however, a third and largely unarticulated dualism persists: the split between mind and body regarding leadership work.

The discourse about good or poor leaders, about male or female leaders, seldom considers the body type of the leader, the sexuality of the leader, or the 'body work' that leadership requires. If you look closely at studies and discussions of leadership, you find that attention is focused on what leaders think and say and not much attention is paid to what they emote, enact or embody. There seems to be an assumption that the work of leading and managing in school and university settings is work of the mind rather than the body.

Reliance on the Cartesian split between mind and body has contributed to a focus in the school leadership literature (and in much of what most people know about school leaders) on the mental, rather than the bodily, aspects of what transpires when people perform leadership roles. Feminist insights about embodiment (such as those offered in Horner and Keane 2000), however, stress that all of us come to our leadership work as embodied individuals. We are seen by others, and by ourselves, as either male or female, belonging to a particular ethnic/racial group or groups, short or tall, attractive or unattractive, and as matching or not matching dominant images for the roles we take on. Moreover, we use our bodies to carry out much of our leadership work, not just our minds (for further discussion see Reynolds 2002a).

Educational scholars Eisner and Powell (2002: 134) have indicated the important role that 'somatic forms of knowledge' play in the work that people do. Such forms of knowledge come about when people use their physical body as a source of information. Linking mind and body in our investigations of leadership work allows us to consider the aesthetics of leadership, the art as well as the science of leadership.

In this chapter, I examine aspects of leadership which become visible when we turn away from the traditional mind/body split which has dominated the field of educational administration research. What can we see when we consider leadership as an embodied act? How are women school leaders limited by images of the feminine 'prom queen'? How are male school leaders affected by presumptions about the masculine 'chief executive' image? To address these questions, I draw from several recent feminist studies of school/ university female leaders (Reynolds 2002a) and focus on tensions between the leadership goals of those studied (their desires for their leadership) and the reactions of others to their attempts (how people have reacted to their embodied work).

Images of prom queens and chief executives

In North American culture in the twentieth century, there have been a variety of rituals enacted to introduce females to society once they are of marrying age. Among these rituals, perhaps the most recent has been the high school prom, a yearly dance for graduating students where one of the young women is selected by a panel of judges to be the prom queen. Mechanisms for selecting the queen and the qualities judges look for vary from venue to venue, but usually the queen is the one who is feminine without being blatantly sexual, and pretty by North American standards for beauty. The prom queen is almost always someone who is 'popular' with peers, teachers and parents. Since this is a clearly embodied image, I have selected it in this chapter as an image for considering how women school leaders in this context may be seen to be affected by such notions of embodiment.

The other gendered image I am employing in the chapter is that of the chief executive officer, or CEO. In the twentieth-century North American context, the head of large corporations is often given this title and the people chosen for such roles during this period have almost always been men. While the mechanisms for selecting the CEO vary from venue to venue, usually the CEO is seen by others to be someone who is competitive, smart, well-connected, able to be tough when necessary, attractive, and projecting 'presence' and/or power. While the sexuality of the male CEO is usually not an overt consideration, I am prepared to argue that indeed what society might deem 'conventional sexuality' is usually expected of the CEO. We see this when sexual scandals emerge, such as the one surrounding Bill Clinton, the US President, and Monica Lewinsky in the 1990s. The CEO image can be helpful as we think about how male school leaders may be seen to be affected by such notions of embodiment.

In my study of Canadian women and men school principals across two generations (Reynolds 2002b), I noted some changes over time in the ways these female and male leaders were treated within the same school board as they moved into leadership roles. In this chapter, I consider how those data reveal insights about embodiment and leadership. The women leaders I interviewed who became school principals in the 1940s and 1950s, were, in my view, 'dutiful daughters' because they persistently took on tasks in schools which 'fatherly' male administrators asked of them. In this period, if women married, they were automatically fired by the board. Clearly limited by their female bodies, women in this era could not properly put themselves forward for leadership, nor could they continue to work as teachers or as leaders once they were married, a status which openly confirmed their sexuality. Those women who did not marry and who had leadership skills were only offered leadership roles in single-sex girls' schools. Like the stereotyped image of the female prom queen, these women were not overtly sexual, they were 'popular' with male leaders who appointed them to principalships in the all-girls' schools, and they did what was asked of them.

Male leaders in the same 1940s and 1950s generation in my study reported that it was very important for them to be married before they could hope to put themselves forward for a leadership role in schools. I argue here that this married status was necessary to ensure the 'conventional sexuality' required in the masculine CEO image. Since many of the men I interviewed were ex-military men, they also can be seen to have had the 'body type', usually tall and athletic, which matched the image of the powerful CEO. Several of these men admitted that being a male in elementary schools made them a bit of an 'oddity' because all of the other teachers were female. Here, we see that simply having a male body for many of these men was enough for them to be seen by others as an able leader in an elementary school.

Women in the same study who became principals a generation later in the 1960s and 1970s, reported having had a difficult time crossing what they called the 'gender line' from teaching into the principalship. In this period, they were able to put themselves forward for promotion to co-educational schools, at both elementary and secondary levels. However, if they were pregnant, called themselves feminists, or in other ways drew attention to their female body, these women reported having had to struggle for acceptance from their male superiors, their male and female peers, and many parents in their school community. The women in this era who had childcare responsibilities which required overt body work (such as breastfeeding or caring for a sick child) talked about trying to carry out these responsibilities in a hidden fashion. I argue here that for women school leaders in this period, this 'hiding' of their bodies and their body work was a form of disembodiment. Several of these women, for example, talked about trying to 'never let them see you sweat'. They also reported that others frequently pointed out how 'tired' they looked. Clearly, prom queens were not supposed to sweat or look tired. It seems as if, in this era, these women leaders felt pressure to appear as if they were not exerting themselves in embodied ways.

Men in the same study, who became principals in the 1960s and 1970s, reported very little change from what men claimed in the earlier generation. The CEO image for male leaders seems to have remained more consistent and less challenged over time than the image of the female prom queen. Men were still moving rapidly into principalships in elementary schools, even though there were more women in the teaching profession. These men also reported that, in this era, persistent work by the women teachers brought to an end the 'automatic' higher salaries offered to men in schools simply because they were men. Some of these men explained that this higher salary had been tied to assumptions about their need to support a family with their wages. It was also tied to the work expected of men teachers supervising in the schoolyard or in such 'dangerous territory' as the boys' basement, and in coaching sports teams. All of these forms of work can be clearly argued to be embodied. Over these two decades, however, women teachers began to share this 'body work' and to demand equal payment and a 'living wage', which matched that of men doing teaching work.

Insights from other studies

Jill Blackmore (1999) talks about 'troubling women' in leadership roles in Australian schools today. She argues that in today's era of 'new managerialism', there has been a regendering of many school leadership roles, such as the vice-principalship and the principalship in primary schools. Women who fit female stereotypes, such as that of the prom queen, are more likely to gain support from their staff and parent communities than women who do not match the standard expectations for women. Those who try to break the usual 'gender scripts' are seen as trouble. Blackmore discusses ways in which schools are more reactive in today's contexts. Without adequate resources, leaders are required to be highly accountable. They must work in teams, manage diversity, and deal with localized decision-making involving parents. Blackmore (2002a: 66) suggests that all of this requires males or females who are school leaders to have a more 'managed self' than one which would be 'self-actualized'. Is this another description of disembodiment? Clearly, in the following quote, Blackmore suggests that it might be:

> Strong women often are seen as difficult, dangerous, and even deviant, because they 'trouble' dominant masculinities and modes of

management by being different. This difference can become exaggerated if they exercise a different voice and insist on declaring their femaleness in what were historically male domains. ... Feminist leaders can be particularly disruptive, because they frequently try to change organizational cultures and structures as well as individual attitudes in order to achieve more inclusive workplaces and gender justice.

(Blackmore 2002a: 53)

In her study of women educators in Alberta in the 1990s, Beth Young (2002) argues that some women are choosing to manage the new educational environment by either declining to take on leadership roles and/or by accommodating their family responsibilities by taking on 'part-time' work in schools. In each of these routes, women avoid an actual collision with the organization by choosing to limit their participation. Rather than denying their embodiment as females, some women divide their lives into zones of activity and place limits on what they are willing to take on in each zone. Lest we think that this is an ideal solution, Young warns:

Whatever the motive or the positive or negative outcomes of the decisions by individual teachers, our research suggests an array of micro-politics and moral issues ... many of which are related to gender. ... Both teachers and administrators have told us about highly politicized staffing negotiations between principals and teachers in the name of program needs. Teachers and administrators claim that these negotiations contribute to job intensification and complexification in relation to teachers' work and the work of the principal.

(Young 2002: 86)

Following Young's research, it seems that rather than some women worrying about being the prom queen, some women teachers choose not to go to the prom. For others, a collision with the organization when they are leaders means that their attendance at the prom no longer seems like a good idea. In a case study of women who have left leadership roles in colleges and universities, either voluntarily or involuntarily, Schmuck *et al.* (2002) write about how women can be at odds with their organization in ways that lead to 'exit' decisions. The cases described highlight the dilemmas encountered by some female leaders as they strive to work in embodied ways to enact what they think a female leader should do. In each of the cases described, superiors, peers, or both, did not share the woman's views. The four women studied called themselves feminists and offered some advice to others who might someday find themselves in collision with their institution. They advised creating alliances, both inside and outside the organization; celebrating small changes; picking battles carefully; connecting with family and friends for fun, joy and support; and knowing when to leave while considering all the personal positives that can be entailed with a decision to leave.

In her case studies of three women principals in New Zealand, Strachan (2002) argued that feminist leaders and those who work with them could hold sometimes very unrealistic expectations of 'sainthood'. In describing the successful enactment of the transformative agendas of the women she studied, Strachan acknowledged that many people did not actually like these women, even though they gave them a degree of respect and admitted that what they had accomplished was beneficial for the school. Strachan put it this way:

> To drive for change, they were passionate and feisty. Even though those with whom they worked may have supported their agenda, those very same qualities also at times made them difficult to work with. ... In being feisty, formidable and determined, the women in the study risked the censure of others. They were certainly not saints. However, many of those with whom they worked, while acknowledging this unsaintliness, at the same time realized the necessity of their single-mindedness to achieve their transformative agendas.
>
> (Strachan 2002: 123)

Would the women in Strachan's study be voted prom queen? Likely not. Did they get things done? Yes, they did.

Valerie Hall (1996) felt that school administration for the women school heads she studied in the UK was like 'dancing on the ceiling', clearly an embodied act. Hall, like others who have studied women school leaders (for example, Kinnear 1995; Blount 1998), has described how many of these women declared that they were not feminists. Indeed, many women leaders have claimed adamantly that they are not any different from male leaders and they do not want to be. For some women, then, one way to get on with leadership is to do so as if they had a male body, or no body at all. Indeed, during the past decades in North America, seminars designed to help women 'dress for success' have been popular. In these seminars, women have been advised that if they desire to attain a leadership role in education, they need to downplay their femininity in a variety of ways. They are told not to wear perfume, jewellery or pale colours, such as pink. Instead, they are encouraged to wear tailored suits, dark colours and 'sensible' shoes. What is the message here about embodiment?

There is a troubling message for me in terms of the literature on school leadership if we continue to ignore or mute themes of gender and the body work of leadership in schools. In a study by the University Council for

Educational Administration of the most published authors in the field of educational leadership between 1986 and 1996 (White and Zirkel 2001), only 31 authors had published ten or more articles in major US refereed journals. Only five of these scholars were women. Have more women been able to contribute to the leadership literature since 1996? Do more recent authors, male or female, consider the body work of leadership? In the studies mentioned in this chapter, researchers clearly indicate that there is no single female or male response to leadership or to particular historical contexts within which leadership is taken up by either men or women. What is clear, however, is that valuable additions can and must be made to our literature base on school leadership by considering sexuality, body images and the body work entailed in being a school leader in a given setting.

10 Transgressing Heteronormativity in Educational Administration[1]

James W. Koschoreck

Introduction

The overwhelming heteronormativity presumed in the field of educational administration poses challenges both for scholars and practitioners who strive to transgress the societal expectations that constrain the expression of sexually diverse populations. In this chapter, I use information gathered through personal interviews to examine multiple ways in which the normalization of sexuality might be interrogated. I argue that lesbian, gay, bisexual and transgendered faculty and administrators can more effectively contravene the normalizing practices of heterosexism by refusing to remain silent about issues of sexuality. Additionally, I include some implications for practising researchers and administrators for those who are seeking to challenge the heterosexist norms.

In these first few years of the new millennium the voices of queer educational administrators and researchers continue to be muffled by the overwhelming bellowing of the heteronormative order.[2] While it is undoubtedly true that an increasing number of LGBTQ[3] issues are being discussed both at national and regional educational conferences and in scholarly books and journals, the marginalization of these topics means that students, teachers and administrators in the public schools continue to experience intolerable levels of discrimination and harassment as a result of their actual or perceived sexual differences. According to a recent study published by the Human Rights Watch (2001), verbal and sexual harassment of LGBTQ students occurs across the USA with alarming frequency. Furthermore, the failure of teachers and administrators to adequately address these issues of abuse and to provide supportive educational information leads to a hostile school climate that undermines the emotional stability of LGBTQ students and contributes to depression, alcohol and drug abuse, school drop-outs, risky sexual behaviours and elevated levels of suicide attempts (Human Rights Watch 2001: 68–76).

What follows is in essence a montage of my own experiences as an out, gay male academic, along with findings from interviews I conducted with a gay male educational administrator. Each of us has come to an understanding that sexuality matters, whether it is given explicit voice or silenced.

Authority and legitimation

Issues of legitimation surrounding the production of academic texts have long occupied scholars in many disciplines. Countless theoretical elaborations concerning alternative modes of validity provide a normative framework within traditional modes of enquiry. The unrelenting focus on validity stems primarily from the epistemological assumption that the relationship between research data and analysis and an external reality can and should result in the production of an authoritative text that truthfully mirrors some aspect of the presupposed external real. That the issue around such fundamental assumptions remains unresolved even in the various forms of postpositivist research has been the subject of much recent academic debate (Denzin 1997; Scheurich 1997).

While it is beyond the scope of this discussion to reproduce at length the details of the argument that suggests that the 'masks of validity' (Scheurich 1997: 80) continue to function as a barrier in the production of knowledge, suffice it to say that continued efforts by postmodernists and critical poststructuralists (for example, Lather 1993) to reappropriate the concept of validity have not gone unchallenged. Scheurich's (1997: 87) contention that 'both conventional and post positivist validity practices (unconsciously) inscribe a two-sided "truth" or "trustworthiness" map' that privileges one side of the map over the other causes him to suggest that 'what is called for here, then, in the absence (fear) of silence, is a Bakhtinian dialogic carnival, a loud clamour of a polyphonic, open, tumultuous, subversive conversation on validity as the wild, uncontrollable play of difference' (Scheurich 1997: 90).

In the spirit of contributing yet one more tune to the already cacophonous multi-logue on legitimation, I should like to advance my own 'ephemeral practices of validity' (Lather 1993: 686). I recently came across a collection of essays entitled *Perversions: Deviant Readings* (Merck 1993). In the introduction to this collection, Merck tells us a number of ways that the word 'perversion' has come to be understood. Interpreted alternately as a 'deviant sexuality', an 'opposition to what is expected or accepted' or a 'defection from doctrine' (Merck 1993: 1–3), the term 'perversion' ultimately derives from the original Latin *perversus* meaning 'turned the wrong way'. Citing Christian Metz, a film theorist, as having said that 'lost objects are the only ones one is afraid to lose, and the semiologist is he [sic] who rediscovers them from the other side', Merck justifies the 'deviant readings' as precisely coming from the other side (Merck 1993: 10). Whether from the vantage point of a deviant sexuality, in opposition to the accepted, or as a defection from doctrine, Merck's readings are legitimated as an authoritative production of one who seeks to find 'lost objects' from 'the other side'.

As a mode of resisting normalization, then, I believe that the idea of perverse validity corresponds to the larger project of seeking in difference a way to disrupt the normative narrative, whether it be locally determined or civilizationally embedded in our assumptions about the world we live in. The implications for research of applying the notion of a perverse validity are challenging, to be sure. The very acts of interrogating and disrupting normalizations of any sort can often lead to a reinscription of the selfsame processes of inclusion/exclusion that the researcher set out to trouble in the first place (Scheurich 1997). The unsuccessful operationalization of the project, however, need not invalidate the intent.

Popkewitz (2000) cautions us that educational reform can occur only when researchers and educators illuminate the issues of power that are entrenched in school practices. In discussing, for example, the contemporary policy notions of urban and rural schooling, he troubles these commonsensical categories by noting that they correspond more to a social space that bounds the child rather than an actual geographical differentiation, claiming that the terms serve more 'in the sense of ordering, dividing, and normalizing the inner capabilities and characteristics of the child' (Popkewitz 2000: 22). Applying the notion of perverse validity might help to create a critical knowledge of the ways in which notions of sexuality, leadership, teaching, curriculum and identity intersect with systems of inclusion/exclusion.

Britzman (2000) challenges us to reconsider the importance of sexuality in the delivery of education. Claiming that 'education's present structure and modes of thought resist ethical actions and can be viewed as criminally negligent in its censorship of safer sex education, in its eschewal of difficult ideas, and in its incapacity to notice its own harm' (Britzman 2000: 35). Her desire is to open a space for the conversation that would allow for the complexities of sexuality to inform our vision of education. Rofes (2000) discusses the importance of bringing the fullness of his person to the classroom as a pedagogical act of resisting the heteronormative order. While some might view this approach as an inappropriate use of his academic position, he defends his decisions and actions by stating that if critical pedagogy is about collectively gaining a deep understanding of how social and political forces interact with our everyday lives and help to produce our identities, social practices and communities, then silencing, avoiding or depersonalizing/disembodying sex may function powerfully to affirm and reify a dangerous and oppressive status quo (Rofes 2000: 147). His refusal to remain silent about issues of sexuality represents a profound commitment to transgress the normalizing practices of heteronormativity.

Confessions of a gay school administrator

I first met Jack[4] two years ago when I arrived at the University of Cincinnati. I was apprehensive about moving to a predominantly conservative midwestern city as I knew that in the early 1990s the voters of Cincinnati had passed a resolution (Issue 3) that would prohibit the enactment of any law designed specifically to protect the rights of lesbians and gay men. As I felt myself moving into dangerous, conservative territory, Jack appeared in my life as the proverbial breath of fresh air. The information represented below resulted primarily from a formal two-hour interview. I have also filled in spaces with knowledge gleaned over two years of knowing Jack. I have chosen to represent Jack's voice in the multiple snippets that follow in order to hear as much as possible of what he has to say. I have also tried to maintain Jack's original voice.

Jack discusses why he became an administrator

> I guess I've always sought out leadership roles as a child, as a teenager, and as a college student. In college I was involved in a variety of organizations and activities and always sought out the leadership role. It goes back to helping people, I think, because I felt like my ideas were good and valid. I felt I could help make the organization better through building with others.
>
> As a teacher, I sought out leadership roles. The principal would say, 'I'd really like you to chair this committee', or 'I'd like you to serve on this curricular committee', or 'Could you do this?' I guess the decision to go into administration was another example of leadership opportunity to help build a better school for the kids and the organization.

Jack begins to transgress the heteronormative order

> I remember once as an administrator, the first year I started, there was a little boy in first grade with a horrible behavioural problem – acting out physically, verbally, emotionally. In addition to those issues he got the teachers' attention because he was identifying as a girl. He wanted to go to the girls' restroom; he wanted to wear girls' clothes at Halloween. He would tell stories of how he dressed up as a witch or as Barbie one other year. He wanted to be like Brittany Spears. So the gender identity piece was a piece of him. That wasn't the whole piece.

He was being raised by his grandmother. She would come in for conferences. He really was a behavioural problem. Being a gay male, I was very interested and very sensitive to all this. He was special to me because here was the first time that I could have impact on a little boy's life to make sure that he is given the support that he needs. I didn't want anything to happen to him because he was very sensitive, and I didn't want teasing to happen.

He was safe in first grade. The teacher was really good, the kids were good to him. So when he transitioned into second grade I wanted to make sure that he had a safe teacher, someone who would accept him. So I wanted to make sure he had a teacher that would welcome him and love him and care for him. I wanted to make sure that he had kids in his class from his first-grade class that knew him and loved him and took care of him. So that happened. We put him in a very supportive environment with kids that he knew and liked him because that's who he was. That happened again in third grade and fourth grade. There was always a group of kids that would watch out for him, would stick up for him on the playground.

In the back of my mind I thought, 'Do they think I'm paying too much attention to this case?' I had a whole list of cases, specific cases who had issues and problems. Was I spending too much time on this one? But I thought it didn't matter. It doesn't matter if I'm gay or straight.

As far as they care, I'm just a sensitive person who's watching out for him and this whole other list of kids who had a variety of needs.

Commentary

Learning to transgress the heteronormative order is at best a process that occurs by fits and starts. Those of us who are inclined to challenge societal expectations for our sexualities face considerable obstacles every step of the way. As we move from the self-interested focus to create supportive, nurturing spaces for ourselves towards the ethical responsibility of finding ways to alter the negativities faced by other LGBTQ people, the barriers seem to proliferate. The overshadowing conservatism of educational administration assures that the path towards social justice will be 'fraught with creepy detours' (Britzman 1997: 34).

So if we know in advance that we are likely to encounter resistance, refusal and creepy detours along the way, how can we prepare ourselves for the journey? Fortunately, several 'maps' have already been prepared to assist us in subverting the normalizing practices of heteronormativity.

Sears (1997) has compiled a list of strategies designed to resist hetero-sexism and homophobia. Claiming that the most significant tactic an LGBTQ person can use is to be open about his/her sexuality with family, friends and colleagues, and to speak frankly and repeatedly about the harmful consequences of heterosexism, Sears appears to presume that the battle against heterosexism and homophobia can predominantly be won by breaking down the walls of ignorance that allow non-gay people to persist in their prejudicial biases against the LGBTQ collective. Basing his argument on research from the social sciences that finds that individual attitudes are greatly affected by personal relationships, Sears' key proposition relies on a sort of ripple effect as changed attitudes reach progressively wider circles of individuals.

Luhmann (1998: 143), on the other hand, argues that 'this approach is grounded in a set of assumptions common to lesbian and gay politics that follow from the notion that homophobia is little more than a problem of representation, an effect of lacking or distorted images of lesbians and gays'. She asserts, moreover, that this type of approach 'looks to expand the definition of *normal* to include lesbians and gays, rather than attacking and undermining the very processes by which (some) subjects become normalized and others marginalized' (Luhmann 1998: 143, emphasis in original). Although she offers valuable insights into how pedagogy might be queered by shifting from a content-driven focus to a 'conversation about what I can bear to know and what I refuse when I refuse certain identifications' (Luhmann 1998: 153), she clearly admits that the queer pedagogy she proposes is likely incapable of eradicating anti-heterosexist thought. Her insistence on querying the issues, in spite of this, responds to an ethical commitment to interrogate the systemic effects of heteronormativity.

Finally, De Castell and Bryson (1998) boldly defy the tendency in our research to ignore the queer other with a list of recommendations for educational researchers that would help us to subvert heterosexist assumptions in the elaboration of our enquiry projects.[5] The implication is that educational administrators and researchers have at their disposal a number of 'guide-books' to assist them in their journey on the circuitous – and sometimes dangerous – path of transgressing heteronormativity. As it stands, none of the maps are complete, and none will relieve them of the ethical obligation of discovering their own way. We must commit, then, at this moment to continue to engage in the dialogue about how we are all negatively affected by heterosexism, to trouble the 'taken-for-grantedness' of the hetero/homosexual categorization of individuals, and to be willing to experience the messiness of the journey.

Notes

1. A previous version of this chapter was published in *Leading and Managing* (2002) 8(2): 135–143, and is published here with permission.

2. Several years ago De Castell and Bryson (1998: 245), 'troubled by the absence or invisibility of lesbian students, teachers, administrators and, indeed, researchers in educational research accounts, sought to examine the underlying causes for this absence/invisibility. It is certainly worth asking, given the dialogical character of so much current educational research, whether researchers who are not themselves gay or lesbian are just not privy to this kind of information about their subjects: they do not have the 'radar' so they do not see it and the students and teachers, wisely I suppose, do not volunteer the information, and so the troublesome question is never 'in evidence'. It is worth asking this because maybe this absence is not insignificant. Maybe it matters *enormously* to what is discovered who is doing the research, from what identity position – and this is certainly not something we hear much about at educational research conferences. Perhaps it is something that is apparent only to people who cannot actually go into a school and do research in person, because, being openly and visibly lesbian, access to the school would be refused – and we say this from experience (De Castell and Bryson 1998). But whether apparent to most people or not, it surely matters that only heterosexual or faux-heterosexual people are usually welcome to do school-based educational research. And it surely matters if these same heterosexual people are either unable or unwilling to see or to report the presence of gay and lesbian subjects in their research population. 'The school's deep investment in the business of providing youth a strongly reinforced socialization into *the heteronormative order*, to the extent that this concern shapes perceptions and invisibilities, is an investment that constrains what can be said and what must be silenced' (De Castell and Bryson 1998: 247, my emphasis).

3. Lesbian, gay, bisexual, transgendered and questioning.

4. As is customary, I have changed the names of persons and places throughout this section in order to preserve the confidentiality of my participant.

5. In order to accomplish the interpretation of data collected from my participant, I utilized one of the most well-known methods for coding and analysing qualitative data, an approach that has come from a paradigm often referred to as 'grounded theory' (Strauss and Corbin 1998). Often referred to in the literature as 'the constant comparative method of analysis' (Glaser and Strauss 1967, quoted in Strauss and Corbin 1998: 62), grounded theory is characterized by the simultaneous processes of asking questions and making comparisons. Primarily an inductive approach, grounded theory purports to generate theory through a systematic reflection on the raw data.

11 Leadership and Aboriginal Education in Contemporary Education: Narratives of Cognitive Imperialism Reconciling with Decolonization

Marie Battiste

Like a river that winds its path around an environment, bubbling and diving in different places, aboriginal education has had a bewildering path. Aboriginal peoples in North America have always had their own ways of teaching, learning and knowing. In the treaty process, the British sovereign promised them they could maintain their own knowledge, sciences and humanities. Most of the First Nations treaties required the Crown to fund their parents' choice for education so that children could learn new skills and abilities to complement their Aboriginal knowledge system. However, federal governments in North America provided formal Eurocentric-based education, beginning with day schools, horrendous residential schooling, and massive, destructive adoptions to non-First Nations families. All of these forms of education sought to destroy Aboriginal knowledge and languages and replace them with an Anglo-centric ideology and identity.

When all these failed, the federal government in Canada contracted education services for First Nations children with provincial educational systems. This new attempt also failed, and the few first-generation First Nations educators demanded Indian control of Indian education. First Nations acquired some control over their band school, but were forced to comply with the provincial curriculum and English instruction. Discourses for analysing these fatal policies have generated a profusion of studies. This chapter addresses four narratives of cognitive imperialism generated by recent studies. Combining notions of race and gender, these narratives have shaped contemporary educational responses to Aboriginal students and contributed to today's Aboriginal identity crisis.

I seek to address how to decolonize these four narratives to achieve effective educational strategies. As a Mi'kmaw educator in Canada, I offer some thoughts about these narratives and a required healing process. Over the past

25 years, I have experienced many of the issues in Aboriginal education as a female student, teacher, principal, curriculum developer, administrator and professor. My course of rediscovering and shaping Aboriginal education has been a long rewarding path, and I have been part of many transformative ideas and developments. I have attempted to design approaches to enable education to be a spirit nourishing and transforming learning experience for Aboriginal students. I have always been aware of the systemic bias of the modern education system with its cognitive imperialism and its Eurocentric, patriarchical, exclusionary and hegemonic foundation. At different times, I felt close to understanding what needed to be done in and with schools. I have experimented with many features of language and cultural education, as well as with teaching anti-racism. Of late, I have been raising the issue of the lost capacity of indigenous knowledge and humanities in contemporary schooling and urging educators to make needed educational reform. In particular, I think it is vitally important that teachers address the politics of knowledge.

Narratives of cognitive imperialism

Narrative 1: The urgent crisis

The federal and provincial governments in Canada have created educational systems that have failed and are failing Aboriginal students. In 2000, only 37 per cent of First Nations students completed high school, compared with 65 per cent of the general population (Auditor General of Canada 2000). According to the Royal Commission on Aboriginal Peoples, only 9 per cent of First Nations students (primarily female) enter university and only 3 per cent of them complete their university degree programme (RCAP 1996 Vol 3: 440). Despite the many changes that have been made to Canada's educational system over the years, it will take First Nations students more than twenty years of accelerated and restorative education to catch up to the national average for high-school graduation. These statistics represent a significant educational failure, in particular for male students, and the need to improve them presents a significant challenge. It is a crucial test of the resolve of many educators, policy-makers and First Nations people.

These education failures are in crisis because of the current growth rate for aboriginal populations, which is nearly three times faster than the non-aboriginal population in Canada. Educational planners and administrators remind us of the related cost of a continued high failure rate. Educational planners are beginning to explore educating Aboriginal students and developing capacity; however, their focus remains on integration and assimilation based on Canadian values. Most of their efforts are to supply Aboriginal teachers to schools. This narrative calls for individual capacity development, but ignores the hostile Eurocentric, racialized environment teachers and students have to navigate and survive. It also often ignores gender issues in educational settings.

Narrative 2: The racialized environment

Almost all education systems view Aboriginality as a race rather than as an intellectual heritage that is taught and learned. As a result of the past policies of residential schools, adoptions, urbanization and language loss, Aboriginal heritages and languages have been oppressed and are becoming extinct. The teachings and values of Aboriginal knowledge (including languages) are not reflected in most education systems. Few bridges have been constructed between Aboriginal knowledge and Canadian knowledge. Little discussion of Aboriginal knowledge is included in the existing curriculum. The existing educational systems remain systemically inequitable to Aboriginal students.

Aboriginal teachers, both males and females, report various experiences in schools, particularly being aware of the multiple forms of racism and racial superiority expressed in the schools. However, racism is often dismissed even when clear examples are offered. Educators often refuse to recognize and identify racism as a social construct.

Failing to confront their racialized environment, school systems frequently hire Aboriginal teachers with racialized identities to communicate with students. Administrators often assume that the presence of these teachers will offer solutions. Administrators frequently assume that Aboriginal teachers have innate knowledge, tools, protocols and capabilities that other educators lack. Sometimes they do, but most of the times they do not. Aboriginal teachers are a diverse lot and they represent many experiential locations. Regardless of gender or origin, every educator, including Aboriginal educators, is marinated in the same Eurocentric, gendered and racialized educational institutions. Some First Nations teachers may bring Aboriginal knowledge to the institutions, but their training in Aboriginal pedagogy is generally non-existent.

Narrative 3: Additive projects

Many schools seek Aboriginal leaders, outside experts or counsellors to be on planning committees and to participate in other policy-directing activities. This is good practice in that this can counter speaking 'for' Aboriginal people, and replace it with speaking 'with' Aboriginal people about what is best for their children. Such reforms are additive, however, not structural, meaning that people can be added to committees, organizations, advisory groups and school boards without ever making any substantive changes to the system. It adds to the decision-making and disciplinary regime but does not disrupt it.

Cultural relevance, inclusion and neo-assimilation are regarded as the cornerstones of an informed contemporary education. Many additive projects have become synonymous with multiculturalism. As an educational practice, however, these approaches do little to resolve the gendered and racialized cognitive imperialism of the curriculum. Additive projects are a management technique for cultural diversity. This technique in Canada has attempted to treat minority issues from women's issues of the 1970s to the gay rights issues of the 1990s. Now this technique is being used for Aboriginal educational issues.

Many educators look to Aboriginal teachers to help them make the curriculum less exclusive. The strategy of hiring such teachers seeks to correct a perceived 'lack in' sensitivity, experience or knowledge among the staff and the 'lack of' materials or pedagogy. Typical solutions offered by such teachers are as fragmented as the cultural units that are added to the prescribed curriculum. While the hiring of Aboriginal teachers bolster positive self-representations of fairness, tolerance, autonomy and respect, the teachers themselves often do little more than add diverse voices to contemporary education intolerance. These additive units leave intact the structural bias of the Eurocentric curriculum.

Often, teachers are willing to identify Aboriginal culture as objects of art but refuse to deal with Aboriginal knowledge. They find Aboriginal ecological or spiritual traditions problematical, while celebrating Christian traditions of Christmas, Easter and other religious traditions. They may recognize colonialism as a history of Indian/white relations but refuse to teach Aboriginal peoples' constitutional rights. They may recognize the lack of Aboriginal content in the curriculum but reject the unbalanced politics of knowing and knowledge production in society.

Cross-cultural add-on units or even a course in native studies can be additive projects. Such courses are usually offered in schools with a large population of Aboriginal students. Perceived as a problem solely for Aboriginal students, courses in native studies are designed to help Aboriginal people cope with masked racism or colonialism. The native studies narratives in such courses are frequently about Aboriginal/newcomer relations, which inscribe a 'we and them' ideology, affirm colonial binaries and Aboriginal inferiority or victimhood. Such narratives were created by Eurocentric nationalism and have primarily been written by 'white' historians, anthropologists and sociologists, to legitimate their disciplinary knowledge. Native studies courses are rarely about Aboriginal knowledge, despite such knowledge being considered vital for Aboriginal students to obtain academic success.

These additive projects avoid the overriding issues and questions of legitimation: whose knowledge is included, whose languages are considered as legitimate vehicles for carrying the knowledge? Can Aboriginal teachers who have been marinated in Eurocentric education be equipped to make decisions for the collective, community or nation? How will their choices be made, and what governs those choices?

Eurocentric or the 'western' knowledge operates in Canadian education as 'depoliticized' knowledge, whereas indigenous knowledge is treated as if it is a 'product of local backward tribes' or of cultural learning styles. Hence, educators tend to treat indigenous knowledge based on difference and/or the politics of Indian/white relations (that is, native studies).

Narrative 4: Aboriginal identity crisis

As a result of cognitive imperialism, the persistent assimilation strategies of the existing education system, and the reality of systemic sexism, racism and discrimination, male and female Aboriginal students are thrust into a perpetual state of identity chaos, struggling with perceptions of inferiority, incapacity and dependency that affects their ability to succeed. This educational environment has powerful results in creating despair and damaging effects on Aboriginal individuals and communities. With large populations of Aboriginal students under stress, they are seen as needing psychological help. This in effect individualizes their problems, rather than examining the systemic problems that cognitive imperialism creates.

Identity-building is tantamount to human rights and self-actualization. It is a quest for individual identity development. However, given the trauma and crisis that Aboriginal students have experienced and continue to experience, identity and self-esteem are not easy targets.

Decolonizing Canadian education

Colonialism as a theory of relationships is embedded in power, voice and legitimacy. It has racialized Aboriginal peoples' identity, marginalized and delegitimated their knowledge and languages. The imperialistic system of knowledge that is considered as the mainstream, functions like a 'keeper' current in a rapidly flowing river. The keeper current drags a person to the bottom and then to the top, but if the person fights against the current they usually drown.

Decolonization is a process of unpacking the keeper current in education with its powerful Eurocentric assumptions and its narratives of race, gender and difference in curriculum and pedagogy. It is the channel for generating a post-colonial education system.

Post-colonial theories of indigenous education offer the 'possibility of new readings' on the debates/discussions. These theories offer the reading of the inclusion/exclusion debate as a tension between scorn and desire leading to colonial ambivalence in action. The most effective theories or strategies centre indigenous knowledge as a shared education norm. They stress, that theories of culturalism reinscribe cultural imperialism towards Aboriginal students. Affirmative action or equity of labour is seen to mask the systemic discrimination and practices of cultural imperialism, while elitist research and studies of indigenous education continue the discourse of knowing the indigenous 'other' – by legitimating scientific rationalism.

Decolonizing indigenous education is framed within concepts of dialogue, respect for educational pluralities, multiplicities and diversities. It is about self-determination, deconstructing decisions about curricular knowledge, and re-energizing education and knowledge. It is not a singular or total theory but multiple theories, strategies and struggles. Its outcomes must account for the imposed tragedies and indignities colonial education has placed on Aboriginal people, and the need for systemic healing in educational systems. First Nations educators have embarked on a transformative journey, but one that is not assimilative; rather, it is a therapeutic education process of healing in the relationships among people. We need to restore a balance in relationships and authority over our lives and our future as we live in harmony with each other. We are interdependent in our ecology and environment, and we will have to develop institutions, policies and practices that signal the respect for our diversity and our interdependence. This requires a complex and systemic educational reform which cannot be accomplished in a workshop, course or seminar or an additive component for two weeks. Elizabeth Minnich (1990: 36) offers this insight: 'Old knots and tangles that are in all our minds and practices must be located and untied if there are to be threads available with which to weave the new into anything like a whole cloth, a coherent but by no means homogenous pattern.'

Educators in Canada have a privileged status. The majority are non-Aboriginal teachers and this group provides the norms for the profession and for schools. We have been immersed in Eurocentric thought and education most of our lives and view it as normal. We have not been taught alternatives. Canadian educational institutions have used cultural relevance as an educational tool, but they have not interrogated the existing cultural interpretative monopoly.

Who is to decide or speak for Aboriginal knowledge? Who should speak about questions of curricular content and pedagogy in educational pluralism? When we are thinking about 'mainstream' education, who belongs to the 'main' and who is 'streamed'? What is stereotyped, represented or imagined in the terms 'Aboriginal', 'First Nations' or 'indigenous'? How do we know the 'other', and what methodology do we employ to talk about the 'other'? What role does the 'other' have in self-representing, defining their agenda, and speaking and being heard?

In addressing these questions, educators can bring forth post-colonial understandings and transformative strategies. In so doing, we can centre educational commitment to our responsibilities for the enhancement of humanity and its infinite capacities. Each strategy taken to rebuild human capacity is a decolonizing activity that brings collective hope and provides insights, voices and partnerships that can dispel resignation and despair.

12 Bridge People: Leaders for Social Justice

Betty Merchant

Introduction

This chapter discusses our research efforts to better understand the formation and practice of social justice. It was conducted from the perspectives of eight individuals nominated for participation because of their reputation as stewards of social justice in the communities in which they live.[1] As members of a department of educational administration and policy studies, we are concerned about the preparation of educational leaders in general, and in the development of administrators who are knowledgeable about, and committed to, critiquing educational policies and practices for the purposes of understanding how these policies and practices support or inhibit the provision of just and equitable educational experiences for all students. Thus, we asked our participants how we might improve the preparation of school leaders.

The eight individuals we interviewed were recognized as leaders for social justice and equity in San Antonio, Texas, and the surrounding area. Although they were not all educators, each of them played a significant role in improving access and opportunity for children historically marginalized by mainstream public schooling. Five of these individuals had achieved national distinction for their role in shaping the agenda for educational reform. Our research participants consisted of four public school administrators (three principals and a retired superintendent), three university-level administrators (a university president, a college of education dean and a director of a university policy research centre), and one lawyer in a firm defined by its strong social justice advocacy. Two of the participants were female – the college dean and one of the principals. Two of the individuals we interviewed were white; the other six were Hispanic. The interviews were between 45 and 90 minutes in length and each were audio- and videotaped. All of these tapes were transcribed and reviewed for emergent themes.

The research participants shared a number of characteristics, including:

- a strong orientation to social justice and equity issues instilled early in their lives by parents/significant adults;
- a strong sense of purpose and belief in their ability to succeed;

- powerful experiences of marginalization that shaped their determination to succeed and to improve things for others in similar situations;[2]
- a lifelong commitment to social justice and equity issues that permeates their personal and professional lives;
- a deep appreciation for the value of creating community and high expectations among those with whom they work;
- a humility about their visibility in the community and an appreciation for the role of luck in shaping their professional and personal lives;
- an awareness of the influence of the social/political movements of the 1950s and 1960s and the ways in which their involvement in these movements strengthened their commitment to social justice and equity issues.

The participants in this study reflected a profound knowledge of self, a strong connection to their parents, and an intimate understanding of the political, social, economic and educational inequities in their communities and in the USA. They functioned at the intersection of numerous and conflicting forces with an unshakeable confidence in themselves and a deep sense of social purpose. Although they shared a passion for action, they were also patient and recognized the fact that change is often slow and painful. Although these individuals had either experienced or witnessed deeply hurtful acts of discrimination and other forms of social injustice, they persisted in their efforts to eradicate inequities. In taking this position, the individuals whom we interviewed maintained their viability as persons who communicated effectively between and among groups, for the purposes of improving the lives of the people for whom they advocated. To borrow a phrase from our interview with the college dean, all of these individuals were 'bridge people', and in a very real sense, this accounts for their success in creating more just and equitable conditions for children and families who enjoy few, if any, of the benefits of mainstream society.

As we conducted our interviews and transcribed the tapes, we became increasingly convinced that the most powerful revelations about the formation and practice of social justice were to be found in the words of the participants themselves. In recognition of this, we use their quotes extensively and restrict our comments to a brief section at the end of this chapter.

Early orientation to social justice

All of the individuals we interviewed made explicit links between their commitment to social justice and the modelling provided to them by their parents as they were growing up. Here are several quotations that illustrate this theme:

> I consider myself a tremendously privileged human being because I was raised in a family that apparently must have been motivated by a strong concern for social justice. I don't have histories, but I have a fairly strong sense that it is multi-generational. My dad's large extended family were community leaders in the sense that they were always seen as the people who would come up with the intelligent response and they were also pretty good orators across the board.
>
> (College dean)

> There's a very strong relationship between my childhood and my interest in social justice, and that is, when I was growing up, my father was involved with the civil rights movement in the early 1950s. And Dr Hector Garcia from Corpus Christi established a veterans' organization of Mexican Americans and it was called the American GI Forum, and my dad was one of the first to enlist in this new movement in 1948. . . . I think my dad understood and before you knew it, we understood it and social justice became something for us. And truly, I credit my parents for instilling that in us, and being sure that we understood what our position in society was and to always vow to struggle.
>
> (University president)

> I was influenced, first of all, by my own family – by my father who died when I was 5, but whose legacy I heard, and my mother.
>
> (Female principal)

> The passion [for social justice] is very personal – nothing to do with professional preparation. A lot was expectation from my parents – not that they had much education.
>
> (Male principal no.1)

> It's interesting that people make distinctions and put labels on people. It plagued me quite a bit while growing up . . . inadequate, not feeling 'as good as'. My parents didn't play into this. My father was extremely strong in this – not educated but well read – could read Thoreau. I can remember him reading some of what Thoreau wrote about social justice. I guess it got embedded in me in some place. All those feelings, all those questions, all that introspection . . . make me extremely sensitive to all people.
>
> (Retired superintendent)

[My] family was moderate politically, but both my parents were interested in helping the little guy.

(Lawyer)

We were dirt poor and we were the only family that we knew that were on public assistance. . . . [M]y mom was sort of a union organizer . . . So I learned a lot of community organizing probably from watching my mother. It's one thing to demolish an idea; it's another thing to actually help somebody succeed.

(Policy centre director)

The individuals we interviewed were in their forties and fifties. Their notions of social justice were affected by the events of their time, as illustrated by the following quotes:

I grew up in the 1960s and went to high school and college [during] the growth of the civil rights movement, the [Vietnam] war. In terms of going to college in the 1960s, I was impressed by many of the faculty who were anti-war and I saw the effect of student protests and faculty on the war.

(Lawyer)

And at particular points, important points, in the struggle for des arroyo of the Mexican American community in Texas and the Latino community nationally, I think that I found my voice.

(College dean)

The two quotes that follow illustrate how the activities of the interviewee's parents were consistent with the notion of 'bridge people' who build connections between and among communities:

My mother took me to high school with her to do literacy training in Tijuana twice a week for about two years to a little barn out in the outskirts of Tijuana, where we would work with adults who didn't know how to read. My big sister volunteered for two years as a teacher in a migrant camp in Texas.

(Female principal)

Several of the members of my family, my father in particular, were what I call 'bridge people'. In a completely racially divided environment of the 1950s, they were the Mexicans who would serve on a jury, or they were the Mexicans who might occasionally be invited to a meeting of the hospital board, or something of this order.

My dad only went to the third grade and my mother went to the eighth grade, but nonetheless he and about five or six other gentlemen in the community served this role and what was interesting was how they served it. Because my dad and two of his cousins always went in and gave them hell! Some of the other individuals really were more accommodating and as a result, they made a lot of money, but we felt really good about what we were doing! So that kind of model was there.

(College dean)

Vivid personal experiences of marginalization

The people with whom we spoke recounted vivid experiences of marginalization and/or boundary crossing efforts that played a key role in motivating them to devote themselves to improving the lives of others. Some of these experiences were relatively positive, as the following quotes reveal:

When I was about 7 or 9 years old, we integrated the swimming pool, and then that same summer, we integrated basically the library services, and my parents prepared me for that; they were without incident. So then, I just never felt that there was any need to hesitate to advance rationality because I think social injustice is irrational.

(College dean)

I never felt discrimination during high school. My first taste of prejudice was when I went to college – a predominately Lutheran college. That was my first taste of that. But I think I had been prepared by my teachers [most of whom were Caucasian] to deal with this, so that never really bothered me.

(Male principal no.2)

Other marginalization experiences recounted showed how hurtful such experiences were:

I remember clearly one day when he [my father] took all the kids and we went out to Lake McQueen and we got there and we were kinda – we were hungry. So we got there and we said, 'Hey, Dad, when can we eat?' And so he said, 'Well, let's see what's going to happen here.' So he went over there and said, 'We'd like a table.' It's a big picnic ground – a public part – and they said, 'Well, we don't serve Mexicans here. You have to go elsewhere.' And we just thought, 'Oh my god. ... OK ... so we just tried to just tell him, "Oh, we're not that

> hungry dad – that's OK – don't worry.' But, you know, he was gonna
> confront – he was confronting that segregation, period. This is 1955
> and you know, those things are instilled in you.
>
> (College president)

> Most of my passion comes from my negative experiences. I was born
> in Texas and segregated because I couldn't speak English. ... I was a
> migrant worker [earning] sixty dollars a month.
>
> (Male principal no.1)

> I discovered I was a Mexican when I was about 8 years old. One
> summer, my family and I took off for the coast to Corpus Christi.
> There were courts, or summer cottages, and I was out there playing
> with a bunch of white kids, and at a certain point we wanted to drink
> some water so we snuck into the kitchen to get some water and we
> heard the parents of some of the kids say, 'We better watch it, we
> heard our son is playing with some Mexicans.' We went outside and
> asked, 'Who's a Mexican?' Our idea was, 'Let's go look for them'.
> Later that day, I realized I was Mexican.
>
> (Retired superintendent)

Often, schools provided the context for this marginalization:

> I ... was viewed as a tough case. I mean, we integrated – and we were
> the first group of kids that integrated a junior high school after the
> Brown Decision and they were certain that we would be trouble-
> makers. ... And it was all white and they had not ever had but a very
> token representation of Hispanic kids there – maybe one or two,
> because it was an all-white neighbourhood, but the districts had
> changed. So there was a real struggle, there was a real struggle for
> several years. And my brother is a very bright kid – I think they
> discovered in us some talent and they realized that we were just
> normal kids.
>
> (College president)

Early recognition and support

Two of the individuals we interviewed spoke about the role of their communities in their development of a sense of purpose, negative as well as
positive:

There was discrimination from the majority as well as within our own race. Anyone who wanted to go above and beyond was criticized for being Anglo. ... Some people in the community recognized something in me and started supporting me ... took me to a college homecoming game – set up expectations for me.

(Male principal no.1)

I was raised in a community where people came together ... I think they were pursuing the dignity of the individual and the dignity of the group. And then they acted upon it. ... I grew up with a strong locus of control – the notion that I could act upon the world. I never felt like a victim.

(College dean)

Athletic ability can also attract recognition and support, as was case for the college president:

And I think from then on, when I went on to high school, it was a kind of different setting – within a year, people started, because of my track specialization and abilities, again, people started to come to me and say, 'Wow! You know, you're really good and you're gonna go to college. You're gonna get a track scholarship, so you're gotta get ready. You gotta get ready for college...'

I remember an occasion when I was a senior and I had about 60 scholarships. I had the best time in America – the best time in a mile in America. I had about 60 scholarships, and one of them was to the University of Texas. And one of the counsellors had said, 'Well, I don't know – this is a big, big jump for this kid, from a vocational school to the University of Texas' ... but my coach thought, 'Well, I think that's where he should go', so apparently they were having some discussion about this. So one day, my coach said, 'Well, you got to come in the morning to take a test.' ... I took a test and walked out of that and by the afternoon, they had the results back. I had taken an IQ test and my coach said, 'Well, you passed the test.' And I said, 'Really?' He said, 'Yes.' I said, 'What kind of test was this?' 'It was an IQ test.' And I said, 'Well, how do you know I passed?' And he said, 'Well, you have a higher IQ than I did when I went to college.' So I said, 'Can I go to the University of Texas?' He says, 'Yeah, you can go.'

Lifelong commitment to social justice and equity

All of the research participants articulated a lifelong commitment to social justice and equity issues that permeated their personal and professional lives. They described formative events that occurred relatively early in their lives, many of which were credited to luck or destiny:

> By eighth grade, I was the only one left [of the Mexicans]. Some were still behind, others left and married. Only two Hispanics graduated from my class. I was one of the only Hispanics to go to college, despite seeing talents in other Hispanics, including cousins. I promised to improve this situation – I'm not going to be the hinge to the gate – I'm going to open it up. . . . I didn't get hired as a laborer. . . . It was destiny – mystical . . . things happened to prevent me from making a wrong choice. In fact, I got a scholarship – people pushed me in that direction . . .
>
> (Male principal no.1)

> I came from the Edgewood District, but while there I had some excellent teachers who repeatedly told us we were as good as anyone. The idea of college was planted in our minds early on. They worked well beyond the school day . . . they and our parents made us believe we could do this. My own wife is a product of that same school and is now a principal in [College]. She would say one of the reasons that we succeeded is that we had teachers, counsellors and principals who believed in us. I don't remember them saying, 'If you go to college' but 'When you go to college', not 'If you take these tests' but 'When you take your tests'. As far as becoming an educator, I can very quickly look back at my former high school band director and he's the reason why.
>
> (Male principal no.2)

> I've always felt that I needed to provide some kind of leadership somewhere. I became a principal when I was 25. I was one of those Teachers of America – nominated two years in a row, and I got selected. After my third year of teaching, I became a principal of a junior high. I just get a real charge out of working with the parents and working with the teachers. I get a lot of satisfaction from a child bringing me a little piece of paper, saying 'You really helped me out'. [Shows a photograph of a boy in a football uniform with the inscription, 'Thank you for being there. I will do my best'.] This is my

evaluation here – that paperwork is going to get faded and yellowed, but this picture here is what it's all about.

(Male principal no.1)

The people we interviewed also identified observations and insights gained while in college that further strengthened their resolve with respect to addressing social justice issues:

Universities were also a negative – the extent to which universities were dedicated to making money. I don't think the professor [in law school] did much regarding social reform. They were not particularly interested in the area. . . . None were dedicated to changing the world through law – they were dedicated to changing their clients.

(Lawyer)

The university constructed this marketing campaign and recruitment campaign that drew out from all these inner-city schools, extra-ordinary people, and then routinely failed them. And it was clear to me that the university didn't have any understanding of who these people were and that I would have an opportunity to directly chal-lenge the system. And I went out and I found, in fact, that much of what the university was doing in 'good faith' was, in fact, harmful to the people they were trying to serve.

(Policy centre director)

Creating community and maintaining high expectations

When the people we interviewed talked about their commitment to creating a sense of community and high expectations among those with whom they worked, it was clear that educators had a powerful effect in this regard, both positively and negatively:

Aside from my family, the other people who have affected me were other educators. In Las Cruces, I had a principal who said he'd take the children home after school. I was floored by this! How relaxed and comfortable he felt in the community and to see how comfort-able the parents felt when they came to the school – a warm, sup-portive school environment. When I first started teaching as a bi-lingual teacher, I asked a teacher how many children would learn to read; the teacher said, with no hesitation, 'All of them.'

(Female principal)

Each of the individuals we interviewed defined social justice in a manner that reflected the knowledge and sensitivities they had acquired within their family, community, school and national contexts. These definitions guided their actions and sustained them in times of difficulty and hardship:

> In terms of where you get that 'fire in the belly', I think that 'fire in the belly' comes from the capacity to recognize the injustice but also having cultivated a kind of basic self-confidence and a basic self-assurance. We don't develop a fire in the belly about social injustice in the absence of the cultivation of a strong philosophical base, a sense of competence and a sense of security in the individual. It involves self-examination; it involves teaching – not just to skills or to knowledge – but to the development of the total human being. And I can't imagine that you can educate leaders without attending to that.
>
> (College dean)

> The incredible pain of knowing that somebody has the privilege to determine what someone else's life should be like. ... That even on the worst days, you can do something really important just by virtue of your privilege and those experiences. And they also get me through real hard periods. Now I understand because of accident and because of my commitments to things even on the worst days, I have the power to do things that matter and almost no one has the right to do that. So you have this special burden and ... the understanding of how many other people weren't helped just fires me up.
>
> (Policy centre director)

Conceptualizing educational administration as a mechanism for social justice

Many of those we interviewed express that school administrative work was a route to improve social justice:

> And I will tell you, I've spent a lot of time over the last ten days asking myself, 'How do we prepare teachers and other educational professionals and leaders who will fight for kids? Who will just damn well fight for kids?' Because the reality is that once you understand that, for the human beings upon whom we are acting as educators in whatever role, we have only two choices. We either fight for their success or we accept their failure. And if we accept their failure, then they accept their failure. They think their failure is inevitable. But as

long as ... we are still fighting for the success of that one individual, then they can't accept failure.

(College dean)

I think that it is a very hard task for school administration programmes to produce advocates for social change because schools are principally socializing instruments. It's how we prepare people to live in our world and there are almost no cultures that have the confidence and security to prepare people for change. ... So one of the jobs of school administrators is not to produce, as a set, people who will push the system too far. But there have to be people who understand what the driving engines are that move us toward justice. That's the most you can expect. In order to make progress, you need stability but you also need catalysts for change. So I think it's complicated.

(Policy centre director)

I do think that a lot of times people in the school are not sufficiently educated as to being leaders, although they are seen as such. [They are] not encouraged to use their expertise to change communities. In rural Texas, teachers are the largest core of college graduates in their communities. If they get involved, this adds a lot. In urban areas, often teachers and administrators are too focused on local school district policies and raising test scores and forget they are a large core of professionals. Administrators, principals, counsellors, most are focused on their particular membership and don't use their membership for social change. I think sometimes they lose their opportunity to use their expertise to change things.

(Lawyer)

I never had any methods courses that focused on social justice – never did. I remember some professors who used to speak in jest about social justice. ... What we are doing to prepare our kids for what is happening now is the result of a lot of effort over time, and if you don't continue to struggle, we're going to fall behind. We have to look at children – not deny their distinctions. How do we get administrators to understand that they are not just dealing with the children in front of them, but to the generations that come after them? One of the biggest disappointments I have is when I come across Hispanic administrators who turn their back on these issues because they were socialized into a white model ... you're always Mexican – sorry! If you're an Anglo living in Texas and have been told, 'You know, those people are not very good', how do you change this? And make sure that you're not treating them as 'less than'?

(Retired superintendent)

One principal made an interesting distinction between 'advocate' and 'practitioner':

I don't know if I'm an advocate, but I'm a practitioner of that philosophy [social justice]. If I were an advocate, I'd be all over the place. ... The passion is very personal – nothing to do with professional preparation. If you're in the [principal's] position because of professional preparation, you won't have that personal passion. Then this becomes a burden. Where does my personal passion come from? Salary? Working with kids! If no passion – burnout. I want to restate: 'It's all personal – nothing to do with professional preparation'.

(Female principal)

Incorporating a social justice focus into the preparation of educational administrators

Our interviews revealed several suggestions for improving the preparation we provide school leaders:

[The preparation of administrators] involves self-examination; it involves teaching, not just to skills or to knowledge but to the development of the total human being. And I can't imagine that you can educate leaders without attending to that. I remember, for example, during the early part of the civil rights movement, there were educational leadership programmes that took people in preparation, or for example, people who were aspiring to become superintendents; they required that people live – actually live – I know there was one programme that required them to live in the ghetto in Chicago for two weeks. They actually lived with families and then they examined and then they reflected on that experience. You're not going to cultivate that kind of examination through just the examination of theoretical principles and you're never going to cultivate it if you have exclusively a skills or knowledge perspective. But it begins with the human being understanding their own place in the world and then developing a sense of confidence about their capacity to influence the world.

(College dean)

I think that very few people get to have the privilege of working on things they really care about; very few people get to choose what they actually do and whether their work is connected to their values. That's so lucky to have it. One group of people who have that privilege are faculty. Faculty have the enormous privilege of working on problems that they alone feel are important. And second, they get to work with the most likely leaders of the next generation; these are extraordinary privileges. Very few faculties take advantage of the privilege or understand these responsibilities. So faculty speak in the language of myth and privilege but don't, in fact, work on things that are easy to work on from where they are situated. And this I find infuriating and this related to administration programmes. People just fall into, 'I'll just publish these three papers and I'll run these courses.' So individual faculty are blessed with the possibilities of being activists and getting paid for it. That's such a sweet thing. Universities have been constructive players in moving society forward; that is not true today and departments need to think about that.

(Policy centre director)

When we look at professional standards for administrators, if social justice isn't part of the curriculum, it's kind of outside of the curriculum. Their handle on being able to address social justice issues – [it's] not there. ... For example, as an administrator, you're going to hire a school nurse. Who would you look for? In this community, we need a nurse who's bilingual, but that's not enough. We also need someone familiar with the community who can refer parents to needed resources.

(Female principal)

It's going to have to be both nature and nurture. [The] student's dedication to some sort of social activism. ... [I]f they've been working on something for several years – at least worked in an area where they're at a very low pay level and working on social issues – I think that's very important ... [they're] more likely to continue this. I know how to work with people who are educators who are truly ignorant of some of the inequities in society. They have not really been focused on inequities. In the old days most of them didn't understand, didn't understand the relationship between the two. Teaching and building this into the curriculum would be helpful. Bringing in critics of the system would be important. ... Bring in people with some kind of interest in changing them and then give them some exposure to changing things. [It is] also important to bring in outside critics like me. There's no one professor who can expose you to the variety, the problems, tracking, misuse of testing, and so on, and very few professors can expose students to all of that as well as the rest of the curriculum.

(Lawyer)

Striving for social justice without bitterness

As illustrated in the following quote, it is important not to let bitterness creep in:

> One thing I learned from my parents, really, was that it sort of was – we had to struggle, we had obstacles, we had challenges, and we would rise up to it. But they never hated anybody. And they taught me, they taught me to love and they taught me not to hate. So there wasn't any bitterness. I mean my dad didn't drive away from that restaurant, saying, you know, 'That rude woman who ...'. He knew that she was given instructions and I think he knew that she was pained by it, that it wasn't something she wanted to do – to tell this family, 'You're not good enough to be in this restaurant.' You know, 'Your brown skin means you can't be here.' It wasn't her – she knew she had her instructions and so you would never question whether it was hate in that. It was kinda like, you know, everyday we're taught that there's a long journey here and we're taking steps every day to correct these injustices and we didn't worry about hating. And so I don't really have any bitterness – I dread the thought of having any vengeance or revenge in my heart. You know, I don't have that, and I hope I never do.

(College president)

Authors' reflections

The individuals we interviewed for this study stressed the role of family members and specific critical incidents in their youth as powerful factors in developing a commitment to social justice. To borrow the expression of the college dean, their passion for equity grew from 'a spark in the belly' to a 'fire in the belly'. This fire was not one of bitterness or hate, but one of compassion and warmth, which allowed them to reach out to others as 'bridge people', for the purposes of improving the lives of all those with whom they worked.

Each of the Hispanic interviewees conveyed in one way or another the sentiments of male principal no.1: 'When I look at these faces, I look at me.'

This raises some difficult questions about whether direct personal experiences are a prerequisite to developing a commitment to social justice and whether we, as university faculty, can develop a sensitivity in students who have not yet had the kinds of marginalizing experiences described by the individuals who participated in our study. This is further complicated by the extent to which faculty members understand the experience of marginalization.

All of the people we interviewed felt that school leadership preparation programmes could increase students' awareness of the struggles faced by individuals whose experiences and opportunities are unfairly mediated by their race, ethnicity, income level, extent of English language fluency, gender and any other characteristics that place them at the margins of mainstream society. They suggested a number of ways in which this could be accomplished, all of which are feasible within a fairly traditional framework of professional preparation programmes. For example, several interviewees suggested that we design field experiences for students that would take them out of their comfort zones and into neighbourhoods in the community that they knew little or nothing about; experiences that would challenge their taken-for-granted notions of how the world works. The lawyer took this a step further by challenging us to incorporate political activism into the preparation of educational leaders. He and others in the study reminded us of the link between social justice and political action that is virtually absent in professional preparation programmes. Others stressed that the students in our programmes need to develop a sense of shared responsibility for the learning of all children as well as a confidence in their ability to address the needs of all children. The people we interviewed reminded us that it is important that we and our students realize that social justice is not solely the concern of marginalized groups, but an issue that concerns all of us, and without our combined efforts, social injustices will continue to occur.

The participants in our study felt that, in order to move from an intellectual appreciation of social justice to the development of a genuine commitment to social justice and equity, university faculty will have to aggressively integrate these concepts and practices into all aspects of their preparation programmes. We must move beyond classroom discussions that treat these issues in a theoretical and abstract manner, to providing experiences that will enable students to recognize and combat the inequities that permeate the very systems and institutions in which they work. An important component in this process is the development of good communication skills and the ability to interact effectively with a broad range of people. This skill, in particular, is critical to the development of 'bridge people' who, as so powerfully evidenced by the individuals in this study, play a crucial role in addressing the inequities of the communities in which they work.

Out of the deepest respect for the individuals who participated in this research, we end this chapter with a quote from the retired superintendent that conveys the power of education as a mechanism of social justice:

> A friend of mine was sharing with us that there was a debate between him and a medical doctor about which doctorate was more important [the MD or the PhD]. And he said that the medical doctor told him it was the medical doctorate. And my friend said, 'You know, you can only fix people to live – we give people reason to live'.

Notes

1. Our research was supported by funds awarded by Catherine Marshall and provided by the Ford Foundation.
2. All but one person described a lack of bitterness over these events/interactions, acknowledging the social/political realties of the contexts within which they experienced these things, and articulating a generous sense of compassion that characterizes their lives and relationships.

13 'The Emperor has No Clothes': Professionalism, Performativity and Educational Leadership in High-risk Postmodern Times

Jill Blackmore

Leadership has been positioned as the solution, the central structural and cultural focus in the recent trend to supposedly more autonomous self-managing institutions. Any quick survey of airport, university or local bookshops indicate numerous populist experts advocating different modes of leadership ranging from the more macho titles of *Ready/Aim/Fire: strategic leadership*, to more seductive titles of *Intelligent Leadership* (Mant 1997) and *Emotional Intelligence* (Goleman 1995). This focus on leadership was replicated in education during the 1990s where leadership supplanted management and administration in the lexicon of educational reform, and when management principles of efficiency and effectiveness became educational rules. Yet leadership is in crisis in the new millennium. There is a lack of public trust in leaders in politics, business and religion, as self-interest – the retention of power no matter how high the levels of greed and sexual impropriety, protecting 'one's own' before the rights of others displayed by those in official leadership – has become the main game. Justice Marcus Enfield (1997) commented that, at the very moment when we need a 'strong, moral and passionate leadership which will educate the public about human rights and our obligations towards fellow human beings', we are witnessing leadership which follows market polls and which cuts back the human rights infrastructure and gives over responsibility to the market. And yet we cling to particular leadership models of the 'emperor' dressed up as strong, macho and protective as a solution to our woes rather than seeing them as the problem. Leadership continues to be treated as an individualized and decontextualized practice. Yet the past decade has seen shifting boundaries and new sets of relationships that create new demands, problems and possibilities for leadership work.

I consider the implications for leadership as part of a wider professional enterprise to promote a deliberative democracy in the context of the rise of the performative state, new knowledge economies and the new work order (Gee and Lankshear 1995). I explore a number of interrelated themes;

the changing nature of educational professionalism in the context of the ongoing search for a professional knowledge base, the rise of the performative state, and finally, the enduring masculinism of executive power. I argue that because leadership theory in education tends to draw more from management than from social theory, it continues to treat organizational life as apolitical, and leadership as a generic set of attributes somehow detached from wider social relations and the material conditions of educational work. The effect is that leadership research fails to address fundamental issues about changing relationships between the individual, education and society, the changing nature of knowledge and the materiality of educational work, and how this impacts on what it is to be 'a professional' educator in 'postmodern times' (Hargreaves 2003; Lingard *et al.* 2003).

While I appeal to notions of professionalism, as a feminist I am equally cautious about the capacity of professionalism as a concept and a practice to necessarily, without significant reconceptualization, to do the required political work to sustain the practices of a deliberative democracy. Traditional forms of professionalism have actively excluded 'the other' to the norm of white middle-class maleness, failing to 'represent' the wider populations that the professions claim to serve. Professionals also should not be cast as being either overly altruistic, as many elite professions claim, or overly self-interested, as promoted in recent New Right discourses about the producer capture by the professions. In that sense, I am advocating a new form of professionalism that differs from both the elitist and 'masculinist' professionalism of the twentieth century and the view of politically neutralized technical professionalism currently being promoted in the context of the permeation of new managerialism through the public sector. New demands will be made upon the profession as the very nature of both career and profession will be transformed in the wider context of a new 'education order' in the context of knowledge-based economies.

The emperor shops for another grey suit: the search for a knowledge base

During much of the twentieth century, since the emergence of educational administration as a field of theory and practice in the 1920s, there has been an ongoing pursuit for a knowledge base, a theoretical 'suit' that can be adjusted to 'best fit' the practice of educational administration and leadership (Scheurich 1995). The field of educational management, as that of management theory itself, has been in a continual state of anxiety, as they do not have the solution because of the lack of exclusive knowledge and capacity for prediction. Management theory does not have the knowledge base of natural science: it has a high level of uncertainty (Kerfoot and Knights 1996).

Indeed, 'its deployment in exercises of power often produces self-fulfilling effects that give it the appearance of predictability. This is because management exercises hierarchical power over subordinates who, in turn, often secure employee compliance given the unequal control of resources in conventional organizations' (Kerfoot and Knights 1996: 89).

The focus on leadership in educational administration historically arose out of the search for this field of practice to make it 'different' from teaching. Teaching, owing to its numerical feminization and focus on caring, was viewed as a 'quasi' profession (Brown and Anfara 2002). Educational administrators sought to establish a distinctive disciplinary field of practice and theory, and legitimacy was to be gained by assuming the mantle of other disciplines and outside the field of education, whether it be from scientific management in engineering in the 1920s, the theory movement derived from the natural sciences in the 1950s, or the political theory given the rise of the new social movements of the 1970s, the shift to focus on performance outcomes (for example from curriculum to assessment) in the 1980s, and then the adoption of private industry principles of efficiency and management techniques through the new public administration in the 1990s (Blackmore 1996).

Representations of leadership similarly shift from the leader being portrayed as a rational decision-maker, to that of transformational leadership drawn from McGregor Burn's conceptualization arising out of the black civil rights movement of the 1960s; and then leaders as visionary change agents in the 1970s with the rise of the new social movements. The paradigm wars of the 1980s arose from changing social and political context that challenged the dominance of white middle-class male worldviews with the emergence of alternative, more radical knowledge and ways of viewing the world as articulated by the new social movements of black civil rights, feminism, environmentalism, student activism and, more recently, multiculturalism and post-colonialism. These demanded representation, recognition and inclusivity (Harding 1998). Not surprisingly, the 1980s saw the emergence of a proliferation of new descriptors of leadership: transformational, instructional, emancipatory, feminist, ethical – but all were still largely counter-hegemonic leadership discourses to the dominant practice of 'administration as a science'. We then had entrepreneurial leadership in the 1990s with the rise of educational markets and new managerialism (Beck and Murphy 1994; Blackmore 1996).

Parallel claims for representation and recognition were occurring within the professions after the 1970s. This expanded with the growth of the welfare state and a new generation of highly qualified 'baby boomers'. Women teachers gained equal pay as a necessary condition of teaching being perceived as a profession among equals, and notions of professionalism and unionism were not seen to be mutually exclusive. Indeed, strong teacher unions promoted debate over educational issues (for example curriculum, assessment) and sought to self-regulate the profession through registration in many instances. Some education systems, as in Victoria, Australia, empowered teachers and parents locally through moves to increased participation in school-based decision-making. This trend was informed by a parallel movement in certain universities in Australia and the UK around action research informed by texts such as *The Socially Critical School* (Kemmis and Carr 1984).[1] Collegiality underpinned notions of teacher professionalism and risk-taking innovation in curriculum, pedagogy and even school organization (for example mini schools, vertical schools) were the main game (Fielding 1999; Hargreaves 1999; Little 1999).

Globalization and the radical restructuring of education brought new anxieties with new risks. It also brought new challenges to professionalism. Education has been positioned as critical to addressing postmodern issues of cultural diversity and the new post-Fordist work order in the context of the democratization of knowledge production and dissemination. Indeed, as strategic responses to economic globalization and the rise of the information society in which knowledge becomes central, anglophone nation-states repositioned education as central to national productivity. Education became a commodity.[2] While this could be seen to locate education professionals as knowledge workers and central to national growth, government and educational managers in organizations are also seeking to manage knowledge production, and therefore to more closely direct professional expertise towards particular national or organizational ends.

At the same time, the more competitive environment created by scarce and more insecure access to training and employment, together with neo-liberal policies promoting individual choice and user-pays, have encouraged more instrumental attitudes to education as a form of individual positional good that serves the utilitarian needs of the corporate and globalized marketplace. Corson (2002) suggests that there is no encouragement in new education instrumentalism for scepticism about the common sense. In this context, more inclusive notions of leadership have been marginalized in the 1990s with the rise of managerialist and market-orientated versions of entrepreneurial leadership that have selectively co-opted localized and more communitarian impulses (for example school-based decision-making) of these earlier counter-hegemonic discourses and realigned them with neo-liberal concepts of individual choice and self-management. We now see more devolved systems of education claiming to facilitate increased parental choice, provide flexibility to meet local student and community needs, and to impart local ownership of decisions. Yet recent studies of decentralized systems indicate that devolution of responsibility has been accompanied by strong central policy frameworks, financial arrangements and multiple accountabilities that re-regulate and increase control by the centre (Macpherson

1998). Devolution has meant the school principal's work is increasingly about personnel management, financial management, resource management, image management and fund-raising, in addition to, and sometimes instead of, teaching and learning (Blackmore 2004b). The move to learner-centredness in a workplace where life pathways are tenuous and flexibility is the main game, has been increasingly construed in more competitive terms. The focus on quality in teaching and learning arises from the desire to be seen to perform in a more service-orientated and client-driven education industry in which parents and students increasingly know what they want, and expect to get it.

However, the position of the professional educator is being challenged by the promises of new modes of communication, information production and dissemination. The professions, both of academics and of teachers, already under challenge as definers of what constitutes valued knowledge (for example curriculum), and how that knowledge is disseminated (for example pedagogy) by feminist, post-colonial and indigenous movements, have also been repositioned. Some argue that the very nature of knowledge itself is changing, away from disciplinary-based knowledge formation to transdisciplinary-based knowledge formation, with a focus on problem-solving that collapses old theory/practice dichotomies, rendered obsolete, and there is a need for a critical interdisciplinarity in a new knowledge society (Barnett 1997). The early twenty-first century has also seen new discourses of teacher leadership emerging (Lingard *et al.* 2003). The growing interest in learning, information management and network theory is converging with research in the cognitive sciences to develop new notions of individual and organizational learning theory that are emerging in notions such as distributed learning and distributed leadership (for example Gronn 2000; Spillane *et al.* 2004). Cognitive science and network theory point to the need for collective and distributive leadership in order to capture the experiential knowledge base of an organization and harness it for organizational purposes. The focus here is on professional autonomous workers reliant upon collegiality for improvement, and modes of collegiality based on sharing of information that is contingent on trust (Gronn 2000; Von Krogh *et al.* 2000; Spillane *et al.* 2004). Leadership is about managing knowledge, as information and communication are now central to power (Mant 1997). But again these descriptors are more about 'how to' rather than 'what to do', identifying attributes of individuals or organizations and not focusing on relationships.

The central tension here is between the capacity of management to capture the creative intellectual work required to maintain productivity and the desire to manage it and direct it to organizational ends (Blackmore and Sachs forthcoming). The conditions in which innovation are more likely are less open to control. Those in formal leadership positions in education are therefore situated as managing the significant transitions in terms of what constitutes professional knowledge and new relationships between management and expertise. The issue is whether teachers, and indeed academics, will be situated in the new work order as symbolic analysts – those who conceive and manage work – or as the technicians who provide expertise, or as the service workers who service management. In this context, is a knowledge base in educational administration desirable or possible for the profession? Scheurich (1995: 25) argues that a positivist and functionalist paradigm, which excludes interpretive, critical, feminist theories (and which, I would suggest, is also highly Ameri-centric), dominates any knowledge base that currently exists and post-colonial theories. Does this mean educational administration/teaching is not a profession if there is no formalized standardized knowledge base? Perhaps the status for the education profession rests in the public's eyes in providing an excellent and fair public education system. Yet the trend to standardization works against recognition of the complex nature of problems that require a diversity of answers and no one training programme will do (Donmoyer 1995). Improving the status of the profession through developing a knowledge base does not necessarily improve the conditions of schooling and what happens in schools unless there is a greater recognition of diversity and difference within the field of administration itself. Indeed, the trend to internationalize professional standards through international professional bodies to increase individual mobility and the 'quality movement' generated by the focus on outcomes in schools and higher education, exacerbate these tendencies.

The emperor dresses up in an Armani suit: performative professionalism

The postmodern shift from Fordism to post-Fordism informed by the logic of manufactured uncertainty entails the transformation of institutions, social structures and relations to deal with complexity, contingency and fragmentation. Postmodern depictions of the new social order also tend to promote seductive discourses about flexibility, diversity, autonomy, individualization and reflexivity (Bauman 2001). They predict the reorganization of advanced capitalism away from modernist organizational structures (hierarchical, pyramid-shaped, gender division of labour, rule-governed, culturally homogeneous, white-male-dominated, unresponsive to markets and clients, institutionally bounded, strong demarcations between the public and private, limitless mass markets, one size fits all) towards postmodern organizational structures and cultures (flatter, devolved, autonomous work units, team-based, flexible, adaptable and multi-skilled workers, culturally diverse, family-friendly, client-responsive, reliant upon innovation and people to add value, limited niche markets, customized individualization, networked).

Accompanying this is a wider psychic shift impacting on the social formation of identity, culture and community, produced by dual processes of individualization and new forms of interdependency (Bauman 2001).

Against this discourse of optimism runs another. The dominance of the combination of radical neo-liberal market discourses and new public administration in particular, together with social neo-conservatism, have transformed educational work and notions of 'the public' through a process of corporatization. The new public administration was the neo-liberal response to economic globalization that put pressure upon the state through international monetary markets (World Bank, International Monetary Fund) and its ideological dominance in global education policy communities (Henry *et al.* 2001). This economic orthodoxy which travelled rapidly through the policy texts and discourses of global policy elites, imposed the principles of private management on public administration to make the nation-state leaner and meaner, more internationally competitive, and safer for mobile capital (Clarke and Newman 1997). Market and management principles now permeate educational practice in self-managing schools in the UK, New Zealand and Australia. Relations between states, within nation-states, and between the state and the individual have changed with the shift from welfare to post-welfarism, generated by discourses of self-help and self-management, and have absolved government of the responsibility for education, health and welfare (Gewirtz 1998). The paternalistic welfare state of the twentieth century, and the professions that grew with the rise of state bureaucracies, sought to protect individuals from the market. Now the state protects the market against restrictions (for example, World Trade Organization). Now the post-welfare-state tends to mediate global markets, national interests being seen to coincide with the market. Civic society is now about management and markets, and civil society is about participation and democratic life. Yet this is the moment when the state's intervention in the market is critical to protect individuals and groups to create more inclusive societies through access to education and other forms of cultural capital (Deetz 1992).

The performative state also seeks to steer from a distance by focusing, through policy, on outputs (usually reduced to that which is most easily quantified in terms of standardized tests and academic exit exams), not inputs (and the need to address significant structural inequalities here) or processes (around complex issues of participation, inclusivity and diversity). One could say that the dominant paradigm in educational policy and its incredible fixation on school effects and outcomes exemplifies those shifts – paying little attention to substantive issues of structural inequality, neglecting the impact of intensification of teachers' work, reducing student participation and retention rates, failing to resource pastoral care, all of which impact on student performance. A new range of disciplinary practices has emerged to satisfy this craving for data. While policy steers, performance management, quality assurance and performance indicators are the pedals of this new engine of management. The audit (or for schools, the review), standardized tests and final exit scores for access to university, are tools of the new accountability. They provide a level of visibility that satisfies the media and markets while being seen to manage risk. The audit is part of the network of control that defines what counts, and how it is counted, being at the same time 'a language, arch-commentary and social constructor of consciousness, society and environment that creates the limits, and sets the boundaries of entitlement' (Power 1999: 142). A side effect of the new drug of the audit is that auditing becomes a form of gesture politics that puts organizations on the defensive. Schools that are seen to be failing are blamed, rather than systems failing in their lack of support (Myers and Goldstein 1997). Ultimately, the audit provides 'deluded visions of control and transparency which satisfy the self image of managers, regulator and politicians but which are neither as effective or as neutral as commonly believed' (Power 1999: 143).

Professionals during the 1990s were repositioned outside the state by New Right discourses about producer capture that positioned professionals as self-interested when they opposed the introduction of new public administration based on efficiency, markets and managerialism (Clarke and Newman 1997). New Right politics strategically manufactured distrust in the professions, who were the main defence of 'the public' (Apple 1998). In the case of Victoria from 1992 to 1999, in order to implement neo-liberal market ideologies in education, health and welfare, the Kennett government excluded professional and voluntary bodies from policy formation, discredited professional expertise through a reliance upon market surveys to inform government policy (for example, sentencing by judges), restructured or removed funding from any independent tribunals that oversaw state activities and were staffed by 'old' public service professionals (auditor-general and free legal services), and actively sought to undermine unionism (Blackmore and Thorpe 2003).

The twin processes of corporatization/managerialization and marketization are captured through the notion of performativity. Performativity is the product of systemic and organizational foci on measurable outcomes, the end result, the visible, rather than the process or performances required to get to that end. One side of performativity is the bottom line of efficiency; the other side is about image and 'being seen to be doing something' (Blackmore and Sachs forthcoming). The image is like a simulacrum in which the real disappears and it all becomes fabrication (Ball 2000). Performativity is also a 'system of regulation, of organizations and of the self, providing a measure of worth and of productivity against which individuals are judged' (Ball 2000: 3). A corporate culture was produced in public bureaucracies by new employment contractual arrangements for senior education bureaucrats and performance management contracts for principals. This 're-engineered' loyalty upwards to the employer (government/central bureaucracy) and away from loyalty to a wider constituency of the public (Blackmore 1999). The individualization permeating public sector management was propagated through discourses supplanting notions of provider/client rather than public servant/citizen, and responsibility for outcomes was dispersed due to the proliferation of the outsourcing of core work to private tender and downloading responsibility to under-resourced public schools, funded according to enrolments and therefore competing with each other in deregulated markets (Wylie 1998; Yeatman 1998; Woods *et al.* 1999).

Public sector professional reconstruction has been achieved through retrenchment, outsourcing, reduced costs and increased surveillance (Bottery and Wright 1996). In this context, in which performativity rules, individuals internalize the goals and missions of organizations through systems of terror and reward, continually remaking themselves in the image(s) of the corporation to meet market and managerial demands, to become what Casey (1995) refers to as 'designer employees' (see also Du Gay 1996). Loyalty is now only upwards, loyalty to immediate supervisor, through a hierarchy of performance management, appraisal and reward systems. The new contractualism discourages opposition from within or without, expects agreement, silences debate and casts a veneer of neutrality over what is highly political. At the same time, performance management and audit cultures co-opt longstanding professional concerns over being accountable to students and parents, improving practice through reflection rather than measurement, being informed both by research and through experiential learning in making professional judgements, and working collaboratively by a new discourse about being professional (that is, maintaining technical expertise, adhering to professional standards, promoting efficient and effective use of resources, promoting evidence-based practice, and teamwork). What are missing in the new rhetoric of technical or performative professionalism are any spaces for professional judgement and autonomy and any pursuit of moral and substantive values such as social justice.

These new accountabilities are upward to managers and outward to markets. Within organizations, the dual performative demands of markets and management create a sense of ambivalence for educational professionals. Auditing and accountability imply a lack of trust in the professions. While education professionals wish to be accountable, the natures of these new disciplinary technologies are often not particularly representative of the core work of teaching and leadership (Robinson 1994). Standardized test scores have little capacity to provide a full picture of the complexity of the type of multi-literacies required in the new work order (for example cultural, technical, numerical, citizenship, social, linguistic and/or visual literacy) expected in a culturally diverse knowledge based society (New London Group 1996).

The performative technologies create a sense of dissonance between what teachers and principals in schools called 'performative' work and 'real' work. Not only are the data and reporting required an inadequate representation of the complexity of their core work, but the process of production is counter-productive in the sense that reporting and performance requirements create categories, establish priorities and work with assumptions that do not make sense of the problems and issues teachers face (Thomson 1998). Indeed, the performative exercises required of schools and teachers change the very nature of that work through the intensification of labour, what is taught, how it is judged and with what effect (Blackmore and Sachs forthcoming). Performativity can also lead to a form of fabrication to fit the categories of documents and reports, or the standardizing tendencies of management through best-practice rhetoric and normalizing images of good schools promoted through markets. Performing schools compete in local and national sports, entertainment and high-stake tests. The focus on teacher, school and student attributes fails to attend to the complex range of judgements based on ethical principles, values and interpersonal relationships as well as intuitive professional knowledge acquired through experience and reflection that form the basis of teachers' and leaders' daily actions.

In their text on identity and primary teaching, Menter *et al.* (1996: 120) argue that marketization drives the necessary destabilization of traditional bureaucratic professional work cultures that characterized pre-reform provision. Managerialism becomes a key feature in securing the processes of transition. We have gone from managed capitalism, in which the professions and the state were key aspects of that management in the educational settlement of the post-war period, to deregulated capitalism where the state and the professions, through their technical expertise, mediate and facilitate market relations. Within public sector organizations such as schools, the new managerialism has seen the reassertion of executive prerogative, an emerging divide between managers and teachers (Mahoney and Hextall 1997; Blackmore and Sachs forthcoming). The new managerialism delivers a form of class relations that actually challenges traditional notions of professional power, the basis of the 'new middle class' of the twentieth century, substituting it with a new managerial class whose disciplinary base is that of management theory. Management assumes a form of generic sets of transferable competences and inherent logics that often bear little relationship to the core work of what is being managed. Management, according to Clarke and Newman (1997: 52), has 'filled the discursive space in which change is conceived, defines the terrain and direction of change. It expresses the imagined futures and ways of getting there. It establishes the limits of the possible and the imaginable, and above all, the sayable.'

So there is little comfort in the modes of entrepreneurial leadership in the 1990s that have been more about control, authority, hierarchy and subordination than democratic process, compassionate authority and co-operative learning. Indeed, leadership in the context of greater uncertainty is becoming more about risk aversion and control, creating a counterproductive psychic economy of distrust. At the same time, there is a dispersion of management throughout schools down to teachers, leading to their co-option in these new forms of professional control. Entrepreneurial leadership in the performing school is about being opportunistic, managing risk and producing not the best, but the right, representations according to the norms laid down by management and markets about what constitutes a good school, effective leadership and educational success in which the identity of the principal as success or failure is linked to that of the school (Gleeson and Husbands 2001; Thomson 2001).

The emperor's old grey suit replaced by a black pinstripe: 'recuperative masculinities'

Organizational and leadership theory continues to ignore how radically changing relations in workplaces, in the social relations of gender, the collapse of boundaries between family and work, and the production of new work identities and collective possibilities (Gee and Lankshear 1995). The 1990s saw fundamental transformations arising from globalizing forces including increased mobility of capital, people, goods, images and ideas producing tendencies towards both political, cultural and localized diversity and the homogenizing dispositions of new managerialism, markets, transnational capital and western cultural hegemony. On the one hand, we see significant debates around the politics of recognition of difference with rising grassroots awareness of the need for reconciliation in Australia and in South Africa, the articulation of postmodern discourses of diversity and the highly visible presence of individual women in executive leadership. Changing social relations of gender that have produced different notions of family and home, put new demands on education from early childhood through to the role of professional training and education in universities. On the other hand, life is marked by increased risk and interdependency, although risk is greatest for those with the least cultural, social and educational capital. The trend is for more casualized jobs for many and the portfolio career for the mobile few, with educational outwork becoming increasingly more common in schools and universities.

Various reports depicted the 1990s as a decade of women in leadership. We are told that we are in postmodern, post-feminist and post-Fordist times. And yet statistics tell us is that while women are increasingly entering the ranks of middle management (school principals) in many educational systems, they have not gained access in the numbers expected, have not gained dominance in executive positions, and where they have gained access the climate is still very chilly (Ozga and Walker 1999). This is indicated by the revolving door syndrome where executive women exit large corporations for self-employment. The Australian Affirmative Action Agency reported that, in 1987, women held 23.7 per cent of management positions and that in 1998 this had fallen to 23 per cent. Newspaper headlines in Australia as elsewhere state 'Still No Room at the Top', Women Reject Big Corporations (Carson 1999). In non-government schools, women are 65 per cent of profession but only 43 per cent of principals. And in 2003, in many countries there were fewer eligible teachers applying for the principalship – with women indicating high levels of disinterest (NASSP 1998; Blackmore 2002b; Lacey 2002).

So why, in a period of rapid social, political and economic turmoil, has there been so little change? Chisholm (2000: 1) points to the paradox that in rapidly changing societies, such as South Africa which is undergoing significant change and where groups with an emancipatory agenda enter the state, 'the possibilities for altering organizational culture and structural conditions [appear] to be strong'. But, despite the powerful agenda of social justice that has shaped the recomposition of the state and the bureaucracy, new discourses of leadership undermining the position of women have emerged. Whereas the former has seen the appointment of women and blacks to key leadership positions, the latter has paradoxically associated masculinity with economic rationality, being strong, making 'hard decisions, the "hard" knowledge areas of science and technology, and "entrepreneurship"' (Chisholm 2000: 1).

Educational restructuring has facilitated a re-masculinization of executive power as masculinity and capitalism take on a new mode of control. New transnational masculinity (Connell 1998) is also about the 'colour of competence', where the hegemonic image of leadership is white, male, middle class and heterosexual. The dominant construction of 'good' leadership continues to have both racialized and gendered connotations.

The literature tends to suggest that there is a complex array of factors – the relationships between the institution of schooling and its organizational structures, the life trajectories of educators and their professional identities, and the changing social relations of gender – that explain the current disinterest in the principalship, particularly by women. In particular, the literature points to competing personal and professional priorities, issues of quality of life, and a sense that the rewards (intra-psychic and professional) are not sufficient (Blackmore 2004b). Women who are leaders in schools but not in the principalship, comment that they do not want to 'become like that' or did not want to make decisions, which were 'antithetical' to their professional, personal and ethical beliefs. They saw leadership in schools as about business management and image management, not about what was the core work of their profession: leading to improve teaching and learning (Blackmore 1999).

Young women teachers tell us that the intensification of their work means they are even less able to consider moving up the organization as demands of home and school are so great (Lacey 2002).

The reconstitution of professionalism in current times indicates its enduring 'masculinism' and 'whiteness' revitalized through the wielding of executive power, the recycling of old images of leadership with the corporatization of education and the rise of recuperative masculinity (Lingard 2003). Professions have historically been about exclusion, utilizing a range of mechanisms such as credentialing and certification, to restrict access, and premised upon faith in science and expertise, control over a specific practitioner expertise and knowledge base, and the capacity for self-regulation (for example professional bodies setting standards of practice and fees). Traditional male-dominated professions such as law and medicine gained prestige through their capacity to exclude female practitioners in the late nineteenth century in the field of education, health and welfare (administration/teaching, medical and nursing, psychologists and welfare). This exclusion came about through the seemingly neutral bureaucratic processes embodied in the 'rational man in the grey suit' (Morgan 1995; Blackmore 1999). The feminized quasi-professions of the public sector were an extension of the domestic female role servicing the real professions. Feminization of the profession was associated with de-professionalization, a discursive association that is currently being recycled around the crisis of 'what about the boys' and suggestions that boys need more male role models.

Recent literature around the restructuring of work and the professions indicates a trend to re-masculinization at the executive level due to a structural backlash. Lingard (2003) refers to how this 'recuperative masculinity' politics has emerged out of the context of radical market reform, new modes of governance, and the feminist backlash culturally encouraged by neo-conservative social policies. New forms of paternalism, entrepreneurialism, careerism and personalism are coming together to produce a form of competitive corporate masculinities in designer suits (Collinson and Hearn 1996). Control no longer derives from the natural authority of being male, but a particular masculinity gains ascendancy: 'Coterminous with the language and practices of strategic management, competitive masculinity sustains and reproduces a variety of behavioural displays consonant with entrepreneurialism, risk taking, and an instrumental orientation towards others' (Kerfoot and Knights 1996: 87).

At the same time, performativity encourages managing from a distance, an emphasis on efficiency as a bottom line to the exclusion of emotional and ethical values, and control, although through consent and through the soul and not coercion. The modern corporation is a site of 'rational control', a masculine enterprise. The new careerism is represented as that of the globally mobile multinational masculinity, embodied in the homogenizing western global uniform of the black pinstripe suit of the entrepreneur, a mode of masculinity that excludes many men as well as women (Connell 1998). It is a mode of masculinity associated with personal sacrifices of family, leisure and even physical and mental health. At the same time, these new masculinities, as their older versions, are reliant upon the hidden services provided by women in the household that facilitate their personal success, mobility and capital accumulation (Mulholland 1995). What is different about this transnational masculinity is that it no longer has loyalty to country although the means of regeneration of white male executive power is through the practices of homosocial reproduction: working with those who look and are like themselves (Connell 1998; Sinclair 1998).

The corporate leader is still modelled on particular hegemonic male images of being strong, able to make the hard decisions, being independent, taking unilateral action, and so on. This dominant hegemonic masculinity excludes alternative approaches and images as weaker and lesser (for example gay, indigenous or Asian masculinities), in particular, feminist modes of femininity. This is not to argue that all men fit this image, or that all women do not, as there are instances of women who work well in such environments. Not all men are macho, hard-nosed, and hyper-rational and claim to represent the universal interest, just as not all women are caring and sharing (Blackmore 1999). The issue therefore is to broaden notions of masculinity and femininity beyond macho white male leadership, to encourage and accept a wider repertoire of leadership images, practices and worldviews, to debate what leadership is about and for whom, rather than consider matters of style and image (Deem and Ozga 1997).

The emperor has no clothes: leadership, standards and technical professionalism

In schools, the issue of teacher professionalism and what it means has emerged as a key issue for the next decade. In Australia, discussions about teacher professionalism are being driven by public government, as employer of most teachers, and not the profession (MCEETYA 2003b). It is evident in the interest of government in professional standards, accreditation and the rise of quasi-autonomous or statutory authorities dealing with registration and accreditation such as the Ontario College of Teachers in Canada, the Scottish Teaching Council, the Teacher Training Agency in the UK, the professional standards push in the USA and the new Victorian Institute of Teachers in Australia. University faculties that provide teacher education are also driven by student and employer demand and standardizing practices arising from the imposition of new quality assurance agendas focusing on generic graduate skills and attributes. The focus is on professional standards for teachers and for principals as the response to the new demands of the job. Teacher professional associations in Australia are seeking to use standards to develop teacher expertise in particular disciplines (for example maths, science, English) through reflective practice, postgraduate courses and networking and to develop a professional knowledge base and contribute to more 'generic' skills and understandings. At the same time, the professional standards debate is being driven largely without regard to the wider material conditions of teachers' work and public schooling and without reference to the industrial relationships that have radically changed the relationship between teachers and their employers (for example, increased principal control over teachers' careers). But does this focus on standards increase the status of teaching as a profession? Standards in themselves merely guarantee baseline benchmarks and espouse wider sets of attributes, even if linked through career progression and credentials. But this requires systemic commitment to rewards for professional learning (see Blackmore 2002b).

What notion of professionalism will the next generation of teachers encounter? In the next five years the influx of new teachers will be similar to that seen in the early 1970s. But this time they enter a system where teaching is being casualized, and, some argue, de-professionalized, with the creation of new types of teachers (aides, assistants), more hierarchical and performance-based career structures, and increased external regulation of the profession. This is in a wider context of increased individual competitiveness between schools and teachers, where expertise is marketable and treated as a commodity. Having emerged from a highly competitive school system and higher education system into a deregulated and casualized labour market, the next generation of teachers will then be presented with a view of professionality emphasizing the competence and standards of individual teachers, a further tendency towards individualization. Will this mean that there is less of a collective sense of being a professional or what Brennan (1996) calls democratic professionalism? This means having loyalty to, and concern about, more than one's classroom, one's school, one's discipline, or even one's system and involves a broader commitment to a set of professional ideals and education as a field of ethical and democratic practice.

The twentieth-century notion of 'the public' is being replaced by a market and a managerialist economy of educational work that is infused with different values and priorities. Education as a public activity has been discursively reconstituted through the language of purchaser/provider, audit, performance and risk management, and generic multi-skilled managers are *the* new profession. These new 'professional' managers have been given significant executive powers to shift organizational cultures. They have 'the right to manage', producing in public sector organizations a new divide between management and educational worker. Indeed, professional educators are increasingly perceived to be redundant when they do not 'fit' or when their expertise is no longer required. Kerfoot and Knights (1996) suggest that the rational detachment encouraged in the ways in which management is conceived, leads to a form of estrangement resulting from extreme rationality and a belief in one's own competence and power.

The current generation of principals sits uneasily, bridging this divide, expressing considerable ambivalence about the tensions this creates for their leadership habitus (Blackmore and Sachs forthcoming). As yet, principals are not part of this new 'professional managerial class' whose disciplinary base derives from human resource management, accounting and business. The new managerial class's knowledge base is not imbued with the same under-standings about obligations and responsibilities to 'the wider public' and lacks the tradition of seeking to redress social inequality and promote social justice that exists in the professional disciplines of health, welfare and edu-cation (Townley 1994; Gewirtz 1998). Technical professionalism is premised upon expertise and not public trusteeship, about being professional in terms of being competent (Brint 1995). The tension between this new managerial leadership and educational professionalism is most evident in the job de-scriptions of leadership work; these reflect system-wide priorities of economy, efficiency and performativity. They focus on performance management and outcomes, financial management and industrial relations in which people management and innovation are low on the list. There is a dissonance be-tween the organizational descriptors of what principals are expected to do and be, and what teachers and parents see as the key aspects of good leadership.

These trends are not specific to Victoria, or to Australia. Studies indicate the push for technical modes of professionalism (Mahoney and Hextall 1997). Johansson *et al.* (2000: 4) reflect:

> Deregulation and decentralization, new laws and new national cur-riculum seem to have changed work-conditions for principals dra-matically during the last decades. Different discourses of change are competing in society, and new contexts of meaning are challenging established roles and identities. The discourse is not restricted to a Scandinavian society, but is also influenced by a global discourse of educational leadership and administration, which seems highly dominated by research within an American context. For instance, new public management, with a focus on accountability, effective-ness, competition and local democracy frames the nature of school leadership in new ways where managerial aspects are emphasized.

Corson (2002) refers to how utilitarian attitudes to schooling are being gen-erated in Canada by parents, students and employers, and these limit the democratic possibilities of education in terms of citizenship formation and social-capital-building. The standardizing effects of markets and management have effectively normalized and systematized differential treatment of particular marginalized social groups, marked by the exclusion in Ontario's New Right government (as in Victoria in the 1990s) of words like democracy, equity, multiculturalism and anti-racism, accompanied by the denigration of the humanities for its lack of use value. Standardized curriculum and assessment restricts possibilities for non-standard students.

The corporatization of education marked in the 1990s by the twin strategies of managerialism and marketization has revitalized particular aspects of old modes of leadership. The rise of education markets, despite the discourses about choice and meeting diverse client desires, have had normalizing tendencies, encouraging conformity rather than diversity, when what we need are innovation and risk-taking. Organizations that engage with self-improvement publicly do so at great risk, as discourses about failing institutions quickly dampen down any transparent processes of self-reflection and reflexivity. Performativity requires being seen to be performing well at all times. The market is a harsh critic. Nor does the client-driven sector encourage parents to actively become involved in schools, or to work with teachers to resolve problems. The market only offers parents the option to exercise the choice to exit, not voice (Blackmore 2004a). Paradoxically, organizational responses to postmodern discourses about diversity, heterogeneity, uncertainty, reflexive individualism and ambiguity have been to increase control, standardize, and develop more intrusive work and management practices that lead us to manage ourselves better to fit a range of organizational needs and images. Education is no longer viewed as a site of innovation and social change.

New state formations and accumulation regimes have produced 'a stripping out of meaning from what were once central concepts in the organization of public life (for example citizenship, equality, justice – but also closer to my theme, professionalism) and their replacement with "hollowed out" concepts like client, consumer, stakeholder, quality, excellence, leadership, performance' (Ozga 1995: 6). Neo-liberalism has, through these new governed mentalities, produced 'new relations between expertise and politics' especially in the realm of welfare and education where the sense of obligation and of seeking justice for all is central. The corporatization of education has worked towards a consensus politics of schooling that is numbing in its standardizing dispositions, and that lacks the moral imperative of a dissensus politics that argues that debate and disagreement are central to strong democracies (Fazzaro and Walter 2002: 28). Hanlon (1998) refers to the 'struggle for the soul of professionalism'. Ball (2000: 2) argues that it produces a new form of social and moral regulation that 'bites deeply and immediately into the practice of state professionals – reforming and re-forming meaning and identity – producing or making-up new professional subjectivities'.

Sennett (1998) talks about the corrosion of character that is occurring: of how the new worker has to respond to what the boss and customer wants, adopting and adapting to their wishes. Pollitt (1990) sees the 'old' professionals as being repositioned as being 'on tap' and not 'on top' in this new regime, thus challenging strong professional cultures built on shared knowledge and an understanding that they have particular responsibilities towards and understandings about 'the public'.

Leadership in the context of the rise of technical professionalism as a response to greater uncertainty has become more about risk aversion than risk-taking in a low-trust and high-risk society (Bishop 1999). Educational leadership needs to get beyond the current fetish about style and performativity, to reject the neo-modernist emphasis on standards and get back to the substance of leadership: leading for whom and for what. Equity is particularly risky work in this context, as it means addressing and reflecting on institutional priorities and practices in a transparent way: confronting the problems and asking hard questions. Taking risks requires environments of collegiality and professional trust that have not been evident in recent years. Performativity does not allow this type of leadership work, and indeed is seen to be highly dangerous for leaders and for institutions. If leadership is reduced to technical expertise and not to substantive positions of value, if leadership is reduced to looking after one's own school without concern for education in the wider sense and educational equality, then leadership will become self-serving and inward to protect 'our own' to the neglect of 'others'. The post-modern tensions for self-managing schools within market systems is between 'the independent impulse underlying their formation and operation and the common interest vested in their educational benefits and social effects' (Freeman 1999: 2). It is a microcosm of the educational tensions between self-interest and private notions of freedom on the one hand, and civic engagement and mutual responsibility on the other (Freeman 1999: 3).

Get rid of the suit! Who wants to be a leader now?

So, what to do? The changing nature of the conditions and nature of work will create new challenges for the professions. I have already argued that discourses about professionalism, and the increased imposition of external, local, national and, increasingly, global standards on the work of educational professionals will continue to change the field of practice, setting up new controls but also creating new possibilities.

What of the next generation of teacher leaders? Recent reports indicate that the loss of early career teachers is high (MCEETYA 2003a). This is significantly different from the previous generation where teaching was viewed, particularly for women, as a safe and secure career. As work becomes more like a series of projects, security is gained through the accumulation of experience and qualifications in numerous jobs in the form of 'portfolio careers' (Gee and Lankshear 1995). A person's status and credibility will not be gained through their institutional location but more through their mobility and the portability of skills. Professional reputation will be through affiliations and networks with different types of people who share related identities and partial alliances based on projects and interests. Knowledge will also be derived from these communities of practice. The leadership issue is how to develop and sustain the networking within and across communities of practice and with more diverse populations, 'harnessing the power of unfamiliarity' (Gee and Lankshear 1995: 191). Power and reputation in this performative context comes through which networks the individual belongs to, their mobility (virtually and physically), and their capacity to make weak and diffuse links with a diverse range of people. Managers' (principals') roles will be, in this context, to design identities and create bonding, no matter how temporary, between the individual and the organizational goals in terms of shared practices and not shared interests. The problem for managers will be to maintain the attention of not just the consumer but also the worker.

Even if such depictions may be an idealization of post-Fordist work, or, as Connell (1998) points out, more akin to the life of the new global masculinities of the white middle-class male as mobile member of the new global elite, they do raise questions about the future of teaching as a profession. For example, educated women, the traditional, flexible and cheap source of teaching labour, now have greater occupational choices and mobility, deferring marriage and motherhood for independent lifestyles. Men are also making lifestyle choices that are family- and health-related. The conditions of teachers' work and, in particular, the role of the principal is not attractive to many. This is a critical time for teachers and academics, a period in which notions of career and of professionalism are in flux and are highly contested.

In order for teaching to reconstitute itself as a 'new profession', we first have to reclaim education as a site of advocacy and social and political action both within and in relation to communities of practice, and we need to revitalize a sense of collectivity, no matter how temporary or transitory, through new alliances with other professions. This means foregrounding in all aspects of our work the issue of social justice, that is, revitalizing the notions of teaching and leading as passionate work, and also of teachers as leaders (Lingard *et al.* 2003). What I want to argue for is that those in leadership need to get involved in wider debates about our shared educational futures – this means engaging with issues of difference and social justice in ways that moves us forward, rather than backwards. It is about taking a stand – deciding on what we see are important changes and issues to promote educational justice and generating debates about the nature of that society (Gewirtz 1998: 482; Hargreaves 2003). Principals therefore need to engage with the education profession more widely, rather than treating educational administration as a discrete activity.

Leadership should be focusing on clear principles of redistributive social justice, processes of deliberative democracy and inclusivity in ways that foreground the educational (and therefore social and material) needs of the student and local communities. This is about relational work as well as about the fair distribution of resources (Gewirtz 1998). We need to broaden our notion of social justice to take into account both distributive justice (that is, of goods, rights and responsibilities among individuals), and also relational justice that deals with the social, collective and interpersonal (for example violence, care) (Young 1999). In this context, leadership would be less facilitating change determined elsewhere and more proactive, value-driven and about a politics of recognition. Leadership has been denuded of its political content, reduced to a repertoire of skills that do not require political, intellectual or ethical value positions. A politics of recognition would, Gewirtz (1998: 476) argues, 'involve not only a commitment to respond to others and otherness but also a commitment to avoiding practising the power of surveillance control and discipline upon others'.

Second, we need to assume a position of policy activism (Thomson 1999). Yeatman (1998: 1) refers to professional activists as those who were 'highly motivated by some conception of social justice and who sought to make a difference in their policy work'. This required not only a broad commitment to public service, but also, significantly, an alternative vision that they strived for in the long term while they dealt with the pragmatics of the immediate. They used a range of skills, strategies, forms of persuasion and promotion, organization and networks to mobilize people and resources to this end. Sachs (2003) advocates activist professionalism, which is rooted in orthodox notions of professionalism – expertise (technical knowledge over specific field of practice), altruism (ethical concern for clients) and autonomy (need to exercise control over entry into and practice of profession) – but which extends to promoting active trust and generative politics. Active trust involves shared values and principles, building on strategic alliances between groups in a wider educational alliance for collective action to 'improve at the macro level all aspects of education and at the micro level student learning outcomes and teacher status' (Sachs 2000: 6). A generative politics, while in defence of the politics of the public domain, asks: Whose issues are put on the agenda and how do these issues become public? Who provides the moral and intellectual leadership? Who is inclusively promoted? How can trust and collaboration overcome traditional suspicions and reservations? How can alternative forms be established to promote a socially just education? It also requires a sense of the collective and the role of professional organizations, both disciplinary-based and union-based (Louis *et al.* 2000).

Third, this requires us to promote the notion of critical professionality in our mentoring and educating of the next generation of education professionals by encouraging reflective, knowledge-based practice that is informed by strong theory, that provides a range of perspectives as to what counts as research, that includes a multiplicity of knowledges, and that promotes a sense of ethics and a concern for social justice. This means teacher educators and leadership development courses need to focus on decisions that are less about efficiency and more about equity, providing teacher leaders with a capacity to read and do policy and research from a critical frame informed by principled practice (Blackmore 2002b). It also requires development of 'professional learning communities' that are sustainable, in which teachers' professional autonomy and judgement are supported through a multiplicity of leadership roles, images and practices, and a multiplicity of desired social and academic outcomes. This would counter the trend towards standardizing and individualizing teachers' competences (that is, 'performance training sets' of technical professionalism) (Hargreaves 2003: 134–135).

Fourth, this may require us to collectively revitalize the notion of education as being about social change, as the basis for building social capital for a new knowledge society rather than merely responding to markets and management (Cox 1998). Dempster *et al.* (2001: 11) suggests that what characterizes a professional is 'engagement with an element of the client's life in order to bring about changes that are in the client's interests'. That is, professionals work towards making things better, which is a normative concept. Education is premised on passing on something of value and not mere transmission of facts. It is relational work based on important pedagogical moments as part of a process of identity formation. In the notion of service to customers, we have forgotten that students are future citizens and workers with responsibilities and rights. We need to renew trust in education's social as well as human capital-building capacities, and recognize that good leadership is grounded on, and indeed contingent upon, personal and professional relations based on collaborative principles of deliberative democracy and the types of informed, ethical and professional practices where leadership is the practice of many and not a few (Blackmore 2004a).

Notes

1.   As one of the highly qualified baby boomers and a product of the 1960s public schools in Victoria, I enjoyed equal pay for women teachers when introduced in 1970, promoted teacher registration and curriculum reform as a branch union leader in schools, was one of the first teacher representatives on a local school council in 1974, and a member of a team of early career teachers who introduced interdisciplinary general studies based on project work at years 7 and 8. During the 1980s, I was a teacher representative elected onto a local

administrative committee that advised the school principal, and ran a staff development day in 1984 to reframe our curriculum using Kemmis and Carr's *Socially Critical School*. Not surprisingly, my first publication as an academic in the *Journal of Educational Administration* was 'Tensions to be resolved: participative decision making in schools' in 1986. My experience indicated how, in a highly centralized state bureaucracy, curriculum innovation, participation based on inclusivity, and teacher professionalism were possible when teachers and parents were involved in policy-making that was framed by progressive state policies. What was missing and that gave space for more conservative policies and increased accountability was our failure to focus on learning outcomes.

2.   In Australia, education in 2003 is an export industry equivalent to wheat and sheep.

Conclusions and Implications: Towards Emergent Theoretical Perspectives on Leadership, Gender and Culture[1]

John Collard and Cecilia Reynolds

Two decades of research into leadership and gender in education have tended to reflect themes from the broader discourses in fields such as psychology and sociology. They have also alerted us to a worldwide problem of male domination of positions of formal power in professions where the vast majority of employees are women. Feminists have actively contested this tradition and argued for more equitable promotion strategies and recognition of alternatives to authoritarian and utilitarian leadership styles that have been alleged to be favoured by males. However, much of this discourse has been locked within essentialist stereotypes of masculine and feminine gender, which are no longer credible. There is a need for more nuanced theory and research which recognizes that gender is mediated by other factors such as diverse social, system and institutional cultures. Factors such as class, ethnicity and sexuality also need to be recognized as shaping variables. The concept of organizational culture itself also needs to become more sophisticated and resist essentializing tendencies. This perspective challenges current theorists, researchers and practitioners to develop more complex awareness about leadership, gender and culture in educational settings.

This book is a step towards the development of a dynamic and nuanced theory of leadership that recognizes the interactive and dialectical nature of three socially constructed phenomena: leadership, gender and culture. As such, it departs from positivist propositions about leadership. We concur with recent theorists who have concluded that positivist accounts have failed to map this complex territory because they have searched for universal foundations instead of building theory from grounded observation of complex processes. Several chapters in this book delineate some of this complexity. Discussions here move beyond the typologies of gender, which have predominated in the leadership discourse for the past two decades. Such typologies can now be viewed as a necessary step along the way, a preliminary charting of the coastline that now requires more precise definition. We believe that there are multiple forms of femininity and masculinity in pluralist western democracies. These forms are reiterated and even mutate in diverse organizational settings. Finally, we contest that the static and monolithic constructs of culture have influenced the mapping of the leadership terrain without reference to such things as the body, sexuality, race or class. The authors in this book are beginning to map the interactions of more complex processes, which move upon the page and defy the certainties of earlier cartographers who mapped formations we now seek to question and rearrange.

It is over twenty years since Biklen and Brannigan (1980) published one of the first major collections on issues surrounding educational leadership and gender. Their collection of essays *Women and Educational Leadership* was followed by an outpouring of gender-focused research and writing, which continues to this day. Most of this has been written by women and about women in what has been defined as a 'masculinist enterprise' (Ozga 1993). It has ranged from what can now be defined as liberal feminist (Kanter 1977; Biklen and Brannigan 1980; Schmuck 1980, 1987; Hall 1996) to critical feminist (Blackmore 1993, 1995a,b, 1999; Ferguson 1984; Marshall and Rusch 1995), and postmodernist perspectives (Sinclair 1998; Grogan 2000).

Men have remained strangely silent upon the issue educational leadership and gender. With the exception of Connell (1987, 1995), Mac an Ghaill (1994) and Lingard and Douglas (1999), little critical analysis has been written. This could be interpreted as male leaders and educational researchers failing to perceive gender to be problematical within the field. Wolcott's *The Man in the Principal's Office: An Ethnography* (1973) was a seminal study of principal behaviour but failed to acknowledge gender as an important component of his subject's identity. Protherough's (1984) analysis of 'great headmasters' in Britain suffered similar limitations. Marshall and Rusch (1995) labelled this as 'gender blindness' within the discourse, practice and university teaching on educational leadership.

However, if we view the research and theoretical perspectives of both male and female writers in the field, we can also see that themes in educational leadership discourse have mirrored those in the broader fields of gender studies, psychology and sociology. This helps to explain why women have been the pioneers in the field. The women's liberation movements of the 1960s and 1970s laid the ground for them to begin scrutinizing educational leadership from a critical perspective. Although there were minor signs of a male awakening in these decades (Farrell 1993) the impact was marginal, the development of masculinist theory and research in gender studies was slow to develop and is still underdeveloped with the exceptions of Connell (1987, 1995), Hearn (1993), MacInnes (1998), Seidler (1994), Steinberg (1993) and Tacey (1997).

One of the major theoretical problems that has confronted scholars writing about gender is the temptation to assume the validity of essentialist stereotypes about men and women. Gilligan's (1982) famous study of men and women making decisions about abortion was a reaction to the masculinist bias she perceived in Kohlberg's (1980) theory of moral development. Her case studies led her to conclude that women were more 'relational' than men, who were more inclined to make decisions from a platform of cognitively based universal values. Since then, many feminist writers have assumed an unquestionable polarity between men and women. Noddings (1984) developed a thesis that women are more care orientated than men. Belenky *et al.* (1986) went even further to argue that women's ways of knowing are fundamentally different from those of men.

The early writings about masculinity are equally fallacious. Hudson and Jacot (1991) typecast men as instrumental, relationship-phobic, and more orientated to scientific and technological thought than women. Steinberg (1993), following Gilligan, argued that men are fundamentally 'instrumental' and biased towards 'rationality, authority and task orientation' in contrast to women who are naturally more communitarian. Hearn (1993) represented British men as essentially patriarchical in both private and public domains. The Australian guru of masculine psychology promoted a belief that boys and men are essentially different from girls and women (Biddulph 1994).

It would appear that both discourses have been seduced by essentialism in their early stages of development. A belief that men and women are essentially different has assumed the status of a law-like foundation upon which research and theory have been built. It is ironic that this bias became ascendant at the same time as the positivist precepts it resembled were coming under radical scrutiny and rejected as an adequate epistemological framework for scientific and social enquiry (Evers and Lakomski 1996a,b).

The past few years have seen the development of a much more sophisticated theoretical base in the field of gender research. This has tended to link gender to cultural, historical and sociological contexts and issues of power in private, institutional and public domains. More recently, it has been seen to be intimately related to cultural beliefs about sexuality (Sinclair 1998) and some postmodernists are even disputing the validity of the concept of gender as a categorical truth. Connell (1995) has advanced a thesis that there are multiple forms of femininity and masculinity and convincingly illustrated this with case studies of corporate, gay and working-class men in Australia. Edgar (1997) has questioned the macho stereotypes which have been so powerful in Australia. Both MacInnes (1998) and Tacey (1997) tend to view the concept of masculinity itself as being in a transformative stage. Unfortunately, popular psychologists and sociologists appear unaware of such developments. Mackay's (1997) recent analysis of 'baby boomers, their parents and their children' fails to acknowledge the complex understandings we now possess about gender and sexuality. Unfortunately, essentialism also continues to be perpetuated by consultancy companies, publishers, relationship agencies and universities who have a vested interest in portraying Mars and Venus to be doomed to separate orbits for all eternity.

Leadership and gender: initial perspectives

The development of gender perspectives in educational leadership discourse has tended to duplicate the pattern found in the broader academic discourse. Most of the theory written before the 1980s was indeed gender blind and frequently locked into positivist paradigms which sought to develop universal principles for leadership (Halpin 1959; Simon 1976; Hoy and Miskel 1991; Hoy 1996). The first authors to explicitly address the neglect of gender as a key variable tended to write from a liberal feminist perspective which challenged the male leadership dominance in an employment field where the vast majority of employees were women (Biklen and Brannigan 1980). These were promptly joined by researchers from the critical theory perspective (Ferguson 1984) who placed the male dominance of the profession into traditions of exploitation and inequality. However, a full challenge did not emerge until 1987 with Shakeshaft's publication of *Women in Educational Administration*, which documented the history of male dominance in American schools and superintendencies. It was followed by similar works in Britain and Australia (Acker 1989; Adler *et al.* 1993; Blackmore 1993; Ozga 1993; Limerick 1995). With the exception of Blackmore, all these authors accepted gender polarities as unquestioned truths. Some (Helgeson 1991; Adler *et al.* 1993; Shakeshaft 1995) could be accused of female chauvinism as they claimed women leaders possessed educational and relational attributes which made them superior candidates for leadership. At the same time, male leaders were frequently caricatured as essentially bureaucratic and instrumental in their leadership styles. Even Gronn's (1995) excellent critique of transformational leadership as a mythical vogue of the previous two decades, fails to question essentialist assumptions by accepting stereotypical qualities of 'masculine greatness'.

The most extreme example was Gray's (1989) development of male and feminine 'paradigms' in Britain. Following on from the early work of Bem (1978), he argued that women were essentially 'caring, creative, intuitive, sensitive to diversity, non-competitive, tolerant, subjective and informal'. Conversely, men were represented as 'regulatory, conformist, disciplined, normative, competitive, evaluative, objective and formal'. A subsequent feminist polemic (Adler *et al.* 1993) went even further and argued for a feminist leadership style which was 'anti-bureaucratic, relational and organic', as opposed to the bureaucratic instrumentalism of male leaders. It is highly ironic that these authors were writing during the Thatcher regime in Britain, with its emphasis upon the neo-liberal values of control, economic rationalism and performativity. Court (this volume) questions such simplicity by illustrating the differing values in a group of women leaders working together in a New Zealand school. The contradictions suggest that contemporary political cultures may interact with gender to shape beliefs and values (see Davis and Johansson, this volume). A similar conclusion arises from Connell's (1995) account of men in the Australian environmental movement who were submissive to female authority.

There was also a bemusing silence by contemporary feminists about traditions of stern matriarchical leadership in schools. Histories of girls' schools are replete with portraits of female leaders, dating back to the previous century, who are perhaps best described as 'steel magnolias in velvet ghettoes' (Collard, this volume). There is also growing contemporary evidence that women leaders can be authoritarian, bureaucratic and misuse power in the ways depicted by Ferguson (1984) and others. Marshall and Rusch (1995) have written about 'women who lead like men' and Wajcman (1998) felt compelled to entitle her research *Managing like a Man: Women and Men in Corporate Management*. By way of contrast, there are also histories (Webber 1981; Gamble 1982; Hansen 1986; Bate 1990; McConville 1993) where male bureaucrats and patriarchs contrast sharply with other men who demonstrated the compassionate and relational qualities which Gilligan (1982) and Noddings (1984) defined as essentially feminine. Bate's (1990) history of Geelong Grammar complicates the field further by raising questions about the sexuality of one of the early leaders in the school. It implies that interaction between gender and sexuality may be one of the 'sacred silences' in the educational leadership discourse, which also needs to be explored (Koschoreck, this volume). The inconsistencies suggest the limitations of the essentialist assumptions from which many previous authors have worked. They clearly indicate that leader gender is not an all-determining variable. The forces that shape leaders' beliefs and behaviours are much more complex than a single-factor theory can explain.

Recent research

It was not until the mid-1990s that the stereotypes began to be challenged by researchers developing grounded theory based on case studies and careful historical analysis (Reynolds 1995; Coleman 1996; Hall 1996; Kruger 1996). These women were the first voices to point to the need for a more nuanced and finely tuned approach to the field. They argued for closer attention to historical context, family histories, ethnicity and cultural norms at both social and institutional levels to truly understand gender patterns in educational leadership. Ribbins (1996) placed heavy emphasis upon context as a key variable and Mac an Ghaill (1994) was the first to recognize that there was more than one type of masculinity and male sexuality in British schools. Once again, the pattern mirrors that in the broader field of gender studies and validates Connell's thesis about multiple forms of femininity and masculinity. Perhaps these studies even go one step further in recognizing that institutional histories and cultures shape differences between leaders, whereas his work was more focused upon broader social cultures.

The work of Reynolds (1995) in Canada, Hall (1996) in Britain, and Kruger (1996) in the Netherlands, provide useful illustrations in this regard. One of the most sophisticated analyses in the field to date is Reynolds' analysis of life histories of two generations of male and female principals in elementary and primary schools in Ontario from 1940 to 1980. Her work illuminates the interactions between broad social norms, systemic structures and institutional cultures in Canada in that period. She argues that the 'rules of control' within the school system reinforced traditional social spheres for men and women into segmented roles in schools where 'women taught while men managed'. Ozga (1993) had produced a similar thesis in Britain in 1993, but did not have the fine-grained personal histories to support her case study accounts. Reynolds concluded that the low representation of women in the principalship was congruent with social rules for locating women in the 'private sphere' and men in 'public leadership'. Female teachers may have escaped the confines of the domestic hearth only to be constrained in classrooms that continued to imprison them in nurturant traditions. Conversely, men who entered teaching as a profession were promptly promoted from the domesticity of the classroom to public positions of leadership. This was particularly apparent in elementary schools and remains a feature of the principalship in many countries. Schools as social and cultural systems tend to replicate broad social patterns or gender roles.

In Australia, Collard (2003b,c) has demonstrated this gender pattern in government school systems, although the Catholic and independent sectors do not conform to this pattern. Catholic schools have strong traditions of female leadership through religious congregations and, even though there has been a radical decline in the proportions of congregational leaders in Catholic schools since the 1970s, religious orders have fostered the development of female principals. This helps to explain why there is a slightly higher proportion of female than male leaders (51 per cent to 49 per cent) in Victorian Catholic schools. The other explanatory factor is that the majority of Catholic schools in Australia are parochial primary sites and this is somewhat compatible with Reynolds' thesis, for they too can be seen as confined within the nurturant sphere of early childhood education. Blackmore's (1999) thesis that 'emotional labour' in schools is perceived as 'women's work' is also relevant in this regard. We need to ask whether the principalship in primary schools requires more emotional labour than in secondary sites. If this is true, the elevation of women to leadership roles has not necessarily challenged traditional 'rules of control'. The situation in Sweden as described by Davis and Johansson, and by Franzén in this volume provides evidence of this. In the 1990s, Sweden emerged as one of the few countries where the majority of principals were women. However, this outcome has been in part achieved by reclassifying as principals kindergarten directors, the vast majority of whom were female.

Principalship in the independent sector is dominated by men in boys' only and coeducational sites. However, this is not so in girls' schools, where Theobald (1996) has documented the existence of a tradition of strong female leadership, often emanating from the 'cottage industry origins' of such institutions. Some may argue that such women are marginalized within the sector and in the broader schooling landscape. This may be so, and compatible with traditions of gender segmentation in the broader society. However, both the school histories and Collard's (2003b) study of some current women leaders suggest they are anything but compliant with social rules for 'submissive femininity' (Connell 1995). They frequently emerge as strong, passionate educational leaders and there is ample evidence that many do not conform to the essentialist stereotypes propagated by earlier theorists. Indeed, some also emerge as authoritarian, controlling and skilful manipulators of collegial cultures, which subordinate women teachers. Some obviously 'manage like men' in the ways described by Marshall and Rusch (1995) and Wajcman (1998). Others share some of the characteristics of the 'troubling women' who have disturbed educational waters in Australia in recent decades by contesting and resisting patriarchal values and traditions (Blackmore 1999).

Hall's (1996) study of six female principals in England points to a range of familial and cultural factors which equipped her subjects with confident leadership repertoires. Her subjects contested the proposition that masculine institutional and systemic structures deter women from seeking leadership positions. This notion had inspired much of the theory and work of previous authors (Kanter 1977; Shakeshaft 1987; Acker 1989). She also disputed the proposition of Marshall and Rusch (1995) that her subjects 'led like men'. Hall was also the first to acknowledge level of schooling as an influential factor. She noted similarities between female and male headteachers at the primary level, which belie oppositional stereotypes. Collard (2001) found a similar pattern in his broad study of 370 Australian principals. Both authors therefore point to the importance of institutional culture. As Collard has argued previously, primary school cultures and structures may draw both men and women towards values consensus and similar leadership styles. He found even stronger evidence for this in Catholic primary schools, where it appears sectoral culture is a unifying influence (Collard 2003b).

In the Netherlands, Kruger (1996) developed the concepts of 'gender own' and 'gender other' cultures. Kruger was referring to whether the dominant culture in a school can be classified as masculine or feminine. She argued that women find greater difficulty working in masculine regimes, whereas men are more likely to experience stress in feminine regimes. The histories of boys' schools and the critiques of the 'macho myths' they perpetuate in Australia tend to support this view (Edgar 1997). The argument that girls' schools develop cultures and role models which encourage female leadership is a contrasting claim. Collard's research (2003a,c) lends limited support to this thesis. He found that the morale and wellbeing of female principals in independent boys' schools was less robust than for women in other types of schools in the sector. However, he also found convergence between the values of male and female leaders in girls' schools in both the Catholic and independent sectors. The first finding is consistent with what he also discovered in Catholic primary schools and may well be an artefact of the extensive values education this sector conducts for teachers and principals. Independent schools in Australia are not 'systemic' in the same sense as those in the government and Catholic sectors. This therefore suggests another possible interpretation. The men who chose to become principals in girls' schools in either of the non-government sectors may have been attracted by the institutional cultures of the schools themselves. If so, it is natural that their values and leadership styles would be in close harmony with those of female leaders from similar schools.

The more complex findings regarding leadership and gender in the past few years are also consistent with other contemporaneous developments in leadership theory and research (Ribbins 1996, 1999; Pascal and Ribbins 1998). These developments suggest that educational leaders must pay explicit attention to context at three different levels: the macro or societal level, the meso or institutional level, and the micro or individual level. They reflect a more comprehensive theoretical and research framework than that which characterized previous research in the field. Indeed, they comprehend and embrace the variables identified by Reynolds (2002a) and Kruger (1996). Ribbins' work also draws attention to institutional histories and cultures that exert a strong influence upon those who gain leadership positions. The class and ethnicity dimensions of particular schools and leaders (see Merchant and Battiste, this volume) are also identified as important factors.

Future directions?

It is clearly time that the essentialist approaches which characterized the first two decades of research into educational leadership and gender be replaced by a more nuanced theory which recognizes the complex range of variables that influence the values and behaviours of male and female leaders. Such theory must also be informed by recent developments in the fields of gender studies, psychology and sociology that have questioned the typologies developed by earlier scholars. The most sophisticated and grounded studies in all four fields clearly indicate that essentialist theories about males and females radically oversimplify complex cultural phenomena. It is apparent that, following Ribbins (1996, 1999), Blackmore, and others in this volume, there are macro social, cultural and political forces at work. At the meso or institutional level, contextual factors such as class, race, organizational history, structural variables and culture all play a part. Then there are the individual histories and experiences of the leaders themselves which all contribute to how they lead. Single-factor theories about leadership and gender have been discredited and training programmes, which rely upon them, need radical revision.

The more sophisticated awareness of the concept of multiple femininities and masculinities that has penetrated our discourse also challenges us to become more precise. We now have a theoretical framework to help us understand what all practitioners in education have known for a long time: all men and all women do not lead in the same way. The diversity among women leaders has been understated. So has that among men, and we need to heed Shakeshaft's (in Collard 1996) comment that American education systems privilege white, middle-class, heterosexual men over other forms of masculinity. It is clear that some groups of men suffer similar barriers to accessing leadership as Kanter defined for women in 1977. Nor can we assume that women in education operate on a level playing-field. Class, race and sexuality can still pose formidable obstacles to women who aspire to lead. So can the existence of dependent children and elders. Darley and Lomax (1995) quote a female headteacher from Britain who commented that the only women who have time to be principals are 'single, divorced, lesbian or nuns'. Shakeshaft (in Collard 1996) points to how the increased representation of women in leadership along the eastern seaboard of the USA has mainly advantaged single and divorced women. The growth in representation has not been matched in areas of rural America where 'rules of control' operate to protect leadership positions as male preserves.

Darley and Lomax (1995) have suggested that the role of headteachers in Britain may no longer be a one-person job. They point to the difficulties men with dependants experience as they attempt to juggle personal and professional responsibilities. Collard's (2003c) study into principal wellbeing found echoes of this concern among Australian men. Many, especially those from Catholic and independent sectors, complained of the impossibility of 'balancing' the demands upon them. This clearly prompts us to reconsider whether the concept of the single, formal leader has outlived its usefulness and that more creative structures need to be developed for a role that has become increasingly complex (see Court, this volume).

The complexity of the interactions between gender and culture also challenges us to develop more sophisticated concepts of culture than the reductionist definitions, which dominate the discourse. Clearly, 'the way we do things around here' (Caldwell and Spinks 1988, 1998) is limited to what has been identified as the 'manifest level of organisational culture': the patterns of language, behaviour, symbols and rituals (Lundberg 1988). Stereotyped lists of cultural characteristics of the type popularized by Hofstede (1980) in the corporate sector, or the cross-cultural perspectives currently penetrating the educational discourse (Walker and Dimmock 2000) do not comprehend all the forces at work. More sophisticated and fine-grained approaches to research questions are also needed if we are to adequately explain differences within gender groups. As we move towards gaining deeper insights about leadership and gender we will also inevitably be drawn towards enriched understandings of culture regarding such elements as race, class and sexuality. There is an interactive dialogue where various levels of beliefs, cultures, histories and even organizational pathologies influence male and female leaders. It is indeed time for new research that recognizes the diversity of this terrain.

Note

1. An earlier version of this chapter was published in *Leading and Managing* (2002), 8(2): 110–122, and is published here with permission.

References

Acker, S. (1989) *Teachers, Gender and Careers*. New York: Falmer Press.

Acker, S. (1999) *The Realities of Teachers' Work: Never a Dull Moment*. London: Cassell.

Acker, S. (2003) The concerns of Canadian women academics: will faculty shortages make things better or worse? *McGill Journal of Education*, 38: 391–405.

Acker, S. and Armenti, C. (forthcoming) Sleepless in academia. *Gender and Education*, 16: 1.

Acker, S. and Feuerverger, G. (2003) Hearing others and seeing ourselves: empathy and emotions in a study of Canadian academics. *Journal of Curriculum Theorizing*, 19(4): 49–64.

Adler, S., Laney, J. and Packer, M. (1993) *Managing Women: Feminism and Power in Educational Management*. Buckingham: Open University Press.

Albino, J. (1992) Women as leaders: the dirty word they must learn. *Education Digest*, 58(3): 33–36.

Albrecht, L. and Brewer, R.M. (1990) *Bridges of Power*. Philadelphia: New Society Publishers.

Allvesson, M. (1997) Kvinnor och ledarskap—En översikt och problematisering, in A. Nyberg and E. Sundin (eds) *Ledare, makt och kön: rapport till utredningen om fördelningen av ekonomisk makt och ekonomiska resurser mellan kvinnor och män*, pp.154–189. Stockholm: Statens offentliga utredningar.

Angus, L. (1989) 'New' leadership and the possibility of educational reform, in J. Smyth (ed.) *Critical Perspectives on Educational Leadership*, pp. 63–92. London: Falmer Press.

Antonucci, T. (1980) The need for female role models in education, in S.K. Biklen and M.B. Brannigan (eds) *Women and Educational Leadership*, pp. 185–192. Lexington, MA: Lexington Books.

Apple, M. (1998) How the conservative restoration is justified: leadership and subordination in educational policy. *International Journal of Leadership in Education*, 1(1): 3–17.

Apple, M. (2000) Between neoliberalism and neoconservatism: education and conservatism in the global context, in N. Burbules and C. Torres (eds) *Globalization and Education: Critical Perspectives*, pp. 57–78. New York: Routledge.

Arendt, H. (1969) *On Violence*. New York: Harcourt, Brace, Jovanovich.

Arendt, H. (1972) *Crises of the Republic: Lying in Politics, Civil Disobedience or Violence, Thoughts on Politics, and Revolution*. New York: Harcourt, Brace, Jovanovich.

AUCC (Association of Universities and Colleges of Canada) (2002) *Trends in Higher Education*. Ottawa: AUCC.

Auditor General of Canada (2000) *Indian and Northern Affairs Canada: Elementary and Secondary Education*, Report to the House of Commons, ch. 4. Ottawa: Minister of Public Works and Government Services Canada.

Austin, A.G. (1977) *Australian Education 1788–1900: Church, State and Public #Education in Colonial Australia*. Carlton: Pitman.

Australian Bureau of Statistics (1998) *Census of Population and Housing: Selected Family and Labour Force Characteristics*. Canberra: ABS.

Avolio, B.J. and Bass, B.M. (1988) Transformational leadership, charisma and beyond, in J.G. Hunt, B.R. Baliga, H.P. Dachler and C.A. Schriesheim (eds) *Emerging Leadership Vistas*, pp. 29–49. Lexington, MA: Lexington Books.

Bachrach, P. and Baratz, M.S. (1962) Two faces of power. *American Political Science Review*, 57: 947–952.

Ball, S. (2000) Performativities and fabrications in the education economy: towards the performative society. *Australian Educational Researcher*, 27(2): 1–25.

Barcan, A. (1980) *A History of Australian Education*. Melbourne: Oxford University Press.

Barnett, R. (1997) *Higher Education: A Critical Business*. Buckingham: Open University Press.

Bartol, K.M. (1978) The sex structuring of organizations: a search for possible causes. *Academy of Management Review*, 3(4): 805–815.

Bate, W. (1990) *Light Blue Down Under: The History of Geelong Grammar School*. Melbourne: Oxford University Press.

Bauman, Z. (2001) *The Individualised Society*. Oxford: Polity Press.

Beck, L. (1994) *Reclaiming Administration as a Caring Profession*. New York: Teachers' College Press.

Beck, L. and Murphy, J. (1994) *Understanding the Principalship*. New York: Teachers' College Press.

Belenky, M., Clinchy, B., Goldberger, N. and Tarule, J. (1986) *Women's Ways of Knowing: The Development of Self, Voice and Mind*. New York: Basic Books.

Bem, S.L. (1978) *The Lenses of Gender: Transforming the Debate on Sexual Inequality*. New Haven, CT: Yale University Press.

Bem, S.L. (1993) *The Lenses of Gender*. New Haven, CT: Yale University Press.

Berg, G. (1995) *Skolkultur – nyckeln till skolans utveckling!* Göteborg: Gothia.

Biddulph, S. (1994) *Manhood: An Action Plan for Changing Men's Lives*. Sydney: Finch Publishing.

Biklen, S.K. and Brannigan, M.B. (eds) (1980) *Women and Educational Leadership*. Lexington, MA: Lexington Books.

Bishop, P. (1999) School based trust in Victoria, Australia. *Australian Journal of Education*, 43(3).

Bizzari, J. (1995) Women: role models, mentors and carers. *Educational Horizons*, Spring: 145–152.

Blackmore, J. (1993) In the shadow of men: the historical construction of educational administration as a masculinist enterprise, in J. Blackmore and J. Kenway (eds) *Gender Matters in Educational Administration and Policy: A Feminist Introduction*, pp. 27–47. London: Falmer Press.

Blackmore, J. (1995a) A taste for the feminine in educational leadership. Unpublished paper, School of Education, Deakin University, Melbourne, Australia.

Blackmore, J. (1995b) Breaking out from a masculinist politics of education, in B. Limerick and B. Lingard (eds) *Gender and Changing Educational Management: Second Yearbook of the Australian Council for Educational Administration*, pp. 44–56. Rydalmere: Hodder Education.

Blackmore, J. (1996) Breaking the silence: contributions of feminist theory to educational administration and leadership, in K. Leithwood, J. Chapman, D. Corson, P. Hallinger and A. Hart (eds) *International Handbook of Educational Administration and Leadership*, vol. 2, pp. 157–196. Dordrecht: Kluwer.

Blackmore, J. (1999) *Troubling Women: Feminism, Leadership and Educational Change*. Buckingham: Open University Press.

Blackmore, J. (2002a) Troubling women: the upsides and downsides of leadership and the new managerialism, in C. Reynolds (ed.) *Women and School Leadership: International Perspectives*. Albany, NY: SUNY Press.

Blackmore, J. (2002b) Teacher professional standards, point and counterpoint. *Curriculum Perspectives*, July: 34–35.

Blackmore, J. (2002c) Leadership for socially just schooling: more substance and less style in high-risk, low-trust times? *Journal of School Leadership*, 12: 198–222.

Blackmore (2004a) Leading as emotional management work in high risk times: the counterintuitive impulses of performativity (being seen to be good) and passion (to do good). *Journal of Educational Change*, Special Issue, in press.

Blackmore, J. (2004b) Restructuring educational leadership in changing contexts: a local/global account of restructuring in Australia. *Educational Management and Administration*, Special Issue, in press.

Blackmore, J. and Sachs, J. (2000) Paradoxes of leadership and management in higher education in times of change: some Australian reflections. *International Journal of Leadership in Education*, 3(1): 1–16.

Blackmore, J. and Sachs, J. (2001) Women leaders in the restructured university, in A. Brooks and A. Mackinnon (eds) *Gender and the Restructured University*, pp. 45–66. Buckingham: Open University Press.

Blackmore, J. and Sachs, J. (forthcoming) *Passion and Performativity: Gender, Educational Restructuring and Leadership in Universities, Technical and Further Education, and Schools*. Albany, NY: SUNY Press.

Blackmore, J. and Thorpe, S. (2003) Media/ting change: the role of the print media in educational reform in Victoria. *Australia Journal of Education Policy*, in press.

Blount, J.M. (1996) Manly men and womanly women: deviance, gender role polarization, and the shift in women's school employment 1900–1976. *Harvard Educational Review*, 68(2): 318–339.

Blount, J. (1998) *Destined to Rule the Schools: Women and the Superintendency, 1873–1995*. Albany, NY: SUNY Press.

Bolton, E. (1980) A conceptual analysis of the mentor relationship in the career development of women. *Adult Education*, 30: 195–207.

Boston, J., Martin, J., Pallot, J. and Walsh, P. (1996) *Public Management: The New Zealand Model*. Auckland: Oxford University Press.

Bottery, M. (1992) *The Ethics of Educational Management, Personal, Social and Political Perspectives on School Organization*. Trowbridge: Cassell.

Bottery, M. (1993) The management of schools and citizenship. *Citizenship: The Journal of the Citizenship Foundation*, 3(12): 6–7.

Bottery, M. and Wright, N. (1996) Cooperating in their own de-professionalisation: the 'public' and 'ecological' roles of the teaching profession. *British Journal of Educational Studies*, 1: 82–98.

Bourdieu, P. (1990) *The Logic of Practice*. Stanford, CA: Stanford University Press.

Brennan, M. (1996) Multiple professionalisms for Australian teachers in the information age? Paper presented to AERA, New York.

Brint, S.G. (1995) *In an Age of Experts: The Changing Role of Professionals*. Princeton, NJ: Princeton University Press.

Britzman, D.P. (1997) The tangles of implication. *International Journal of Qualitative Studies in Education*, 10(1): 31–37.

Britzman, D.P. (2000) Precocious education, in S. Talburt and S.R. Steinberg (eds) *Thinking Queer: Sexuality, Culture, and Education*, pp. 33–57. New York: Peter Lang.

Brooks, A. and Mackinnon, A. (eds) (2001) *Gender and the Restructured University*. Buckingham: Open University Press.

Brown, K. and Anfara, V. (2002) The walls of division crumble as ears, mouths, minds and hearts open: a unified profession of middle level administrators and teachers. *International Journal of Leadership in Education*, 5(1): 33–50.

Brunetti, W. (1993) *Achieving Total Quality*. New York: Quality Resources.

Brunner, C.C. (1995) By power defined: women in the superintendency. *Educational Considerations*, 22(2): 21–26.

Brunner, C.C. (1998) The new superintendency supports an innovation: collaborative decision making. *Contemporary Education*, 69(2): 79–82.

Brunner, C. (1999) Power, gender and superintendent selection, in C. Brunner (ed.) *Sacred Dreams: Women and the Superintendency*, pp. 63–78. Albany, NY: SUNY Press.

Brunner, C.C. and Schumaker, P. (1998) Power and gender in 'New View' public schools. *Policy Studies Journal*, 26(1): 30–45.

Burbules, N. and Torres, C. (2000) Globalization and education: an introduction, in N. Burbules and C. Torres (eds) *Globalization and Education: Critical Perspectives*, pp. 1–26. New York: Routledge.

Burns, J.M. (1978) *Leadership*. New York: Harper & Row.

Burren, P.B. (1984) *Mentone: The Place for a School*. South Yarra: Hyland House.

Butler, J. (1990) *Gender Trouble: Feminism and the Subversion of Identity*. New York: Routledge.

Caldwell, B.J. and Haywood, D.K. (1998) *The Future of Schools: Lessons from the Reform of Public Education*. London: Falmer Press.

Caldwell, B.J. and Spinks, J.M. (1988) *The Self-managing School*. London: Falmer Press.

Caldwell, B.J. and Spinks, J.M. (1998) *Beyond the Self-managing School*. London: Falmer Press.

Cantor, D.W. and Bernay, T. (1992) *Women in Power: Secrets of Leadership*. Boston: Houghton Mifflin.

Cardno, C. (1990) *Collaborative Management in New Zealand Schools*. Auckland: Longman.

Carson, A. (1999) Business fails women, says agency. *The Age*, 24 August.

Case, M.A.C. (1995) Disaggregating gender from sex and sexual orientation: the effeminate man in the law and feminist jurisprudence. *Yale Law Journal*, 105: 1–105.

Casey, C. (1995) *Work, Self and Society: After Industrialism*. London: Routledge.

Cavalier, R.P. (2000) *Personal Motivation: A Model for Decision Making*. London: Praeger.

Chauncey, G. (1994) *Gay New York: Gender, Urban Culture, and the Making of the Gay Male World 1890–1940*. New York: Basic Books.

Chisholm, L. (2000) Gender and leadership in South African educational administration. Paper presented to Gender and Education Conference, London Institute of Education, London.

Clarke, J. and Newman, J. (1997) *The Managerial State*. London: Sage.

Clegg, S.R. (1989) *Frameworks of Power*. London: Sage.

Clifford, G. (1989) Man/woman teacher: gender/family and a career in American educational history, in D. Warren (ed.) *American Teachers: Histories of a Profession at Work*, pp. 293–343. New York: Macmillan.

Cohen, S.S. (1989) *Tender Power: A Revolutionary Approach to Work and Intimacy*. Reading, MA: Addison-Wesley.

Coleman, M. (1996) Barriers to career progress for women in education: the perceptions of female headteachers. *Educational Research*, 9(3): 317–332.

Coleman, M. (1998) The management style of female headteachers. *Educational Management and Administration*, 24(2): 163–174.

Collard, J. (1996) Leadership and gender: an interview with Carol Shakeshaft. *Leading and Managing*, 2(1): 70–75.

Collard, J. (2001) Leadership and gender: an Australian perspective. *Educational Management and Administration*, 29(3): 343–355.

Collard, J. (2003a) The relationship of gender and context to leadership in

Australian schools, in P. Begley and O. Johansson (eds) *The Ethical Dimensions of School Leadership*, pp. 181–199. London: Kluwer.

Collard, J. (2003b) Principal beliefs: the interface of gender and sector. *Alberta Journal of Educational Research*, XLIX, (1): 37–54.

Collard, J. (2003c) Principal well-being in complex times. *International Journal of Educational Administration*, 31(1): 2–14.

Collard, J. (2004) Delta: Policy and Practice in Education (forthcoming).

Collinson, D. and Hearn, J. (1996) Breaking the silence on men: masculinities and managements, in D. Collinson and J. Hearn (eds) *Men as Managers, Managers as Men: Critical Perspectives on Men, Masculinities and Management*. London: Sage.

Colwill, N.L. (1995) Women in management: power and powerlessness, in S. Vinnicombe and N.L. Colwill (eds) *The Essence of Women in Management*, pp. 20–34. London: Prentice Hall.

Connell, R.W. (1987) *Gender and Power: Society, the Person and Sexual Politics*. Cambridge: Polity Press.

Connell, R.W. (1990) Gender, state and politics: theory and appraisal. *Theory and Society*, 19: 507–544.

Connell, R.W. (1995) *Masculinities*. St Leonards, NSW: Allen & Unwin.

Connell, R.W. (1998) Masculinities and globalisation. *Men and Masculinities*, 1(1): 3–23.

Cooper, J. and Stevens, D. (2002) The journey toward tenure, in J. Cooper and D. Stevens (eds) *Tenure in the Sacred Grove: Issues and Strategies for Women and Minority Faculty*, pp. 3–16. Albany, NY: SUNY Press.

Corson, D. (2002) Teaching and learning for market-utility. *International Journal of Leadership in Education*, 5(1): 1–14.

Court, M.R. (1995) Young and feminist: negotiating 'identities' in the 1990s. Unpublished MA thesis, Massey University.

Court, M.R. (1998) Women challenging managerialism: devolution dilemmas in the establishment of co-principalships in primary schools in Aotearoa/New Zealand. *School Leadership and Management*, 18(1): 35–57.

Court, M.R. (2001) Sharing school leadership: narratives of discourse and power. Unpublished doctoral dissertation, Massey University.

Court, M.R. (2002) Negotiating and reconstructing gendered leadership discourses. *Leading and Managing*, 8(2): 110–122.

Court, M.R. (forthcoming) Using narrative and discourse analysis in researching co-principalships. *International Journal of Qualitative Studies in Education*.

Cox, E. (1998) Measuring social capital as part of progress and well being, in R. Eckersley (ed.) *Measuring Progress: Is Life Getting Better?* Collingwood: CSIRO Publishing.

Craib, I. (1987) Masculinity and male dominance. *Sociological Review*, 34: 721–743.

Crow, G.M. and Pounders, M. L. (1995) Organizational socialization of new urban principals: variations of ethnicity and gender. Paper presented to the AERA Conference, San Francisco.

Cubillo, L. and Brown, M. (2003) Women into educational leadership and management: international differences? *Journal of Educational Administration*, 41(3): 279–291.

Curriculum Corporation (1996) *Victorian Schools Database*. Carlton: Curriculum Corporation.

Currie, J. and Newson, J. (eds) (1998) *Universities and Globalization: Critical Perspectives*. London: Sage.

Currie, J. and Thiele, B. (2001) Globalization and gendered work cultures in universities, in A. Brooks and A. Mackinnon (eds), *Gender and the Restructured University*, pp. 90–116. Buckingham: Open University Press.

Currie, J., Harris, T. and Thiele, B. (2002) *Gendered Universities in Globalized Economies*. Lanham, MD: Lexington.

Currie, J., Harris, T. and Thiele, B. (2003) Gendered universities in globalized economies: changing the organization. Unpublished paper, Murdoch University, Perth.

Curry, B. (2002) The caged bird sings: on being different and the role of advocacy, in J. Cooper and D. Stevens (eds) *Tenure in the Sacred Grove: Issues and Strategies for Women and Minority Faculty*, pp. 117–126. Albany, NY: SUNY Press.

Dahl, R. (1961) *Who Governs?* New Haven, CT: Yale University Press.

Daly, M. (1979) *Gyn/Ecology*. Boston: Beacon Books.

Darley, J. and Lomax, P. (1995) The continuing role of women as primary school headteachers in the transformed British school system. Paper presented to the AERA Conference, San Francisco.

Darwin, A. (2000) Critical reflections on mentoring in work settings. *Adult Education Quarterly*, 50(3): 197–211.

David, M. and Woodward, D. (eds) (1998) *Negotiating the Glass Ceiling: Careers of Senior Women in the Academic World*. London: Falmer Press.

Davies, B. (1989) *Frogs and Snails and Feminist Tales: Preschool Children and Gender*. Sydney: Allen & Unwin.

Davies, B. (1993) *Shards of Glass: Children Reading and Writing beyond Gendered Identities*. St Leonards, NSW: Allen & Unwin.

Davies, B. (1997) The subject of poststructuralism: a reply to Alison Jones, *Gender and Education*, 9(3): 271–283.

De Castell, S. and Bryson, M. (1998) From the ridiculous to the sublime: on finding oneself in educational research, in W.F. Pinar (ed.) *Queer Theory in Education*, pp. 245–250. Mahwah, NJ: Lawrence Erlbaum Associates.

Deem, R. and Ozga, J. (1997) Women managing for diversity in a postmodern world, in C. Marshall (ed.) *Feminist Critical Policy Analysis: A Perspective from Post-secondary Education*. London: Falmer Press.

Deetz, S. (1992) *Democracy in the Age of the Corporate Colonization*. Albany, NY: SUNY Press.

Dempster, N., Freakley, M. and Pary, L. (2001) The ethical climate of public schooling under new public management. *International Journal of Leadership in Education*, 4(1): 1–13.

Denzin, N.K. (1997) *Interpretive Ethnography: Ethnographic Practices for the 21st Century.* Thousand Oaks, CA: Sage.

Department of Education (1984) *Management and Administration.* Wellington: Department of Education.

Department of Education (1988a) *Administering for Excellence: Effective Administration in Education* (Picot Report). Wellington: Government Printer.

Department of Education (1988b) *Tomorrow's Schools: The Reform of Education Administration in New Zealand.* Wellington: Government Printer.

DEST (Department of Education, Science and Training) (2003) *Higher Education Staff Statistics.* Canberra: DEST. www.dest.gov.au/highered/statistics/staff/03 (accessed 8 December 2003).

Didion, C. (1995) Mentoring women in science. *Educational Horizons*, Spring: 141–144.

Dillabough, J-A. and Acker, S. (2002) Globalization, women's work and teacher education: a cross-national analysis. *International Studies in Sociology of Education*, 12(3): 227–260.

Donaldson, M. (1993) What is hegemonic masculinity? *Theory and Society*, 22(5): 643–658.

Donmoyer, R. (1995) A knowledge base for educational administration: notes from the field, in R. Donmoyer, M. Imber and J. Scheurich (eds) *The Knowledge Base in Educational Administration. Multiple Perspectives.* Albany, NY: SUNY Press.

Doyle Walton, K. (ed.) (1996) *Against the Tide: Career Paths of Women Leaders in American and British Higher Education.* Bloomington, IN: Phi Delta Kappa.

Du Gay, P. (1996) Organising identity: entrepreneurial governance and public management, in S. Hall and P. Du Gay (eds) *Questions of Identity.* London: Sage.

Due Billing, Y. (1997) Är ledarskap manligt, kvinnligt eller något annat?, in A. Nyberg and E. Sundin (eds) *Ledare, makt och kön: rapport till utredningen om fördelningen av ekonomisk makt och ekonomiska resurser mellan kvinnor och män*, pp. 135–153. Stockholm: Statens offentliga utredningar.

Duke, D., Grogan, M., Tucker, P. and Heinecke, W. (eds) (2003) *Educational Leadership in an Age of Accountability.* Albany, NY: SUNY Press.

Dunlap, D.M. and Goldman, P. (1991) Rethinking power in schools. *Educational Administration Quarterly*, 27(1): 5–29.

Eagly, A.H. and Johnson, B.T. (1990) Gender and leadership style: a meta-analysis. *Psychological Bulletin*, 108(2): 233–256.

Eagly, A.H., Karau, S.J. and Johnson, B.T. (1992) Gender and leadership style among school principals: a meta-analysis. *Educational Administration Quarterly*, 28(1): 76–102.

Edgar, D. (1997) *Men, Mateship, Marriage: Exploring Macho Myths and the Way Forward*. Sydney: Harper Collins.

Edson, S. (1988) *Pushing the Limits: The Female Administrative Aspirant*. Albany, NY: SUNY Press.

Eggins, H. (ed.) (1997) *Women as Leaders and Managers in Higher Education*. Buckingham: Open University Press.

Ehrich, L. (1995) Professional mentorship for women educators in government schools. *Journal of Educational Administration*, 33(3): 27–33.

Eisler, E.W. (1995) From domination to partnership: the hidden subject for organizational change. *Training and Development*, February: 32–39.

Eisner, E. and Powell, K. (2002) Art in science? *Curriculum Inquiry*, 32(2): 131–160.

Ekholm, M., Blossing, U., Kåräng, G., Lindvall, K. and Scherp, H-Å. (2000) *Forskning om rektor – en forskningsöversikt*. Stockholm: Skolverket, Liber.

Emmet, D. (1954) The concept of power. *Proceedings of the Aristotelian society*, 54: 1–26, reprinted in J. R. Champlin (ed.) *Power*. New York: Atherton Press.

Enfield, Justice Marcus (1997) The New International Order: the human dimension. *Background Briefing*, Radio National, Sunday Oct 12.

Enomoto, E., Gardiner, M. and Grogan, M. (2000) Notes to Athene: mentoring relationships for women of color. *Urban Education*, 35(5): 567–583.

Equal Opportunities Commission (2001) *Women and Men in Britain: professional occupations*. Manchester: EOC. *www.oec.org.uk/cseng/research/wm_professional_occupations.pdf*. (Retrieved 30 March, 2003).

Etzioni, A. A. (1961) *A comparative analysis of complex organizations*. New York: Macmillan.

Eveline, J. (2000) Sex matters: a case of gender and authority in Australian university leadership. Paper presented at the European conference on Gender and Higher Education, Eidgenossische Technische Hochschule, Zurich, September 12–15.

Evers, C.W. and Lakomski, G. (1991) *Knowing Educational Administration: Contemporary Methodological Controversies in Educational Administration*. Oxford: Pergamon.

Evers, C.W. and Lakomski, G. (1996a) Postpositivist conceptions of science in educational administration: an introduction. *Educational Administration Quarterly*, 32(3): 341–343.

Evers, C.W. and Lakomski, G. (1996b) Science in educational administration: an introduction. *Educational Administration Quarterly*, 32(3): 379–402.

Evers, C.W. and Lakomski, G. (1996c) *Exploring Educational Administration: Coherentist Applications and Critical Debates*. Oxford: Pergamon.

Evetts, J. (1994) *Becoming a Secondary Head Teacher*. London: Cassell.

Fagenson, E.A. (1993) *Women in Management: Trends, Issues, and Challenges in Managerial Diversity*. Thousand Oaks, CA: Sage.

Fahlgren, S. (1998) *Diskursanalys, kunskap och kön*. Umeå: Institutionen för socialt arbete, Umeå universitët.

Fairclough, N. (1995) *Critical Discourse Analysis*. London: Longman.

Farrell, W. (1993) *The Liberated Man*. Berkeley, CA: Berkeley Publishing Group.

Fazzaro, C. and Walter, J. (2002) Schools for democracy: Lyotard, dissensus and education policy. *International Journal of Leadership in Education*, 5(1): 15–32.

Fennell, A.H. (1999) Power in the principalship four women's experiences. *Journal of Educational Administration*, 37(1): 23–49.

Ferguson, K.E. (1984) *The Feminist Case against Bureaucracy*. Philadelphia: Temple University Press.

Fielding, M. (1999) Radical collegiality: affirming teaching as an inclusive professional practice. *Australian Educational Researcher*, 26(2): 1–34.

Firestone, S. (1971) *The Dialectic of Sex: A Case for Feminist Revolution*. New York: Bantam Books.

Fitzpatrick, K. (1975) *PLC Melbourne: The First Century*. Burwood: PLC.

Fogarty, R., f.m.s. (1957) *Catholic Education in Australia 1806–1950*, vols 1–2. London: Melbourne University Press.

Fogelberg, P., Hearn, J., Husu, L. and Mankkinen, T. (eds) (1999) *Hard Work in the Academy*. Helsinki: Helsinki University Press.

Follet, M.P. (1924) *Creative Experience*. New York: Longmans, Green & Co.

Ford, P. (1997) Gender difference in leadership style: does it make a difference?, in C. Connors and T. d'Arbon (eds) *Change, Challenge and Creative Leadership: International Perspectives on Research and Practice*, pp. 224–235. Hawthorn: ACEA.

Forslund Söderberg, M. (2001) *Kvinnor och skolledarskap*. Stockholm: Skolverket, Liber.

Foster, W. (1989) Towards a critical practice of leadership, in J. Smyth (ed.) *Critical Perspectives on Educational Leadership*, pp. 39–62. London: Falmer Press.

Foster, M. (1999) Race, class, and gender in education research: Surveying the political terrain. *Educational Policy*, 13(1): 77–85.

Foucault, M. (1977) *Discipline and Punish: The Birth of the Prison*. New York: Pantheon Books.

Foucault, M. (1980a) *Power/Knowledge: Selected Interviews and Other Writings 1972–1977*. London: Harvester Wheatsheaf.

Foucault, M. (1980b) Truth and Power, in C. Gordon (ed.) *Power/Knowledge: Selected Interviews and Other Writings 1972–1977*. New York: Pantheon Books.

Franke, K.M. (1995) The central mistake of sex discrimination law: the disaggregation of sex from gender. *University of Pennsylvania Law Review*, 144: 1137–1182.

Franzén, K. (1998) *Finns det skillnader mellan maligt och kvinnligt skolledarskap*. Uppsats, p. 852. Samhällsvetenskapliga Institutionen, Karlstad universitet.

Fraser, N. (1997) *Justice Interruptus: Critical Reflections on the 'Postsocialist' Condition*. New York: Routledge.

Fraynd, D. and Capper, C.A. (2003) 'Do you have any idea who you just hired?!?' A study of open and closeted sexual minority K-12 administrators. *Journal of School Leadership*, 13(1): 86–124.

Frazer, E. and Lacey, N. (1993) *The Politics of Community: A Feminist Critique of the Liberal–Communitarian Debate*. New York: Harvester Wheatsheaf.

Freeman, E. (1999) Community as incentive in the formation of charter schools. Paper presented to the AERA Conference, Montreal.

French, R.P. Jr and Raven, B. (1979) The bases of social power, in D. Cartwright (ed.), *Studies in Social Power*. Ann Arbor, MI: Institute for Social Research.

Gamble, L. (1982) *St Bede's College and its McCristal Origins*. Burwood: Brown, Prior, Anderson.

Garber, M. (1992) *Vested Interests: Cross-dressing and Cultural Anxiety*. London: Routledge.

Gardiner, L. (1977) *Tintern School and Anglican Girls' Education 1877–1977*. East Ringwood: Tintern CEGGS.

Gardiner, M., Enomoto, E. and Grogan, M. (2000) *Coloring Outside the Lines: Mentoring Women into School Leadership*. Albany, NY: SUNY Press.

Gee, J. and Lankshear, C. (1995) *The New Work Order*. Sydney: Allen & Unwin.

Gewirtz, S. (1998) Conceptualising social justice in education: mapping the territory. *Journal of Education Policy*, 13(4): 469–484.

Gilligan, C. (1982) *In a Different Voice: Psychological Theory and Women's Development*. Cambridge, MA: Harvard University Press.

Glass, T., Bjork, L. and Brunner, C.C. (2000) *The Study of the American School Superintendency, 2000*. Arlington, VA: American Association of School Administrators.

Gleeson, D. and Husbands, C. (2001) *The Performing School: Managing Teaching and Learning in a Performance Culture*. London: Routledge.

Goleman, D. (1995) *Emotional Intelligence*. New York: Bantam Books.

Gray, H.L. (1989) Gender considerations in school management: masculine and feminine leadership styles, in C. Riches and C. Morgan (eds) *Human Resource Management in Education*. Buckingham: Open University Press.

Greenberg, J.A. (1999) Defining male and female: intersexuality and the collision between law and biology. *Arizona Law Review*, 41: 265–327.

Greenberg, J.A. (2000) When is a man a man, and when is a woman a woman? *Florida Law Review*, 52: 745–768.

Greenfield, T. (1975) Theory about organization: a new perspective and its implications for schools, in M. Hughes (ed.) *Administering Education: International Challenge*. London: Athlone Press.

Grimshaw, J. (1993) Practices of freedom, in C. Ramazanoglu (ed.) *Up Against Foucault*, pp. 51–72. London: Routledge.

Grogan, M. (1996) *Voices of Women Aspiring to the Superintendency*. Albany, NY: SUNY Press.

Grogan, M. (2000) Laying the groundwork for the reconception of the superintendency from feminist postmodern perspectives. *Educational Administration Quarterly*, 36(1): 117–142.

Gronn, P. (1995) Greatness re-visited: the current obsession with transformational leadership. *Leading and Managing*, 1(1): 1–11.

Gronn, P. (2000) Distributed properties. a new architecture of leadership. *Educational Management and Administration*, 28(3): 317–338.

Gupton, S. and Slick, G. (1996) *Highly Successful Women Administrators: The Inside Stories of How They Got There*. Thousand Oaks, CA: Corwin Press.

Habermas, J. (1986) *Legitimation Crisis*. Boston: Beacon Press.

Hall, V. (1996) *Dancing on the Ceiling: A Study of Women Managers in Education*. London: Paul Chapman.

Halpin, A.W. (1959) *The Leadership Behaviour of School Superintendents*. Chicago: Midwest Administration Centre, University of Chicago.

Handy, C. (1992) The language of leadership, in M. Syrett and C. Hogg (eds) *Frontiers of Leadership: An Essential Reader*, pp. 7–12. Cambridge: Cambridge University Press.

Hanlon, G. (1998) Professionalism as enterprise: service class politics and the re-definition of professionalism. *Sociology*, 32(1): 1–13.

Hansen, I.V. (1986) *By Their Deeds: A Centenary History of Camberwell Grammar School. 1886–1996*. Camberwell, Melbourne: Camberwell Grammar School.

Harding, S. (1998) Multiculturalism, postcolonialism, feminism: do they require new research epistemologies? *Australian Educational Researcher*, 25(1): 37–51.

Hargreaves, A. (1999) Fielding errors? Deepening the debate about teacher collaboration and collegiality. *Australian Educational Researcher*, 26(2): 45–53.

Hargreaves, A. (2003) *Teaching in the Knowledge Society: Education in an Age of Insecurity*. Buckingham: Open University Press.

Harstock, N. (1981) Political change: two perspectives on power, in C. Bunch (ed.) *Building Feminist Theory: Essays from Quest*. New York: Longman.

Harstock, N. (1983) *Money, Sex and Power: Towards a Feminist Historical Materialism*. New York: Longman.

Harstock, N. (1987) Foucault on power: a theory for women?, in L. Nicholson (ed.) *Feminism/Postmodernism*, pp. 157–175. London: Routledge.

Hearn, J. (1993) *Men in the Public Eye: The Construction and Deconstruction of Public Men and Public Patriarchies*. London: Routledge.

Hearn, J. (2001) Academia, management and men: making the connections, in A. Brooks and A. Mackinnon (eds) *Gender and the Restructured University*, pp. 69–89. Buckingham: Open University Press.

Helgeson, S. (1991) *The Female Advantage: Women's Ways of Leadership*. New York: Doubleday.

Hemphill, J.K. (1961) Why people attempt to lead, in L. Petrullo and B.M. Bass (eds) *Leadership and Interpersonal Behaviour*. New York: Holt, Rinehart & Winston.

Henkel, M. (1999) The modernisation of research evaluation: the case of the UK. *Higher Education*, 38: 105–122.

Hennessy, R. (1993) *Materialist Feminism and the Politics of Discourse*. New York: Routledge.

Henry, M., Lingard, B., Rizvi, F. and Taylor, S. (2001) *The OECD, Globalisation and Policy Making in Education*. Oxford: Pergamon.

Heward, C. (1994) Academic snakes and merit ladders: reconceptualising the 'glass ceiling'. *Gender and Education*, 6(3): 249–262.

Hibert, K. (2000) Mentoring leadership. *Phi Delta Kappa*, 82(1): 16–18.

Hirdman, Y. (1990) Genussystemet, in *SOU*: 44–76.

Hofstede, G.F. (1980) *Cultures Consequences: International Differences in Work-related Values*. Beverly Hills, CA: Sage.

Holmquist, C. (1997) Den ömma bödeln – Kvinnliga ledare i åtstramningstider, in E. Sundin (ed.) *Om makt och kön – i spåren av offentliga organisationers omvandling. Rapport till utredningen om fördelningen av ekonomisk makt och ekonomiska resurser mellan kvinnor och män 1997*, pp. 147–177. Stockholm: Statens offentliga utredningar.

Horner, A. and Keane, A. (eds) (2000) *Body Matters. Feminism, Textuality, Corporeality*. Manchester: Manchester University Press.

Hoy, W.K. (1996) Science and theory in the practice of educational administration: a pragmatic perspective. *Educational Administration Quarterly*, 32(3): 366–378.

Hoy, W.K. and Miskel, C.G. (1991) *Educational Administration: Theory, Research and Practice*. New York: Random House.

Hudson, L. and Jacot, B. (1991) *The Way Men Think: Intellect, Intimacy and the Erotic Imagination*. New Haven, CT: Yale University Press.

Human Rights Watch (2001) *Hatred in the Hallways: Violence and Discrimination against Lesbian, Gay, Bisexual, and Transgender Students in US Schools*. New York: Human Rights Watch.

Hunter, F. (1953) *Community Power Structure: A Study of Decision-makers*. Chapel Hill, NC: University of North Carolina Press.

Hurty, K.S. (1995) Women principals: leading with power, in D.M. Dunlap and P.A. Schmuck (eds) *Women Leading in Education*, pp. 380–406. Albany, NY: SUNY Press.

Inayatullah, S. and Gidley, J. (eds) (2000) *The University in Transformation: Global Perspectives on the Future of the University*. Westport, CT: Bergin & Garvey.

Isaac, J. (1993) Beyond the three faces of power: a realist critique, in T. Wartenberg (ed.) *Rethinking Power*. Albany, NY: SUNY Press.

James, B. and Saville-Smith, K. (1989) *Gender, Culture and Society*. Auckland: Oxford University Press.

Johansson, O. (2000) Om rektors demokratiskt reflekterande ledarskap, in L. Lundberg (ed.) *Görandets lov – Lov att göra. Skrifter från Centrum för skolledarutveckling*, vol. 1, pp. 149–177. Umeå: Umeå universitet.

Johansson, O. (2001) Swedish school leadership in transition: in search of a democratic, learning and communicative leadership? *Pedagogy, Culture and Society*, 9(3): 387–406.

Johansson, O., Moos, L. and Möller, J. (2000) A Scandinavian perspective on the culture of educational leadership. Paper presented to the AERA Conference, New Orleans.

Johnson, N.A. and Holdaway, E.A. (1991) Perceptions of effectiveness and the satisfaction of principals in elementary schools. *Journal of Educational Administration*, 29(1): 51–70.

Johnsrud, L. (1991) Mentoring between academic women: the capacity for interdependence. *Initiatives*, 54(3): 7–17.

Jones, K.B. (1993) *Compassionate Authority: Democracy and the Representation of Women*. New York: Routledge.

Jones, A. and Guy, C. (1992) Radical feminism in New Zealand: from Piha to Newtown, in R. Du Plessis, K. Irwin, A. Laurie and S. Middleton (eds) *Feminist Voices: Women's Studies Texts for Aotearoa/New Zealand*, pp. 300–316. Auckland: Oxford University Press.

Juran, J.M. (1995) *Managerial Breakthrough*. New York: McGraw-Hill.

Kanter, R.M. (1977) *Men and Women of the Corporation*. New York: Basic Books.

Kanter, R.M. (1979) Power, leadership, and participatory management. *Theory into Practice*, 20(4): 219–224.

Kanter, R.M. (1989) *When Giants Learn to Dance: Mastering the Challenges of Strategy Management and Careers in the 1990s*. New York: Simon & Schuster.

Kelly, R.M. and Duerst-Lathi, G. (1995) The study of gender power and its link to governance and leadership, in R.M. Kelly and G. Duerst-Lathi (eds) *Gender Power, Leadership and Governance*, pp. 7–27. Ann Arbor: University of Michigan Press.

Kemmis, S. and Carr, W. (1984) *Becoming Critical. Education, Knowledge and Action Research*. Geelong: Deakin University Press.

Kenway, J. (1990) *Gender and Education Policy: A Call for New Directions*. Geelong: Deakin University Press.

Kerfoot, D. and Knights, D. (1996) The best is yet to come: the quest for embodiment in managerial work, in D. Collinson and J. Hearn (eds) *Men as Managers, Managers as Men: Critical Perspectives on Men, Masculinities and Management*. London: Sage.

Kinnear, M. (1995) *In Subordination: Professional Women, 1870–1970*. Montreal: McGill/Queen's University Press.

Kirkpatrick, J.J. (1974) *Political Woman*. New York: Basic Books.

Kohlberg, L. (1980) *Essays on Moral Development*. New York: Harper & Row.

Kolodny, A. (1998) *Failing the Future: A Dean looks at Higher Education in the Twenty-first Century*. Durham, NC: Duke University Press.

Kowalski, T. (1999) *The School Superintendent*. Upper Saddle River, NJ: Merrill.

Kruger, M.L. (1996) Gender issues in school headship: quality versus power? *European Journal of Education*, 31(4): 447–461.

Kulick, D. (1987) *Från kön till genus: kvinnligt och manligt I ett kulturellt perspektiv.* Stockholm: Carlssons.

Kvale, S. (1996) *InterViews: An Introduction to Qualitative Research Interviewing.* London: Sage.

Lacey, K. (2002) *Principal Class Leadership Aspirations.* Melbourne: Victorian Department of Education and Training.

Laclau, E. and Mouffe, C. (1985) *Hegemony and Socialist Strategy: Towards a Radical Democratic Politics.* London: Verso.

Lasswell, H.D. and Kaplan, A. (1950) *Power and Society.* New Haven, CT: Yale University Press.

Lather, P. (1993) Fertile obsession: validity after poststructuralism. *Sociological Quarterly,* 34(4): 673–693.

Lenztaguchi, H. (2000) *Emancipation och motstånd.* Stockholm: HLS förlag.

Leonard, R. (1995) *Beloved Daughters: 100 Years of Papal Teaching on Women.* Ringwood: David Lovell Publishing.

Lieberman, A., Falk, B. and Alexander, L. (1990) A culture in the making: leadership in learner-centered schools, in A. Lieberman (ed.) *Schools as Collaborative Cultures: Creating the Future Now.* New York: Falmer Press.

Limerick, B. (1995) Accommodated careers: gendered career paths in education, in B. Limerick and B. Lingard (eds) *Gender and Changing Educational Management: Second Yearbook of the Australian Council for Educational Administration,* pp. 68–78. Rydalmere: Hodder Education.

Limerick, B. and Anderson, C. (1999) Female administrators and school-based management. *Educational Management and Administration,* 27(4): 401–414.

Lindsay, J. (1967) *Picnic at Hanging Rock.* Harmondsworth: Penguin.

Lindvall, K. and Ekholm, M. (1997) Tillsättning av skolledare – rörelser i tiden. *Forskningsrapport,* p. 12. Samhällsvetenskap: Högskolan i Karlstad.

Lindvert, J. (1997) Förändrad skolorganisation – makt och möjligheter, in E. Sundin (ed.) *Om makt och kön – i spåren av offentliga organisationers omvandling: rapport till utredningen om fördelningen av ekonomisk makt och ekonomiska resurser mellan kvinnor och män,* pp. 178–206. Stockholm: Statens offentliga utredningar, Arbetsmarknadsdepartementet.

Lingard, B. (2003) Where to in gender policy in education after recuperative masculinity politics? *International Journal of Inclusive Education,* 7(1): 33–56.

Lingard, B. and Douglas, P. (1999) *Men Engaging Feminisms: Pro-feminisms, Backlashes and Schooling.* Buckingham: Open University Press.

Lingard, B., Hayes, D., Mills, M. and Christie, P. (2003) *Leading Learning.* Buckingham: Open University Press.

Little, J.W. (1999) Colleagues of choice, colleagues of circumstances. *Australian Educational Researcher,* 26(2): 35–44.

Loden, M. (1985) *Feminine Leadership, Or, How to Succeed in Business Without Being One of the Boys.* New York: Times Books.

Louis, K.S., Seppanen, P., Smylie, M. and Jones, L. (2000) The role of unions as leaders for school change, in K. Riley and K. Seashore Louis (eds) *Leadership for Change and School Reform: International Perspectives*. London: Routledge.

Lorber, J. (1994) *Paradoxes of Gender*. New Haven, CT: Yale University Press.

Lugg, C.A. (2003) Sissies, faggots, lezzies, and dykes: gender, sexual orientation, and a new politics of education? *Educational Administration Quarterly*, 39(1): 93–134.

Luhmann, S. (1998) Queering/querying pedagogy? Or, pedagogy is a pretty queer thing, in W.F. Pinar (ed.) *Queer Theory in Education*, pp. 141–155. Mahwah, NJ: Lawrence Erlbaum Associates.

Luke, C. (2001) *Globalization and Women in Academia*. Mahwah, NJ: Lawrence Erlbaum Associates.

Lukes, S. (1974) *Power: A Radical View*. London: Macmillan.

Lundberg, C.C. (1988) Working with culture. *Journal of Organizational Change Management*, 1(2): 38–47.

Mac an Ghaill (1994) *The Making of Men: Masculinities, Sexualities and Schooling*. Buckingham: Open University Press.

McConville, C. (1993) *St Kevin's College 1918–1993*. Carlton: Melbourne University Press.

McDonough, P. (2002) Resisting common injustice: tenure politics, department politics, gay and lesbian politics, in J. Cooper and D. Stevens (eds) *Tenure in the Sacred Grove: Issues and Strategies for Women and Minority Faculty*, pp. 127–143. Albany, NY: SUNY Press.

MacInnes, J. (1998) *The End of Masculinity: The Confusion of Sexual Genesis and Sexual Difference in Modern Society*. Buckingham: Open University Press.

Mackay, H. (1997) *Three Generations: Baby Boomers, their Parents and their Children*. Sydney: Macmillan.

Macpherson, R. (1998) *The Politics of Accountability: Educative and International Perspectives*. Thousand Oaks, CA: Corwin Press.

Mahony, P. and Hextall, I. (1997) Problems of accountability in reinvented government: a case study of the Teacher Training Agency. *Journal of Education Policy*, 12(3): 267–283.

Mant, A. (1997) *Intelligent Leadership*. Sydney: Allen & Unwin.

Marginson, S. (2000) Rethinking academic work in the global era. *Journal of Higher Education Policy and Management*, 22(1): 23–35.

Marginson, S. and Considine, M. (2000) *The Enterprise University: Power, Governance and Reinvention in Australia*. Cambridge: Cambridge University Press.

Marshall, C. and Rusch, E. (1995) Gender filters in the deputy principalship, in B. Limerick and B. Lingard (eds) *Gender and Changing Educational Management: Second Yearbook of the Australian Council for Educational Administration*, pp. 79–93. Rydalmere: Hodder Education.

Martin, F. (1986) Catholic education in Victoria 1963–1980, in Catholic Education (ed.) *Catholic Education in Victoria: Yesterday, Today and Tomorrow*. Maryborough: Hedges & Bell.

Martin, J.R. (2000) *Coming of Age in Academe*. New York, Routledge.

Maslow, A.H. (1968) *Towards A Psychology of Being*. New York: Van Nostrand.

MCEETYA (Ministerial Council of Employment, Education, Training and Youth Affairs) (2003a) *The Demand and Supply of Primary and Secondary Teachers in Australia*. Canberra: CGPS.

MCEETYA (Ministerial Council of Employment, Education, Training and Youth Affairs) (2003b) *Task Force on Leadership and Teaching Quality 2003: Review of Teaching and Teacher Education*. Canberra: CGPS.

Menter, I., Muschamo, Y., Nicholls, P., Ozga, J. and Pollard, A. (1996) *Work and Identity in the Primary School: A Post-Fordist Analysis*. Buckingham: Open University Press.

Merck, M. (1993) *Perversions: Deviant Readings*. New York: Routledge.

Mertz, N.T. and McNeely, S.R. (1998) Women on the job: a study of female high school principals. *Educational Administration Quarterly*, 34(2): 196–222.

Middleton, S. (1998) *Disciplining Sexuality: Foucault, Life Histories, and Education*. New York: Teachers' College Press.

Miller, J.B. (1993) Women and power, in T. Wartenberg (ed.) *Rethinking Power*. Albany, NY: SUNY Press.

Miller, N. (1995) *Out of the Past: Gay and Lesbian History from 1869 to the Present*. New York: Vintage.

Minnich, E. (1990) *Transforming Knowledge*. Philadelphia: Temple University Press.

Möller, J. (2002) Gender and leadership identities: negotiated realities for women as Norwegian school principals. Paper presented at the Annual Meeting of American Educational Research Association, New Orleans, 1–5 April.

Morgan, D. (1995) The gender of bureaucracy, in D. Collinson and J. Hearn (eds) *Men as Managers, Managers as Men: Critical Perspectives on Men, Masculinities and Management*. London: Sage.

Morley, L. (1999) *Organising Feminisms: The Micropolitics of the Academy*. New York: St Martin's Press.

Morrow, R. and Torres, C. (2000) The state, globalization, and education policy, in N. Burbules and C. Torres (eds) *Globalization and Education: Critical Perspectives*, pp. 27–56. New York: Routledge.

Mouffe, C. (1995) Feminism, citizenship and radical democratic politics, in L. Nicholson and S. Seidman (eds) *Social Postmodernism: Beyond Identity Politics*, pp. 315–331. Cambridge: Cambridge University Press.

Mulholland, K. (1995) Entrepreneurialism: masculinities and the self-made man, in D. Collinson and J. Hearn (eds) *Men as Managers, Managers as Men: Critical Perspectives on Men, Masculinities and Management*. London: Sage.

Myers, K. and Goldstein, H. (1997) Failing schools or failing systems, in A. Hargreaves (ed.) *Rethinking Educational Change with Heart and Mind*, ASCD Yearbook. Toronto: ASCD.

NASSP (National Association of Secondary School Principals) (1998) *Is There a*

Shortage of Qualified Candidates for Openings in the Principalship? An Exploratory Study. Arlington, VA: NASSP.

New London Group (1996) A pedagogy of multiliteracies: designing social futures. *Harvard Educational Review*, 66(1): 60–92.

Noddings, N. (1984) *Caring: A Feminine Approach to Ethics and Moral Education.* Berkeley: University of California Press.

Noddings, N. (1992) *The Challenge to Care in Schools: An Alternative Approach to Education.* New York: Teachers' College Press.

Nye, J.L. (1998) The gender box. *Berkeley Women's Law Journal*, 13: 226–256.

Nygren, A. and Johansson, O. (2000) Den svenske rektorn efter 1945 – kvalifikationer, arbetsuppgifter och utmaningar, in L. Moos, S. Carney, O. Johansson and J. Mehlbye (eds) *Skoleledelse i Norden – en kortlægning af skoleledernes arbejdsvilkår, rammebetingelser og opgaver. En rapport til Nordisk Ministerråd, Nord 2000*, vol.14, pp. 258–311. Köpenhamn.

Olofsson, S-S. (1998) Kvinnliga rektorers ledarstil i svensk grundskola. *Studia Psychologica et Paedagogica series altera*, p. 140. Stockholm: Almqvist & Wiksell International.

Ozga, J. (1993) *Women in Educational Management*. Buckingham: Open University Press.

Ozga, J. (1995) Deskilling a profession: professionalism and the new managerialism, in H. Busher and R. Saran (eds) *Managing Teachers as Professionals in Schools*. London: Falmer Press.

Ozga, J. and Walker, L. (1999) In the company of men, in S. Whitehead and R. Moodley (eds) *Transforming Managers: Gendering Change in the Public Sector*. London: UCL Press.

Parsons, T. (1963) On the concept of influence. *Public Opinion Quarterly*, Spring: 36–62.

Parsons, T. (1969) On the concept of power, in R. Bell, D. Edwards and R.H. Wagner (eds) *Political Power: A Reader in Theory and Research*, pp. 251–284. New York: Free Press.

Pascal, C. and Ribbins, P. (1998) Regarding heads: primary lives and careers, in C. Pascal and P. Ribbins (eds) *Understanding Primary Headteachers*, pp. 1–30. London: Cassell.

Pence, L. (1995) Learning leadership through mentorships, in P. Schmuck and D. Dunlap (eds) *Women Leading in Education*, pp. 124–144. Albany, NY: SUNY Press.

Pincus, I. (1995) *Mellan insikt och handling. Jämställdheten, männen och ambivalensen i den kommunala organisationen*. Örebro: Kvinnovetenskapligt forum.

Pitkin, H. (1972) *Wittgenstein and Justice*. Berkeley: University of California Press.

Pollitt, C. (1990) *Managerialism and the Public Services: The Anglo American Experience*. London: Basil Blackwell.

Popkewitz, T.S. (2000) The denial of change in educational change: systems of ideas in the construction of national policy and evaluation. *Educational Researcher*, 29(1): 17–29.

Potter, Z. and Summers, C.J. (2001) Reconsidering epistemology and ontology in status identity discourse: make-believe and reality in race, sex, and sexual orientation. *Harvard Blackletter Journal*, 17: 113–196.

Power, M. (1999) *The Audit Society: Rituals of Verification*. Oxford: Oxford University Press.

Protherough, R. (1984) Shaping the image of the great headmaster. *British Journal of Educational Studies*, 32(3): 239–250.

Pusser, B. (2002) Higher education, the emerging market and the public good, in *The Knowledge Economy and Postsecondary Education: Report of a Workshop*, pp. 105–126. Washington, DC: National Academy Press.

RCAP (Royal Commission on Aboriginal Peoples) (1996) *Report of the Royal Commission on Aboriginal Peoples*, 5 vols. Ottawa: Canada Communication Group.

Regan, H. (1995) Working together: a feminist construction of schooling, in D. Dunlap and P. Schmuck (eds) *Women Leading in Education*. Albany, NY: SUNY Press.

Regan, H. and Brooks, G. (1995) *Out of Women's Experiences: Creating Relational Leadership*. Thousand Oaks, CA: Corwin Press.

Regeringens skrivelse (1998/1999) *Samverkan, ansvar och utveckling. Utveck-lingsplan för förskola, skola och vuxenutbildning*, p. 121. Government official document on school development in Sweden.

Reiger, K. (1993) The gender dynamics of organizations: an historical account, in J. Blackmore and J. Kenway (eds) *Gender Matters in Educational Administration and Policy*. London: Falmer Press.

Reynolds, C. (1995) In the right place at the right time: rules of control and woman's place in Ontario Schools, 1940–1980. *Canadian Journal of Education*, 20(2): 129–145.

Reynolds, C. (ed.) (2002a) *Women and School Leadership: International Perspectives*. Albany, NY: SUNY Press.

Reynolds, C. (2002b) Changing gender scripts and moral dilemmas for women and men in education, 1940–1970, in C. Reynolds (ed.) *Women and School Leadership: International Perspectives*. Albany, NY: SUNY Press.

Reynolds, C. and Young, B. (eds) (1995) *Women and Leadership in Canadian Education*. Calgary: Temeron Press.

Ribbins, P. (1996) Producing portraits of educational leaders in context: cultural relativism and methodological absolutism. Paper presented to the Commonwealth Council for Educational Administration and Management Conference, Malaysia.

Ribbins, P. (1999) On redefining educational management and leadership. *Educational Management and Administration*, 27(3): 227–238.

Richardson, H.H. (1970) *The Getting of Wisdom*. London: Heinemann (first published 1912).

Robins, K.N. and Terrell, R. (1987) Women, power and the 'old boys club': ascending to leadership in male dominated organizations. *School Library Media Quarterly*, 15 (Summer): 205–210.

Robinson, V. (1994) The centrality of the autonomy–accountability dilemma in school and professional development, in D. Hopkins and A. Hargreaves (eds) *School Development Planning*. London: Cassell.

Rofes, E. (2000) Transgression and the situated body: gender, sex, and the gay male teacher, in S. Talburt and S.R. Steinberg (eds) *Thinking Queer: Sexuality, Culture, and Education*, pp. 131–150. New York: Peter Lang.

Rogers, J.L. (1988) New paradigm leadership: integrating the female ethos. *Initiatives*, 51(4): 1–8.

Rosener, J. B. (1990) Ways women lead. *Harvard Business Review*, November/December: 119–125.

Rothschild, J. (1994) The collectivist organization: an alternative to rational–bureaucratic models, in F. Fischer and C. Sirianni (eds) *Critical Studies in Organization and Bureaucracy*, pp. 448–474. Philadelphia: Temple University Press.

Ruddick, S. (1989) *Maternal Thinking: Toward a Politics of Peace*. New York: Ballentine.

Rusch, E.A. and Marshall, C. (1995) Gender filters at work in administrative culture. Paper presented to the AERA Conference, San Francisco.

Russell, B. (1938) *Power: A New Social Analysis*. London: Allen & Unwin.

Russell, R.A. (1995) Beyond survival: women leaders as agents of change. Paper presented to the AERA Conference, San Francisco.

Sachs, J. (2000) Reclaiming the agenda of teacher professionalism, in C. Day, A. Fernandez, T. Hague and J. Moller (eds) *The Lives and Work of Teachers in Changing Times: International Perspectives*. Lewes: Falmer Press.

Sachs, J. (2003) *The Activist Teaching Profession*. Buckingham: Open University Press.

Sandler, B. (1995) Women as mentors: myths and commandments. *Educational Horizons*, Spring: 105–107.

Scheurich, J. (1995) The knowledge base in educational administration: postmodernist reflections, in R. Donmoyer, M. Imber and J. Scheurich (eds) *The Knowledge Base in Educational Administration: Multiple Perspectives*. Albany, NY: SUNY Press.

Scheurich, J.J. (1997) *Research Method in the Postmodern*. London: Falmer Press.

Schmuck, P.A. (1980) Changing women's representation in school management: a systems perspective, in S.K. Biklen and M.B. Brannigan (eds) *Women and Educational Leadership*, pp. 239–243. Lexington, MA: Lexington Books.

Schmuck, P. (1987) *Women Educators: Employees of Schools in Western Countries*. Albany, NY: SUNY Press.

Schmuck, P. (1995) Advocacy organizations for women 1977–1993, in P. Schmuck and D. Dunlap (eds) *Women Leading in Education*, pp. 199–224. Albany, NY: SUNY Press.

Schmuck, P. (1996) Women's place in educational administration: past, present, and future, in K. Leithwood *et al.* (eds) *International Handbook of School Leadership and Administration*, pp. 337–368. Dordrecht: Kluwer.

Schmuck, P. and Schmuck, R. (1990) Democratic participation in small-town schools. *Educational Researcher*, 19(8): 14–19.

Schmuck, P., Hollingsworth, S. and Lock, R. (2002) Women administrators and the point of exit: collision between the person and the institution, in C. Reynolds (ed.) *Women and School Leadership: International Perspectives*. Albany, NY: SUNY Press.

Scholtes, P. (1996). *The Team Handbook for Educators*. Madison, WI: Joiner Associates.

Schramm, S.L. (2000) *Thinking Thrice: A Feminist Response to 'Mentoring' that Marginalizes*, ERIC: ED 446–463.

Scrla, L. (1998) The social construction of gender in the superintendency. Paper presented at the Annual Meeting of the American Educational Research Association, San Diego, 13–17 April.

Sears, J.T. (1997). *Overcoming Heterosexism and Homophobia: Strategies that Work*. New York: Columbia University Press.

Seidler, V.J. (1994) *Unreasonable Men: Masculinity and Social Theory*. London: Routledge.

Seidman, S. (1996) *Queer Theory/Sociology*. New York: Blackwell.

Senge, P. (1990). *The Fifth Discipline*. New York: Currency Doubleday.

Senge, P. (1994) *The Fifth Discipline: Fieldbook*. New York: Currency Doubleday.

Sennett, R. (1998) *The Corrosion of Character*. New York: Norton.

Sergiovanni, T. (1992) *Moral Leadership: Getting to the Heart of School Improvement*. San Francisco: Jossey-Bass.

Shakeshaft, C. (1987) *Women in Educational Administration*. Newbury Park, CA: Sage.

Shakeshaft, C. (1989) *Women in Educational Administration*, rev. edn. Newbury Park, CA: Sage.

Shakeshaft, C. (1992) Skolledaren, in K. Lööv *The School Leader*, 7(8): 4–6.

Shakeshaft, C. (1995) Gendered leadership styles in educational organizations, in B. Limerick and B. Lingard (eds) *Gender and Changing Educational Management: Second Yearbook of the Australian Council for Educational Administration*, pp. 12–22. Rydalmere: Hodder Education.

Shakeshaft, C. (1999) The struggle to create a more gender inclusive profession, in J. Murphy and K. Louis (eds) *Handbook of Research on Educational Administration*. New York: Jossey-Bass.

Shapiro, H.S. (1984) Crisis of legitimation: schools, society, and declining education. *Interchange*, 15(4): 26–39.

Sherman, W. (2002) Women's experiences with a formal leadership program for aspiring administrators. Unpublished doctoral dissertation, University of Virginia.

Shum, L.C. and Cheng, Y.C. (1997) Perceptions of women principal's leadership and teachers' work attitudes. *Journal of Educational Administration*, 35(2): 165–184.

Siegel, R.B. (2002) She the people: the Nineteenth Amendment, sex equality, federalism and the family. *Harvard Law Review*, 115: 947–1046.

Simon, H. (1953) Notes on the observation and measurement of power. *Journal of Politics*, 15: 500–516.

Simon, H.A. (1976) *Administrative Behaviour*. New York: Free Press.

Sinclair, A. (1998) *Doing Leadership Differently: Gender, Power and Sexuality in a Changing Business Culture*. Melbourne: Melbourne University Press.

Slaughter, S. and Leslie, L. (1997) *Academic Capitalism*. Baltimore: Johns Hopkins University Press.

Smulyan, L. (1999) *Balancing Acts: Women Principals at Work*. Albany, NY: SUNY Press.

Söderberg Forslund, M. (2002) *Kvinnor och skolledarskap – en kunskapsöversikt*. Skolverket Stockholm: Liber.

Somerville, S.B. (2000) *Queering the Color Line: Race and the Invention of Homosexuality in American Culture*. Durham, NC: Duke University Press.

SOU (Statens offentliga utredningar: state official commission) (1980) *More Women as School Administrators (Fler kvinnor som skolledare)*, p. 19. Stockholm: Liber.

Sperandio, J. (2003) Secondary schools for Norwich girls, 1850–1910: demanded or benevolently supplied? *Gender and Education*, 14(4): 391–410.

Spillane, J., Halverson, R. and Diamond, J. (2004) Towards a theory of leadership practice: a distributive perspective. *Journal of Curriculum Studies*, in press.

Stalker, J. (1994) Athene in academe: women mentoring women in the academy. *International Journal of Lifelong Education*, 13(5): 361–372.

Stefkovich, J.A. and Shapiro, J.P. (2003) Deconstructing communities: educational leaders and their ethical decision-making processes, in P. Begley and O. Johansson (eds) *The Ethical Dimensions of School Leadership*. Dordrecht: Kluwer.

Steinberg, W. (1993) *Masculinity: Identity, Conflict and Transformation*. Boston: Shambhala.

Stewart, D. and Prebble, T. (1993) *The Reflective Principal: School Development within a Learning Community*. Palmerston North: ERDC Press Massey University.

Stone, C. (1989) *Regime Politics*. Lawrence, KS: University Press of Kansas.

Strachan, J. (2002) Feminist educational leadership: not for the fainthearted, in C. Reynolds (ed.) *Women and School Leadership: International Perspectives*. Albany, NY: SUNY Press.

Strachan, J.M.B. (1999) Feminist educational leadership in a New Zealand neoliberal context. *Journal of Educational Administration*, 37(2): 121–138.

Strauss, A. and Corbin, J. (1998) *Basics of Qualitative Research Techniques and Procedures for Developing Grounded Theory*, 2nd edn. London: Sage.

Stromquist, N. (2002) *Education in a Globalized World*. Lanham, MD: Rowman & Littlefield.

Stromquist, N. and Monkman, K. (eds) (2000) *Globalization and Education: Integration and Contestation across Cultures*. New York: Rowman & Littlefield.

Swoboda, M. and Millar, S. (1986) Networking–mentoring: career strategy of women in academic administration. *Journal of NAWDAC*, 49: 8–13.

Tacey, D. (1997) Remaking Men: The Revolution in Masculinity. Ringwood: Viking.

Tannen, D. (1991) *You Just Don't Understand: Women and Men in Conversation*. London: Virago.

Teese, R. (2000) *Academic Success and Social Power: Examinations and Inequality*. Carlton: Melbourne University Press.

Terry, J. (1999) *An American Obsession: Science, Medicine and Homosexuality in Modern Society*. Chicago: University of Chicago Press.

Theobald, M. (1978) *Rhyton Remembers 1878–1978*. Melbourne: Hawthorn Press.

Theobald, M. (1996) *Knowing Women: Origins of Women's Education in Nineteenth-century Australia*. Hong Kong: Cambridge University Press.

Thomas, S. (1994) *How Women Legislate*. New York: Oxford University Press.

Thomson, P. (1998) Thoroughly modern management and a cruel accounting: the effect of public sector reform on public education, in A. Reid (ed.) *Going Public: Education Policy and Public Education in Australia*. Canberra: Australian Curriculum Studies Association.

Thomson, P. (1999) How doing justice got boxed in: a cautionary tale for policy activists, in A. Reid and B. Johnson (eds) *Contesting the Curriculum*. Sydney: Social Science Press.

Thomson, P. (2001) How principals lose 'face': a disciplinary tale of educational administration and modern managerialism. *Discourse*, 22(1): 1–26.

Times Higher Education Supplement (2003) *Staff Trends*. London: THES. www.thes.co.uk/Statistics/Staff_Trends/gender/professors/99–2000.asp (accessed 30 March 2003).

Townley, B. (1994) *Reframing Human Resource Management: Power, Ethics and the Subject at Work*. London: Sage.

Trounstine, P.J. and Christensen, T. (1982) *Movers and Shakers: The Study of Community Power*. New York: St Martin's Press.

Turner, C. and Myers, S. (2000) *Faculty of Color in Academe: Bittersweet Success*. Boston: Allyn & Bacon.

Ullman, A. (1997) *Rektorn – en studie av en titel och dess bärare*. Stockholm: HLS-förlag.

Valdes, F. (1995) Queers, sissies, dykes, and tomboys: deconstructing the conflation of 'sex', 'gender', and 'sexual orientation' in Euro-American law and society. *California Law Review*, 83: 3–377.

Vidovich, L. (2002) Quality assurance in Australian higher education: globalisation and steering at a distance. *Higher Education*, 43: 391–408.

Vlahogiannis, N.L. (1989) *Prinny Hill: The State Schools of Princess Hill 1889–1989*. Melbourne: The Princess Hill Schools.

Von Krogh, G., Nishiguchi, T. and Nonaka, I. (2000) *Knowledge Creation: A Source of Value*. London: Macmillan.

Wahl, A. (1997) Ledarstil, makt och kön, in A. Nyberg and E. Sundin (eds) *Ledare, makt och kön: rapport till utredningen om fördelningen av ekonomisk makt och ekonomiska resurser mellan kvinnor och män*, pp. 109–134. Stockholm: Statens offentliga utredningar.

Wajcman, J. (1998) *Managing Like a Man: Women and Men in Corporate Management*. Sydney: Allen & Unwin.

Walker, A. and Dimmock, C. (2000) Insights into educational administration: the need for a cross-cultural comparative perspective. *Asia Pacific Journal of Education*, 20(2): 11–22.

Wartenberg, Thomas E. (1990) *The Forms of Power: From Domination to Transformation*. Philadelphia: Temple University Press.

Weber, M. (1924) *The Theory of Social and Economic Organizations*. Glencoe, IL: Free Press.

Webber, I. (1981) *Years May Pass On: Caufield Grammar School 1881–1981*. East St Kilda: Caufield Grammar School.

Weedon, C. (1997) *Feminist Practice and Poststructuralist Theory*. Oxford: Blackwell.

Weiner, G. (1995) A question of style or value? Contrasting perceptions of women as educational leaders, in B. Limerick and B. Lingard (eds) *Gender and Changing Education Management*, pp. 23–39. Rydalmere: Hodder Education.

Whetherell, M., Taylor, S. and Yates, S.J. (2001) *Discourse Theory and Practice*. London: Sage.

White, G. and Zirkel, P. (2001) Publication productivity in educational leadership journals. *UCEA The Review*. University Council for Educational Administration.

Wingård, B. (1998) *Att vara rektor och kvinna*. Uppsala Studies in Education 73. Uppsala: Uppsala University Library.

Winther Jörgensen, M. and Philips, L. (2000) *Diskursanalys som teori och metod*. Lund: Studentlitteratur.

Woden, M. (1998) The labour market for young Australians, in *Youth: Reality and Risk*. Canberra: Australian Government Publishing Service.

Wolcott, H.F. (1973) *The Man in the Principal's Office: An Ethnography*. New York, Holt, Rinehart & Winston.

Woods, P. *et al.* (1999) The impact of school performance of choice and competition. Paper presented to the AERA Conference, Montreal, April.

Wylie, C. (1998) *Self-managing Schools Seven Years On*. Wellington: NZCER.

Wyn, J., Acker, S. and Richards, E. (2000) Making a difference: women in management in Australian and Canadian faculties of education. *Gender and Education*, 12(4): 435–447.

Yeatman, A. (1998) *Activism and the Policy Process*. Sydney: Allen & Unwin.

Yoshino, K. (2002) Covering. *Yale Law Journal*, 111: 769–939.

Young, I.M. (1990) The ideal of community and the politics of difference, in L.J. Nicholson (ed.) *Feminism/Postmodernism*, pp. 300–323. New York: Routledge.

Young, I.M. (1999) *Justice and the Politics of Difference*. Oxford: Polity Press.

Young, I.M. (2000) *Inclusion and Democracy*. Oxford: Oxford University Press.

Young, J.H. (1993) Principals and collaborative curriculum development: does gender make a difference? *The Alberta Journal of Education Research*, 39(4): 433–448.

Young, M. and McLeod, S. (2001) Flukes, opportunities and planned interventions: factors affecting women's decisions to become school administrators. *Educational Administration Quarterly*, 37(4): 462–502.

Young, B. (2002) The 'Alberta Advantage': 'De-Kleining' career prospects for women educators, in C. Reynolds (ed.) *Women and School Leadership: International Perspectives*. Albany, NY: SUNY Press.

Zainu'ddin, A.G.T. (1982) *They Dreamt of a School: A Centenary History of Methodist Ladies' College, Kew, 1882–1982*. Melbourne: Hyland House.

Index

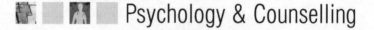

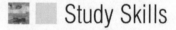